PICTURE IT!

A Comprehension Handbook

Author's Purpose

Inform

Entertain

An author writes for many purposes, some of which are to inform, entertain, persuade, or express a mood or feeling. An author may have more than one purpose for writing.

Persuade

Express

Categorize and Classify

When we categorize and classify, we look at how people or things are related based on their characteristics.

Compare and Contrast

To compare and contrast
is to look for similarities
and differences
in things.

Draw Conclusions

When we draw conclusions, we think about facts and details and then decide something about them.

Fact and Opinion

A fact is something that can be proved true or false. An opinion can't be proved.

Generalize

To generalize is to make a broad statement or rule that applies to many examples.

Graphic Sources

Graphic sources show information in a way the reader can see.

Table

Tables are boxes, squares, or rectangles that catergorize information in rows and columns.

The Case of the
Park Litterbugs

Detective on duty	Day	Garbage found
	Sunday	9
Jaime	Monday	11
Jessica	Tuesday	2
Eric	Wednesday	3
Me	Thursday	5
Ana Luz	Friday	7
Milton	Saturday	15
Libby		

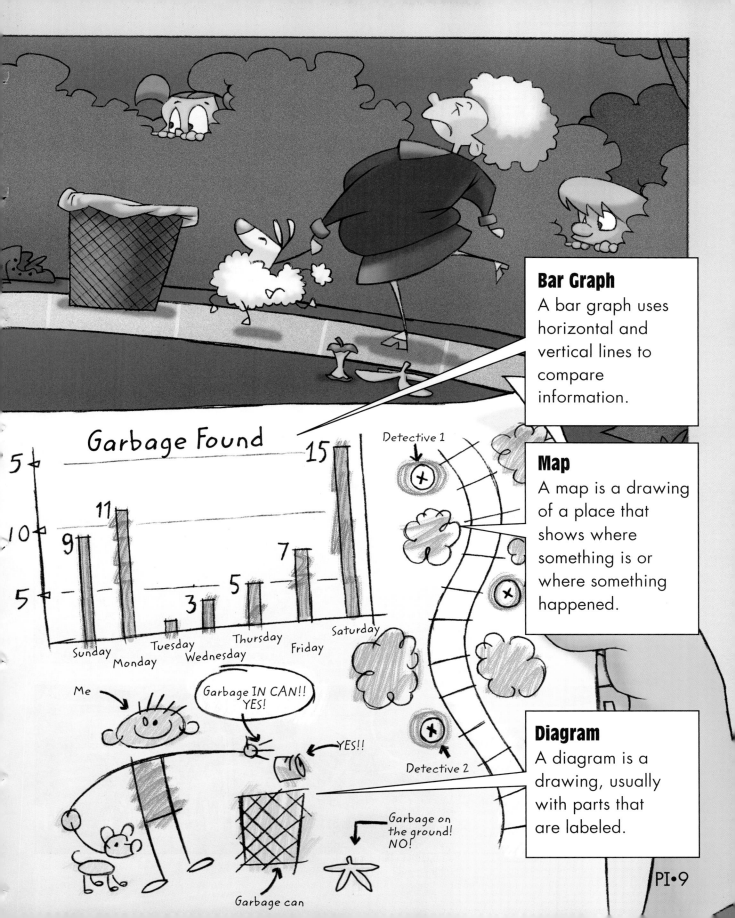

Bar Graph
A bar graph uses horizontal and vertical lines to compare information.

Map
A map is a drawing of a place that shows where something is or where something happened.

Diagram
A diagram is a drawing, usually with parts that are labeled.

PI•9

Room To Grow

Literary Elements

Stories are made up of four main elements: character, setting, plot, and theme. Each of these parts gives you an overall understanding of the story.

Characters

A character is a person or an animal in a story.

Setting

The setting is the time and place in which a story happens.

Plot

The plot is the pattern of events in a story.

The plot starts with a problem or goal and builds toward a climax. The plot ends with a resolution or outcome.

Theme

The theme is the big idea of a story. We look at the plot, setting, or characters to determine the theme of a story.

Main Idea and Details

Main idea is the most important idea about a topic. Details support the main idea.

Sequence

Sequence refers to the order of events in nonfiction. We also use sequence when we list the steps in a process.

ISBN-13: 978-0-328-36593-7
ISBN-10:   0-328-36593-9

2 3 4 5 6 7 8 9 10 V063 17 16 15 14 13 12 11 10 09 08

Reading STREET

Program Authors

Peter Afflerbach

Camille Blachowicz

Candy Dawson Boyd

Wendy Cheyney

Connie Juel

Edward Kame'enui

Donald Leu

Jeanne Paratore

Sam Sebesta

Deborah Simmons

Alfred Tatum

Sharon Vaughn

Susan Watts Taffe

Karen Kring Wixson

PEARSON

Glenview, Illinois • Boston, Massachusetts • Mesa, Arizona
Shoreview, Minnesota • Upper Saddle River, New Jersey

Turning Points

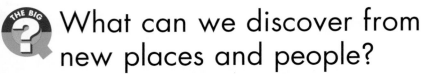 What can we discover from new places and people?

Picture It! A Comprehension Handbook **PI•1–PI•13**
Words! A Vocabulary Handbook **W•1–W•15**

Teamwork

? What is the value
of teamwork?

Picture It! A Comprehension Handbook   PI•1–PI•13
Words! A Vocabulary Handbook   W•1–W•15

Patterns in Nature

 THE BIG ? What are some patterns in nature?

Contents

21

PearsonSuccessNet.com

See It!

- Concept Talk Video
- Background Building Audio Slide Show
- Comprehension Think Aloud Video
- *Picture It!* Animation
- e-Books

Hear It!

- Selection Snapshot and Response
- Paired Selection e-Text
- Grammar Jammer
- e-Books

Do It!

- Online Journal
- Reading Street Pursuit Online Game
- Story Sort
- New Literacies Activity
- Success Tracker

Turning Points

THE BIG ?

What can we discover from new places and people?

UNIT 1

Yang the Youngest and His Terrible Ear   REALISTIC FICTION

What experiences bring diverse people together?

Paired Selection
Gold Mountain   EXPOSITORY NONFICTION

Hurry Freedom   EXPOSITORY NONFICTION

What opportunities can be found in new places?

Paired Selection
The Lure of the West   EXPOSITORY NONFICTION

Grandfather's Journey   HISTORICAL FICTION

What can we learn about the United States as we travel?

Paired Selection
A Look at Two Lands   ONLINE REFERENCE SOURCES

The Horned Toad Prince   MODERN FAIRY TALE

What can we discover in the landscape of the Southwest?

Paired Selection
The Fox and the Tiger   FABLE

Letters Home from Yosemite

NARRATIVE NONFICTION

How does Yosemite reflect the unique qualities of the West?

Paired Selection
Four Days in Yosemite   EXPOSITORY NONFICTION

Turning Points

Build Language
Diversity

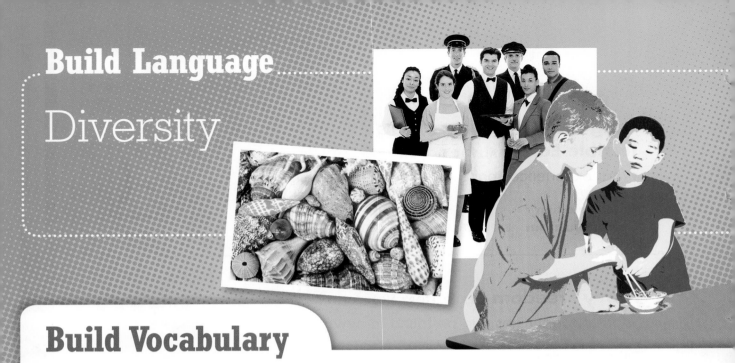

Build Vocabulary

Learn ◎ **Skill** **Suffixes** are word parts that are added to the end of words. Suffixes change the meanings of words. For example, the suffix *–able* means "can be." So the word *washable* means "can be washed."

Practice Use a dictionary to look up this week's Words to Know. Identify which of this week's words have suffixes. Write down the meanings of the suffixes. Then read, "The Big Night" on page 25.

Words to Know	audition	sympathetic	insulted
	rehearsal	audience	praises
	moody	uncomfortable	

On Your Own Read "The Big Night" again. Think about performing in front of an audience. Use words from the Words to Know List to describe how you would feel.

R1.4 Know common roots and affixes derived from Greek and Latin and use this knowledge to analyze the meanings of complex words (e.g., *international*).

The Big Night

Every day for the past month, Katie has been practicing with the school choir to get ready for the big concert tonight. She was as excited now as she was on the first day she had to audition for the choir.

Today was the last rehearsal before the choir took the stage, and the director, Ms. Monroe, was very moody. Everyone knew it was because she was nervous. Katie was sympathetic to Ms. Monroe's feelings. She was nervous too. It was important to Ms. Monroe for the audience to see a great concert.

Not all students were so sympathetic.

"Mark, I can't hear you up there!" called Ms. Monroe. There was an uncomfortable silence in the room. Mark looked insulted.

"Ms. Monroe, I am just trying to save my voice for the show," he said.

"Oh, all right, Mark. As long as the audience can hear you, everything will be fine!" Ms. Monroe decided.

"This is your big night," she reminded the choir. "Smile. Remember everything we have been practicing, and everyone will be singing your praises at the end of the concert!"

 Need a Review?
For additional help with suffixes, see *Words!* on p. W•6.

 Ready to Try It?
Read *Yang the Youngest and His Terrible Ear* on pp. 28–41.

Turning Points

Build Comprehension

Learn ⊙ **Skill Sequence**

- Sequence is the order in which things happen.

- Chronological order, or time order, is one way authors organize text.

- Authors use dates, times of day, and clue words such as *first, next,* and *finally,* to help show the order of events.

- Use a graphic organizer like the one below to put the events of a text in order.

| First Event: Clue Word | → | Second Event: Clue Word | → | Third Event: Clue Word |

Practice   As you read "A New School" on page 27, look for clue words that tell the sequence of events.

On Your Own   **Write to Read** Reread "A New School." List the things you can do to make new friends. What kinds of things would you add to the list?

 Need a Review? See the *Picture It!* lesson on p. PI•13 for additional help with sequence.

 Ready to Try It? As you read *Yang the Youngest and His Terrible Ear* on pp. 28– 41, use what you learned about sequence to help you understand the text.

G5R2.2 Analyze text that is organized in sequential or chronological order.

A New School

Last fall, Tom's family moved to a new neighborhood. Tom was nervous about going to a new school. Before he left for his first day, his father gave him some advice and told him not to worry. Tom was determined to follow his father's advice.

The first thing Tom did was to say hello to other kids, and introduce himself. He asked them what they liked to do when they're not at school. He found that many of the students had the same interests as he did.

Skill What are some clue words that tell the sequence?

The next thing Tom did was to look for after-school activities. Tom liked to play sports, so after school he went to the office to find out about different activities.

Skill When is it a good time to find out about school activities

Finally, Tom invited some of his new friends to come over to his house after school. When Tom's father came home from work, he was happy to find Tom and his new friends playing basketball in the driveway.

"I guess he listened to my advice," Tom's father thought.

Skill Can the order of events be switched around? Why or why not?

Genre

Realistic fiction has characters and events that are like people and events in real life. As you read, think about how the people and events in your life are similar to the characters and events in this story.

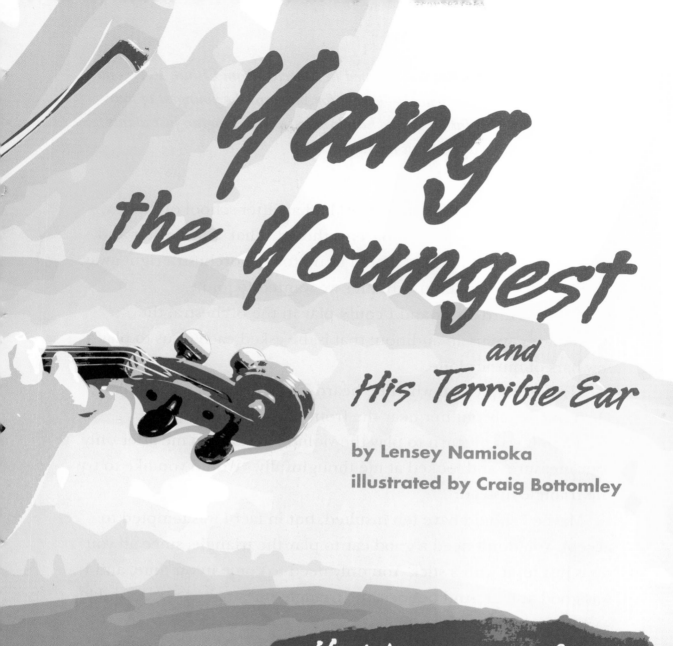

Yang the Youngest and His Terrible Ear

by Lensey Namioka

illustrated by Craig Bottomley

How do you make friends in a new school?

The Yang family has just arrived in America from China. Everyone in the Yang family is musical—except for Yingtao, the youngest of four children. While his father wants him to play violin, Yingtao just wants to fit in and make a friend at his new school.

We discovered that our school had an after-school orchestra, which met twice a week. My parents thought that Third Sister and I were very lucky, and they signed us up for the orchestra right away. They never even asked us whether we wanted to join.

Before Third Sister and I could play in the orchestra, the conductor gave us an audition; that is, he asked each of us to play a few bars of music alone.

He looked pleased when he heard Third Sister play the cello. He immediately put her near the front of the orchestra.

Then it was my turn to play the violin. He stopped me after only four measures and looked at me thoughtfully. "Would you like to try the triangle instead?"

Maybe I should have felt insulted, but in fact I was tempted to accept. You don't need a good ear to play the triangle, since all you do is just hit it with a stick. You only need to come in on time, and I was good at that. And besides, the triangle only makes a small tinkle, so you can't do much harm.

But I knew my parents would be upset. "I have my own violin," I told the conductor unhappily. "My parents will expect me to play it."

He sighed. "Very well. I know what parents are like." He put me in the very last row of the violin section — as far away from the audience as possible.

When I took my place, the boy sharing a music stand with me said, "Hi, looks like I'll be your stand partner."

It was Matthew the boy who had gotten my pen back. I was very glad to see him.

Then the conductor raised his stick and the orchestra began to play.

When playing together with other people, my trick was to draw my bow back and forth, without quite touching the strings. This helped everybody. It helped me; it helped the other players; it helped the conductor; and most of all, it helped the audience.

After a few bars we stopped playing while the conductor tried to cheer up the trombone player, who was making bubbling sounds when he tried to blow.

Matthew turned to me. "You don't play very loudly, do you? I couldn't hear you at all."

"You're lucky," I told him.

He looked puzzled, but I had no time to explain because the conductor raised his stick again.

Matthew played with a dreamy look on his face. I couldn't tell if he was good or not, but he certainly seemed to be enjoying himself.

After the rehearsal the conductor asked Third Sister to stay behind and play a short piece for him. I waited for her outside so we could go home together.

Matthew came up to me while I was waiting. "I heard your sister tell the conductor that your father is a violin teacher."

"Yes, he is," I answered. Maybe this was a chance to get Father another student. "Do you want to take lessons?"

Matthew looked very uncomfortable. "I'd really like to, but my folks can't afford it."

"My father is cheap," I said eagerly, although I didn't actually know how much Father charged. But I felt sure he would love to have a new student, especially someone who really liked music.

When Third Sister came out, she was smiling. "The conductor wants me to play a solo for our first concert!"

I was very happy for her, and even Matthew looked glad. "Hey, that's great!" he said.

"This is my stand partner, Matthew," I said. "And this is my third sister—"

"Hi, my name is Mary," interrupted Third Sister.

I stared at her. I didn't even know she had an American name. She must have picked it without telling the rest of the family. Maybe she felt it would be easier for her new friends to remember.

I'd noticed that many Americans had trouble with Chinese names. When I told people my name was Yingtao, they always asked me to spell it. Even after I spelled it, they had trouble remembering it.

"I heard you play just now," Matthew said to Third Sister. "You're really good!"

Third Sister dimpled again. "I'm terrible. You're just saying that to be nice."

She didn't mean it, of course. That's the way my parents taught us to answer when someone praises us.

"Well, I guess I'd better run," said Matthew. But he didn't seem in a hurry to go.

Neither was Third Sister eager to have him go—not when he had just told her how much he admired her playing. "Would you like to come to our house and meet my elder brother and sister? They also play musical instruments."

Matthew grinned. "Sure if it's okay with your folks."

"My parents would be glad to meet one of Fourth Brother's friends," she told him.

I liked the way she said that—as if Matthew was really my friend, as if I had lots of other friends.

$\mathcal{M}$y parents weren't at home, but we found Second Sister in the kitchen, cutting tea bags. "This is my other sister," I told him. "She plays the viola."

Second Sister looked a little moody but not too moody to greet Matthew politely with "Hello."

I waited to see if she had chosen an American name too. But she just picked up her scissors again.

As we went up the stairs, Matthew looked at me. "What was your sister doing in the kitchen? It looked like she was cutting up tea bags."

"She was."

At the landing Matthew stopped and looked at me again. "What for?"

I was used to seeing Second Sister cutting tea bags, and it had never occurred to me that it might look funny. "When we make tea, we put some tea leaves in the bottom of the cup, and pour hot water over them," I said. "It's ready to drink when all the leaves are wet and sink to the bottom."

"But why do you need to cut the bags?"

"Well, my mother saw some tea for sale at the market one day, and she bought a big box. But it turned out to be all tea bags, not loose tea. So Second Sister cuts up a few bags every day and pours the loose tea into a jar."

It was perfectly obvious to me that tea would steep better when it's loose than when it's tightly packed into a tiny bag.

But I guess Matthew didn't think so. He was still shaking his head and looking puzzled.

I opened the door to the room I shared with Eldest Brother. He was inside, sitting on the floor and screwing knobs into the ends of orange crates. Beside him were a couple of boards and some bricks.

I introduced Matthew, who looked wide-eyed at the crates and boards. "What are you making?"

"I'm making a chest of drawers," said Eldest Brother. "The boards will sit over the piles of bricks to make a top, and the orange crates are the drawers. The knobs make it easier to pull them out."

Matthew peered into one of the crates, which already contained my shirts and underwear. "Why don't you put your clothes in a regular dresser?"

"We don't have enough money to buy much furniture," explained Eldest Brother.

"Gee, I'm sorry," Matthew said, turning red. "I didn't mean to sound rude or nosy." For some reason, he was very sensitive about money.

I had to show Matthew that we didn't mind. Chinese people aren't at all embarrassed to talk about money. When we meet someone, we often ask him how much money he makes.

"That's okay," I told Matthew. "I don't think you're rude or nosy at all."

"My mother was glad when she found all these orange crates she could have for free," Eldest Brother said.

As he continued to put the knobs in, I told him that Matthew loved music.

Eldest Brother looked pleased. "Are you in the school orchestra?"

"I play the violin," answered Matthew. "I'm Yingtao's stand partner."

Eldest Brother stopped smiling. "Did the conductor put you there after the audition?"

I knew why he asked that. He was trying to find out if Matthew was my stand partner because he played as badly as I did.

"I'm a beginner," said Matthew. "I only started playing the violin last fall. The school had an extra violin that nobody else was using, so I asked if I could borrow it."

"Do you take lessons?" asked Eldest Brother.

Again Matthew turned red. "My parents can't afford them," he mumbled. "My father is out of work right now."

I suddenly had an idea. "Maybe you can give him some free lessons," I said to Eldest Brother. "They don't have to be more than fifteen minutes, just long enough to show him what he's doing wrong."

Eldest Brother looked thoughtful. Finally he got up and went to his violin case. "Play something," he said, taking out the instrument and handing it to Matthew.

Matthew swallowed and wiped his hands on his pants. Then he took the violin carefully and looked at it with wide eyes. "Wow," he breathed. "This is beautiful!"

He closed his eyes for a minute and then began to play. From the expression on Eldest Brother's face, I knew that he liked the sound of what he was hearing.

When Matthew finished, Eldest Brother stood silent and then smiled. "It's certainly clear that you have not been playing very long. But you have a nice feel for the violin."

Matthew looked almost scared. "Then . . . then . . ."

Eldest Brother smiled more widely. "All right, I'll give you lessons. We can start after dinner tonight, if you want. Why don't you stay and eat with us?"

Matthew accepted and went to phone his parents for permission. When he came back he asked if he could go to the bathroom.

I was surprised. Did Americans always take a bath before dinner?

"Is it all right if you didn't take a bath just now?" I asked him. "Our tub has something in it."

It was Matthew's turn to look surprised. "I don't need a bath."

"Then why did you tell me you wanted one?" I demanded.

"I just want to go to the toilet," he explained. He began to laugh. "And you thought I actually asked to take a bath? Without someone making me?"

I laughed too. This was not like Jake and the others laughing at me for standing at attention when the teacher came in. We were laughing together because we were sharing a joke. I began to like Matthew very much.

When he came out of the bathroom, he looked shocked. "Was I seeing things, or were there really fish swimming in your bathtub?"

"That's just some carp my mother bought in Chinatown today. We're having them for dinner tonight."

"But they're alive!"

"Of course they're alive!" I snorted. "My mother would never buy dead fish. They're not fresh."

"I've never had live fish," Matthew said, as we went downstairs. "The fish I eat are nice and dead. They come in a can, or they're frozen sticks covered with bread crumbs."

When we came into the dining room, Matthew was muttering, ". . . cut up tea bags, knobs on orange crates, fish in the bathtub . . ."

"Does your friend always talk to himself?" whispered Second Sister as I helped her set the table.

I just smiled. It was a good thing that Second Sister couldn't hear what he was saying.

Matthew was our first American dinner guest. Father nodded approval when Eldest Brother introduced him as my friend and said he had a very good ear.

When we eat dinner, we normally help ourselves to food from the platters in the middle of the table. But since Matthew was my guest, I acted as a host and served him the food.

After a while I noticed that he wasn't eating much. He spent most of the time staring at the chopsticks in my right hand.

"What's wrong?" I asked.

"I've never used chopsticks before," he admitted sheepishly.

"Why don't you give him a fork, Yingtao?" suggested mother.

"No, please," Matthew said quickly. "I really want to learn how to use chopsticks."

So I taught him. I showed him how to grip one of the two sticks steady and jiggle the other stick to close down on the piece of meat.

He managed to eat most of the food I served him, but I noticed he didn't eat much of the fish. "I'm not used to eating someone I saw swimming just a little while ago," he whispered apologetically.

Matthew learned fast, and by the end of the meal he was using chopsticks pretty well. "Hey, this is good finger exercise!" he joked. "I bet it's going to help my violin playing."

"If that's true, then why doesn't Fourth Brother play a little better?" sniffed Second Sister. "He's been using chopsticks since he was two years old!"

Matthew gave me a sympathetic smile. I was used to remarks from my family about my violin playing, but it was nice to have someone who was on my side.

From that day on Matthew was my best friend. I didn't have to stand by myself at recess anymore, and we helped each other a lot in school.

Think, Talk and Write

Talk About It *Yang the Youngest and His Terrible Ear* reminds us that it is not always easy to make new friends. What are some ways to make new friends?

1. Why do you think the author included some of the Yang family's traditions? In what ways do you think the traditions added to the story? **Think Like an Author**

2. What does Yingtao need most at the beginning of the story? How does that change by the end? **Sequence**

3. When summarizing a story, you include only important details. Which two of the following statements would you leave out of a summary of the story? Why? **Summarize**

    a. Yingtao just moved from China to America.

    b. The conductor wanted Yingtao to play the triangle.

    c. Third Sister was asked to play a solo in the concert.

4. Reread the story. Make a list of the words with suffixes and underline the base word in each. **Vocabulary**

Look Back and Write How did Yingtao make a new friend by doing something he was not very good at?

Meet author Lensey Namioka on page 377.

Retell

W2.2.a Write responses to literature: Demonstrate an understanding of the literary work.

Writing

Prompt In *Yang the Youngest and His Terrible Ear,* joining the orchestra helps Yingtao feel comfortable in a new culture. Think about other experiences that might bring diverse people together. Now write a story about it.

Writing Trait

Precise **word choice** helps readers clearly picture the story events.

Student Model

A New Friend for Hanna

Hanna was nervous as she entered her new fourth-grade classroom. **"Will the kids like me?"** she asked herself.

"Everyone, this is Hanna, your new classmate," the principal announced. "Hanna, this is your teacher, Mrs. Hall." **The class was silent.**

"Welcome to our class, Hanna," Mrs. Hall said. "Why don't you tell us about yourself?"

"Well," Hanna began, **"I just moved to California from Illinois last week.** I have a younger brother, and I like to read. The last book I read was <u>Because of Winn-Dixie</u>."

At recess, a girl walked toward Hanna. "Hi, my name is Kate. Have you seen the movie <u>Because of Winn-Dixie</u>?" she asked.

"No, but I'd really like to," Hanna said.

"Great! **Can you come over this weekend to watch it?"** Kate asked.

Characters and events are like those in real life.

Using precise words avoids wordiness.

Declarative and interrogative sentences are used correctly.

Use the beginning of this model to help you write your own story.

 W2.1.b Write narratives: Provide a context to enable the reader to imagine the world of the event.

43

Turning Points

Sequence is the order in which events happen. Writers often use clue words such as *first, then,* and *finally* or dates and times of day to show the order in which things happen.

Time lines can help you picture and remember the order of important events.

 Ready to Try It?
Read "Gold Mountain." Look for dates and times of day that help you understand the sequence.

Concept Link

California has more new immigrants than any other state. Think about what it would be like to move to a new country. Make a list of the challenges an immigrant might face.

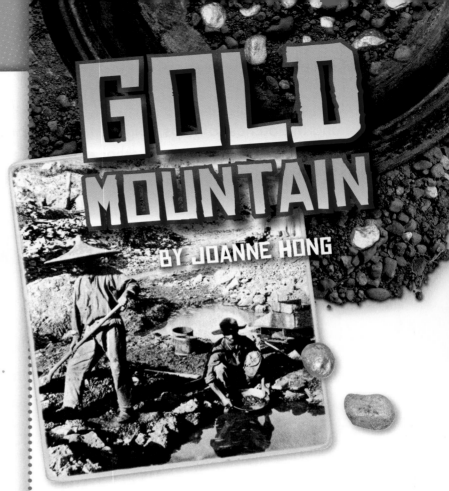

GOLD MOUNTAIN

BY JOANNE HONG

The first Chinese immigrants arrived in California on a ship named *Eagle* in February 1848. They arrived just a few months before gold was discovered in the American River near Coloma. After hearing the news, more Chinese immigrants came to find *Gam Sann*— "gold mountain."

While a lucky few Chinese immigrants got rich in the gold mines, thousands of others worked at low-paying jobs. They fished. They farmed. They helped build the nation's first transcontinental railroad.

With so many Chinese immigrants coming to their state, some native Californians got angry. They felt these immigrants were taking jobs away from them. So in 1882, lawmakers passed a strict law known as the Chinese Exclusion Act. It allowed only a few Chinese immigrants into the United States each year.

In 1910, an immigration station was built on Angel Island to process incoming Asian immigrants. They had to stop there before entering the United States. Many were denied entry and sent straight back to China. Others were forced to remain on Angel Island, living in detention buildings.

In 1943, the U.S. Congress finally put an end to the Chinese Exclusion Act. But even after that, only 102 Chinese were admitted into the United States each year. Lawmakers eventually put a stop to this practice as well.

Reading Across Texts

Think about the first Chinese immigrants in California in 1848. Think about what Yingtao wanted most after moving to America. Use a Venn diagram to compare and contrast the goals of the immigrants and Yingtao's goals.

Writing Across Texts

Using your Venn diagram, write a short paragraph explaining what immigrants might be searching for when they come to America.

CHINESE IMMIGRATION

| 1845 | 1855 | 1865 | 1875 | 1885 | 1895 | 1905 | 1915 | 1925 | 1935 | 1945 |

1848
First Chinese arrive in California.

1865
Central Pacific Railroad recruits Chinese workers to build Transcontinental Railroad.

1882
Chinese Exclusion Act passed.

1910
Immigration station built on Angel Island off the coast of San Francisco.

1943
Congress repeals Chinese Exclusion Act.

Build Language

Opportunities

Build Vocabulary

Learn ◉ **Skill Root Words** A root word is a word from which other words are made. For example, the root of *happiness* is *happy*. As you read, you may come to a word whose meaning you do not know. If you can identify the root, it might help you understand the meaning of the word.

Practice Look for root words in this week's Words to Know. Use a dictionary to write down the meanings of the roots. Then read "A Hard Life" on page 47.

Words to Know	accounts	wages	contractor
	assortment	employment	distinction
	hardware		

On Your Own Read "A Hard Life" again. Choose a root word from one of this week's Words to Know. Use a dictionary to make a list of other words that use this same root.

R1.3 Use knowledge of root words to determine the meanings of unknown words in a passage.

A Hard Life

In 1848, President James Polk reported that the accounts saying that gold that had been discovered in California were true. Soon, people from all over the world flocked to California.

At first, mining gold was easy. All miners needed was an assortment of tools, such as a pick, a shovel, and a pan. By the 1850s, however, gold was more difficult to find. Miners had to design new hardware to help them. The Long Tom was a large wooden rocker into which miners shoveled dirt. Then they rocked the object back and forth to separate dirt from gold.

At the time, average wages for workers were between six and ten dollars per day. Because they could not make enough money mining gold, many people found employment using the skills they brought with them. Some people could make more money as a storeowner or contractor than they could as miners.

Life for miners during the Gold Rush was not easy. Many died from drowning while searching for gold. Others became sick due to a poor diet and unhealthy living conditions. However, a lucky few had the distincion of finding gold and changing their lives forever.

 Need a Review?
For additional help with root words, see *Words!* on p. W•4.

 Ready to Try It?
Read *Hurry Freedom* on pp. 50–61.

Build Comprehension

Learn   **Skill Author's Purpose**

- The author's purpose is the reason or reasons an author has for writing a text.

- An author may write to persuade, to inform, to entertain, or to express ideas and feelings.

- Text features and the language an author uses can be clues to the purpose

- Look at the map on the right. How can this graphic source help you understand the author's purpose?

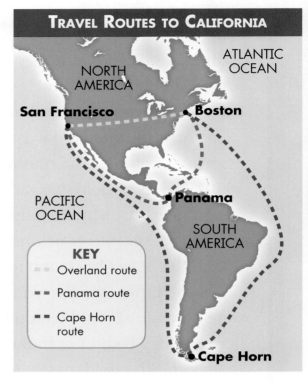

Travelers had several options for traveling to California. Which would you choose?

Practice   As you read "Gold Fever" on page 49, try to determine the author's purpose.

On Your Own   **Write to Read** Reread "Gold Fever." Use both the text and the map above to write a paragraph explaining the author's purpose for writing this passage.

 Need a Review? See the *Picture It!* lesson on p. PI•2 for additional help with author's purpose.

Ready to Try It?
As you read *Hurry Freedom* on pp. 50–61, use what you learned about author's purpose to help you understand the text.

G2R2.3 Use knowledge of the author's purpose(s) to comprehend informational text.

Gold Fever

In January 1848, James Marshall discovered gold in the area that is present-day Sacramento. A year later gold fever spread across the country.

By 1849, people from all over the world rushed to California in search of gold. The journey to California was a long and hard one. Many crossed the deserts and mountains of the U.S. with wagons carrying all the gear, tools, and food needed for six months. Many died from sickness, starvation, and drowning.

Two water routes to California also allowed travel by sea. Some people traveled around South America. It took five to seven months. Others made their way to California on steamships to Panama. The route through the jungles of Panama was quicker, but much more dangerous. After their journey, people arrived on the Pacific Coast tired, hungry, and with little money. They did not know they still had to travel another 150 miles.

Though there was great excitement about finding gold, travelers to California faced many hardships in their search to get rich.

Skill Preview the article. Do you think the author's purpose is to persuade, to inform, to entertain, or to express ideas and feelings?

Skill How does this information reveal the author's purpose?

Skill How can the language that an author uses be a clue to the purpose?

Jerry Stanley

HURRY FREEDOM

African Americans in Gold Rush California

Genre

Expository nonfiction gives information about real people and events. As you read, think about the opportunities that freedom brings.

How does the
search for
gold provide
opportunities
for people?

51

In 1850, an African American named Mifflin Gibbs decided to leave his home in Pennsylvania and go to California. At the age of twenty-five, Mifflin borrowed money from friends, packed a suitcase, and boarded a steamer from New York to Panama. It would take him nearly six months to travel by boat, mule, and foot, and he would spend $800 before he finally arrived in California. Gibbs, and other African Americans, arrived in California with little or no money, but with plenty of hope for freedom and opportunities.

On September 9, 1850, Mifflin Gibbs disembarked from the *Golden Gate,* whose deck was littered with trash. He carried a banged-up suitcase and had the look of a man who needed a new life. Not knowing anyone in San Francisco, he walked the busy streets, apparently without a specific plan or a vision of his future. Although stories of striking it rich had drawn him to California, he never said if he intended to mine for gold. Gibbs was articulate and intelligent and may have viewed California as just a place where he might succeed, if given an opportunity.

This photograph of Mifflin Gibbs was taken when he was in his forties.

San Francisco, 1851. Hundreds of ships lie abandoned in the harbor, their crews having left them for the gold fields.

He quickly discovered that San Francisco might not be the place to turn his life around. Most stores and businesses displayed signs reading "No Negroes" and "No Coloreds Allowed," and whites avoided him as he made his way around the city. He wasn't surprised. With only a few pennies in his pocket, at least he didn't have to worry about being robbed.

View of San Francisco in 1850, the year of Gibbs's arrival.

He kept wandering until he saw several black men talking in front of a hotel on Kearney Street. It wasn't the best looking place, but it was black-owned, and Gibbs entered. The sign above the clerk read "Board $12 a week IN ADVANCE." Gibbs said, "Had I looked through a magnifying glass the letters could not have appeared larger. They seemed to ask, 'Who are you and do you have any money?' It wasn't the first time that he had been totally broke, but it was his first time to be broke three thousand miles from home.

He left the hotel, and after several attempts to find employment of any kind, he approached a house under construction and asked the contractor for work. The man didn't need any help, but Gibbs kept asking for just a few days' work or a few hours'. The wages were ten dollars a day and the contractor finally agreed to give Gibbs two days' work if he would accept nine dollars a day. He agreed, but there was a catch: he had to have his own tools.

Now walking with a purpose, he came upon a large tent with an assortment of hardware and the tools he needed. After telling the merchant that he had no money but had a job, the man looked him over and proclaimed, "All right, take them."

"I felt great relief," Gibbs said, "when I paid the merchant and my landlord on the following Saturday."

It was a start, but Gibbs's job only lasted two days. The white carpenters refused to work with an African American and threatened to strike if Gibbs wasn't fired. He was a good carpenter, at least as good as the others. The contractor didn't want to let Gibbs go and made him an offer. If he could find six carpenters with his skills who would work with him, the contractor would fire his workforce and hire Gibbs's crew. "I could not find the men he wanted," Gibbs said, "or other employment of that kind." He had tools and a few dollars in his pocket, but San Francisco wasn't any different from Philadelphia. He would have to try something else.

Photograph of San Francisco taken in 1851.

Black and white miners working together to open a sluice in Spanish Flat, 1852.

Most black prospectors were in the same situation and some were quick to find a way out. Having failed at mining for themselves, a few hundred went to work for white miners. Many whites believed that blacks had a special gift for finding gold, and they had money to hire people to work for them. African Americans had no special gift, but they took advantage of the belief. They acted as if possessed by magic, and said they had dreams that told of riches for their employers. They earned about eight dollars a day, and by working in choice areas they found gold and kept the belief alive.

When employers mentioned these hired hands, they did so with indifference, almost as an afterthought. An ex-slave named Isadore, an elderly man, pounded rocks with a hand hammer for twelve hours a day and mined an average of seventy-five dollars' worth of gold a day for Franklin Morse. Morse remarked in passing that Isadore "was saving most of the eight dollars in wages to buy his wife's freedom." Another wrote casually, "I hired a Negro man to dig for me. He hopes to redeem his wife and seven children from slavery." The accounts totally missed the drama of the work, work that resulted in freedom.

Slaves in California hit the same wall as the black prospectors from the North. Some were allowed by their owners to go on their own to the gold fields, but the mining associations drove them off and they ended up at the locations where free blacks searched for gold. They had about as much luck, but some succeeded and bought their freedom.

Alvin Coffey was an example. A slave from Missouri, Coffey was brought to California in 1849. After mining for eight months, he earned $5,000, and by washing clothes for miners at night, he earned another $700. Coffey's owner took the money, broke his promise of freedom, and brought Coffey back to Missouri, where he was sold at auction. He asked for a second chance, which his new owner granted, setting the price for Coffey's freedom at $1,500. He had the money after four months of mining, and he was set free.

Alvin Coffey

Slaves also earned their freedom by cooking for whites or finding other jobs. George Washington Dennis was a remarkable example. He was owned by Green Dennis. After they arrived in San Francisco in 1849, Green Dennis formed a partnership with others to operate the Eldorado Hotel. George Dennis was paid fifty cents a day to sweep the floor, which was made of rough lumber.

After working for three months, and collecting five-and ten-cent pieces that had fallen on the floor, Dennis had $1,000, which his owner accepted, granting his freedom. He kept sweeping and eyeballing the floor until he earned another $950, which he used to buy freedom for his mother. Afterward, Dennis hired his mother to serve hot meals at stiff prices: five dollars for a bowl of stew, two dollars for a chunk of corn bread. They netted an average profit of $225 a day, some of which was used to buy relatives out of slavery.

George Washington
Dennis

At least three hundred people worked their way out of slavery in California by finding gold or working at other jobs. They earned $750,000 for their owners and used surplus wages to buy freedom for family members in the South. Meanwhile, slaves continued to arrive in California. The total stayed at about six hundred throughout the Gold Rush period. This included slaves who came with their owners and slaves who came by themselves to earn money for their owners and, perhaps, buy freedom.

An African American prospector works at a sluice box, Auburn Ravine, 1851.

San Francisco, 1849, corner of Clay and Dupont Streets. Gibbs would later establish his boot and shoe business on Clay Street.

After losing his carpenter job, Mifflin Gibbs became a bootblack. Normally, a bootblack polishes shoes. But in San Francisco, a rainy city with hundreds of horses, a bootblack first scraped mud and animal droppings from boots and then applied polish. Gibbs probably chose the job because of the pay. He worked in front of the hotels and earned an average of twelve dollars a day, more than he could have made as a carpenter had he been able to work at that trade.

After nine months of removing muck, he had earned nearly $2,000, ten times what he could have earned in Philadelphia. Gibbs now had hats that were in fashion, several pairs of shoes, and three new suits, which he wore after work. He looked good when he shopped for groceries and personal items in the stores where he was welcome.

Because he was friendly and because clean shoes were much desired, Gibbs came to know hundreds of whites and most African Americans in the city, including William Hall and George Washington Dennis. San Francisco's population grew larger every week, but it was a small city for the five hundred African Americans who lived there. Their neighborhood spanned about three blocks and included the hotel where he now boarded as a resident. Although his work was in the white section of town, his neighborhood was home, a place where friends could meet and talk without looking over their shoulders. Besides new clothes, Gibbs bought a subscription to the *North Star* and was known among his friends as an acquaintance of Frederick Douglass, a distinction of some merit.

The experiences of African Americans in the early years of the Gold Rush ranged from sudden riches to more poverty, the latter being typical. Most found no gold. A few hundred went to work for whites, while others, like Gibbs, seized opportunities in San Francisco.

Think, Talk and Write

Talk About It Moving to a new place is not easy. Think about Mifflin Gibbs's experiences during the Gold Rush. In your opinion, was his struggle worth the move?

1. The author first tells of Mifflin Gibbs's early days in California. Then the author tells about other people. Why does the author include information about other African Americans?
Think Like an Author

2. Do you think the author's purpose in *Hurry Freedom* was to teach readers something? Explain why or why not.
Author's Purpose

3. How did Mifflin Gibbs feel when he first arrived in San Francisco? How did his feelings change by the end of the selection? Use examples from the text to explain your answer. **Answer Questions**

4. What are the roots of of the words *employment*, *contractor*, and *distinction*? **Vocabulary**

TEST PRACTICE ★ **Look Back and Write** Mifflin Gibbs was an African American searching for a better life during the California Gold Rush. Was he successful? Explain your answer.

Meet author Jerry Stanley on page 379.

Summarize

W2.2.a Write responses to literature: Demonstrate an understanding of the literary work.

Writing

Prompt *Hurry Freedom* tells about courageous men who seek opportunity far from home. Think about other times in history when people found opportunity in a new place. Now write an expository composition about it.

Writing Trait

Focus of writing **includes essential information.**

Student Model

Coming to the United States

Li Keng was seven years old in 1933 when her family moved from China to the United States.

The Keng family boarded the steamship, the USS Hoover. It took nineteen long days to cross the Pacific Ocean.

They arrived in San Francisco, California, and then moved to Oakland. Li and her siblings went to school and worked hard to learn English.

The family didn't have much money, but they were able to open a restaurant. **And that's just what her father did!** Li grew up waiting tables. In 1948, the Kengs were finally able to buy a house.

With hard work and dedication, Li and her family had achieved the American dream. **Don't let anyone tell you that you can't do something.** Just like the Kengs, you can do anything.

Expository nonfiction tells about real people, places, and events.

The composition includes essential information.

Writer uses **exclamatory and imperative sentences.**

Turning Points

Use the model to help you write an expository composition.

W1.2.c Create multiple-paragraph compositions: Include supporting paragraphs with simple facts, details, and explanations.

63

Persuasive devices are techniques authors use to make readers think a certain way. Sometimes authors will use the testimony of other people. Sometimes they will use words and phrases that arouse your emotions and promise you great things. Learning persuasive devices can help you understand an author's purpose.

 Ready to Try It?
Read "The Lure of the West." Look for testimonials and promises in the advertisements.

Concept Link

When people moved to California during the Gold Rush, they dreamed of getting rich. Imagine that your family had moved to California during this time. What kinds of opportunities would you expect to find in Gold Rush California?

THE LURE OF THE WEST

By Erin Gerad

Get Rich Quick!

Make thousands of dollars a day from home!

We've all seen advertisements like these in newspapers, in junk mail, or plastered on walls around town. While most people know that it takes a lot of hard work to make money, the hope of "striking it rich" has always been a big part of the American dream.

In fact, it was this hope of striking it rich that set off one of this country's largest migrations of people—the California Gold Rush. In the 1850's, thousands of people became infected with "gold fever." Many were persuaded to move out west by advertisements and stories in newspapers.

Newspapers helped spread gold fever by printing stories about real people who discovered gold. These testimonials were often printed letters from miners to their families back East, telling of gold nuggets as big as eggs. After hearing these stories, many people believed that they too could get rich mining for gold.

Newspapers also carried advertisements for tools and ways to travel to California. Many of these advertisements used words in bold capital letters to lure people to move west. Words such as "INEXHAUSTIBLE GOLD MINES" convinced people that there was plenty of gold and that it was never too late. Some ads offered passage out west on "NEW AND MAGNIFICENT CLIPPER SHIPS."

Unfortunately, what these ads didn't mention were the dangers people faced while traveling to California or how difficult it could be to survive once they arrived. A majority of people would never strike it rich.

AN ACCOUNT OF

CALIFORNIA, AND THE WONDERFUL GOLD REGIONS.

A New Arrival at the Gold Diggings.

WITH A DESCRIPTION OF
The Different Routes to California;
Information about the Country, and the Ancient and Modern Discoveries of Gold;
How to Test Precious Metals; Accounts of Gold Hunters;
TOGETHER WITH MUCH OTHER
Useful Reading for those going to California, or having Friends there.
ILLUSTRATED WITH MAPS AND ENGRAVINGS.

BOSTON:
PUBLISHED BY J. B. HALL, 66 CORNHILL.
For Sale at Skinner's Publication Rooms, 60½ Cornhill.

Price, 12½ cents.

EL DORADO
OF THE
UNITED STATES OF AMERICA.
THE DISCOVERY
OF
INEXHAUSTIBLE GOLD MINES
IN
CALIFORNIA.
TREMENDOUS EXCITEMENT AMONG THE AMERICANS.
The Extensive Preparations
TO
MIGRATE TO THE GOLD REGIONS,
&c., &c., &c.

The great discovery of gold, in dust, scales, and lumps of quicksilver, platina, cinnabar, &c., &c., on the shores of the Pacific, has thrown the American people into a state of the wildest excitement. The intelligence from California, that gold can picked up in lumps, weighing six

Reading Across Texts

Many people move to new places for better opportunities. Think about what it would be like if your family moved to a new state. Discuss how you would feel about moving.

Writing Across Texts Think about the discussion you just had. Design an advertisement to persuade people to move to your area. Include any information you think would make people excited about moving.

Build Language

Traveling America

Build Vocabulary

Learn

◉ **Skill Multiple-Meaning Words** Sometimes a word has more than one meaning. For example, the word *stick* can mean "a long piece of wood" or "to fasten something." You can use context—the words and sentences around a word—to give you clues to the meaning. You can also use a dictionary, which will have a number next to each new meaning.

Practice

Use a dictionary to help you figure out the meanings of this week's Words to Know. Which of these words have multiple meanings? Then read "Becoming American" on page 67.

Words to Know	homeland	towering	longed
	bewildered	sculptures	still
	amazed		

On Your Own

Read "Becoming American" again. See if you can find other words in the passage that have multiple meanings. Use a dictionary to help you write down the different definitions.

Becoming American

People from around the world have been moving to the United States since it became a country. They left their homeland full of hope. Immigrants spent weeks crossing the treacherous ocean. Many arrived in strange cities that did not welcome them. The English language and the new customs in the United States bewildered them. Often they could get only low paying jobs that others did not want.

However, immigrants found much that amazed them. There was real freedom for U.S. citizens. There was a feeling that anyone could work hard and have a better life. Towering buildings called skyscrapers soared into the air. They seemed like sculptures that symbolized the power and promise of the new land.

Energy and growth were all around the immigrants. They learned a new language and new customs. They worked tirelessly and contributed to their new country. Eventually, the newcomers were accepted.

The new life did not take away the pain of loss, though. New Americans longed for the sights and people they had left behind. Having a better life did not still their feelings for their homelands.

 Need a Review?
For additional help with multiple-meaning words, see *Words!* on p. W•10.

 Ready to Try It?
Read *Grandfather's Journey* on pp. 70–81.

Build Comprehension

Learn **Skill** **Sequence**

- Sequence means the order in which things happen. Sequence can also mean the steps people follow to do something.

- Dates, times, and clue words such as *first, then, next, after,* and *last* can help you identify the sequence.

- Sometimes two or more events happen at the same time. Words such as *while, meanwhile,* and *during* can show this.

- Using a graphic organizer such as the one below can help you remember the order of events.

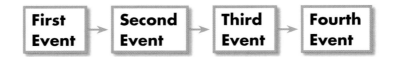

| First Event | → | Second Event | → | Third Event | → | Fourth Event |

Practice As you read "Moving to California" on page 69, look for dates, times, and clue words that reveal the sequence.

On Your Own **Write to Read** Reread "Moving to California." Use the text to make a time line showing when different people immigrated to California.

 Need a Review? See the *Picture It!* lesson on p. PI•13 for additional help with sequence.

▷ **Ready to Try It?** As you read *Grandfather's Journey* on pp. 70–81, use what you learned about sequence to help you understand the text.

🐻 **G5R2.2** Analyze text that is organized in sequential or chronological order.

Moving to CALIFORNIA

Over time, many different groups of people have moved to California and made it their home. Because of this, California has a diverse population.

In 1542, a man from Spain named Juan Cabrillo arrived in California. Many people from Spain moved to California after that. Then, starting in 1841, many farmers from throughout the United States moved to California.

After gold was found in California in 1848, thousands of people from Europe, Asia, and other parts of the world moved there. They hoped to become rich. Many of these people came from China.

By 1852, one out of every ten people who lived in California was from China. But a new law in 1882 said that no one from China was allowed to move to the United States for ten years. During that same time, many people from Japan were moving to California.

Today, more people live in California than in any other state in the United States.

Skill Which of the following events took place first? How do you know?
(a) People moved to California hoping to become rich.
(b) Juan Cabrillo arrived in California.
(c) Farmers moved to California.

Skill Sometimes two events happen at the same time. Which event took place while people from Japan were moving to California?

Skill Which clue word helps you understand the sequence? What date would you put on a time line?

Grandfather's Journey

**written and illustrated
by Allen Say**

Genre

Historical fiction is set in the past. It is a story in which some of the details are factual but in which others are made up or are loosely based on history. Look for the factual details as you read.

**Where does a grandfather's journey take him and
what does he learn along the way?**

My grandfather was a young man when he left his home in Japan and went to see the world.

He wore European clothes for the first time and began his journey on a steamship. The Pacific Ocean astonished him.

For three weeks he did not see land. When land finally appeared it was the New World.

He explored North America by train and riverboat, and often walked for days on end.

Deserts with rocks like enormous sculptures amazed him.

The endless farm fields reminded him of the ocean he had crossed.

Huge cities of factories and tall buildings bewildered and yet excited him.

He marveled at the towering mountains and rivers as clear as the sky.

He met many people along the way. He shook hands with black men and white men, with yellow men and red men.

The more he traveled, the more he longed to see new places, and never thought of returning home.

Of all the places he visited, he liked California best. He loved the strong sunlight there, the Sierra Mountains, the lonely seacoast.

After a time, he returned to his village in Japan to marry his childhood sweetheart. Then he brought his bride to the new country.

They made their home by the San Francisco Bay and had a baby girl.

As his daughter grew, my grandfather began to think about his own childhood. He thought about his old friends.

He remembered the mountains and rivers of his home. He surrounded himself with songbirds, but he could not forget.

Finally, when his daughter was nearly grown, he could wait no more. He took his family and returned to his homeland.

Once again he saw the mountains and rivers of his childhood. They were just as he had remembered them.

Once again he exchanged stories and laughed with his old friends.

But the village was not a place for a daughter from San Francisco. So my grandfather bought a house in a large city nearby.

There, the young woman fell in love, married, and sometime later I was born.

When I was a small boy, my favorite weekend was a visit to my grandfather's house. He told me many stories about California.

He raised warblers and silvereyes, but he could not forget the mountains and rivers of California. So he planned a trip.

But a war began. Bombs fell from the sky and scattered our lives like leaves in a storm.

When the war ended, there was nothing left of the city and of the house where my grandparents had lived

So they returned to the village where they had been children. But my grandfather never kept another songbird.

The last time I saw him, my grandfather said that he longed to see California one more time. He never did.

And when I was nearly grown, I left home and went to see California for myself.

After a time, I came to love the land my grandfather had loved, and I stayed on and on until I had a daughter of my own.

But I also miss the mountains and rivers of my childhood. I miss my old friends. So I return now and then, when I cannot still the longing in my heart.

The funny thing is, the moment I am in one country, I am homesick for the other.

I think I know my grandfather now. I miss him very much.

Think, Talk and Write

Talk About It If Grandfather could describe his journey, what do you think he would say? Look at each picture and tell what Grandfather might be saying about his experiences.

1. Allen Say's paintings are like photographs. Why do you think he made his paintings so lifelike? **Think Like an Author**

2. In your own words, summarize what happened in Grandfather's life from the time he arrived in America until he returned to Japan the final time. **Sequence**

3. Create a graphic organizer for the story to describe what happens at the beginning, middle, and end. **Graphic Organizers**

4. The word *left* on page 79 is a multiple-meaning word. Use what you learned about multiple-meaning words to determine the word's meanings. **Vocabulary**

TEST PRACTICE

Look Back and Write What does Grandfather's journey teach him? Review the story and write a paragraph that describes what he learns.

Meet author **Allen Say on page 378.**

Retell

W2.2.a Write responses to literature: Demonstrate an understanding of the literary work.

Writing

Prompt *Grandfather's Journey* describes different places in America that became important to the author's grandfather. Think about other people who came to America long ago. Now write a story about one person's journey to America.

Writing Trait

Use **precise nouns** to clearly express your ideas.

Student Model

A New Home

Mildred was thirteen years old when she left Poland and traveled to the United States to live with her Aunt Franny in New York City. Franny paid for the journey across the enormous Atlantic Ocean.

As the **steamship entered** New York Harbor in 1906, Milred still remembers the first thing she saw, the magnificent Statue of Liberty. She still talks about what it was like to visit Central Park, splashing in the cool water of the lake and running through the large, grassy park.

When she was fifteen, Milred went to work in a dress factory. By listening to others around her and going to night school, **she learned** English.

Years later, when she was 18 years old, Mildred met a man on a visit to Coney Island. A couple of years later, she married him.

The **United States is** her home, but sometimes she wonders what it would be like if she were still in Poland.

Historical fiction includes historical details to add realism.

Precise nouns express ideas clearly.

Subjects and predicates agree.

Use the model to help you write your own historical fiction.

 W2.1.a Relate ideas, observations, or recollections of an event or experience.

83

Turning Points

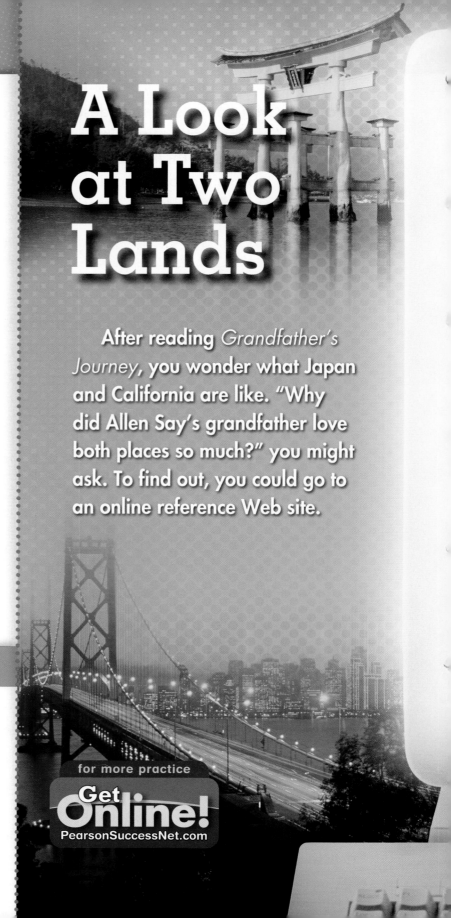

A Look at Two Lands

Online reference sources look a lot like print sources, and they are organized in the same way. Instead of turning pages by hand, you use a mouse to click your way through the information. Other text features include search windows, which allow readers to type in information they are looking for, and links, underlined words and phrases, which also take readers to specific information.

 Ready to Try It?
Read "A Look at Two Lands." Use the text features of an online reference source to locate information.

After reading *Grandfather's Journey*, you wonder what Japan and California are like. "Why did Allen Say's grandfather love both places so much?" you might ask. To find out, you could go to an online reference Web site.

Concept Link

California has more than 1,300 miles of coastline. If you were planning to hike along the coast of California, which part of the state would you choose? What kind of weather would you find?

for more practice
Get Online!
PearsonSuccessNet.com

84

At the site, you find links to a dictionary, an encyclopedia, and other reference sources. You decide to click on the encyclopedia link.

File   Edit   View   Favorites   Tools   Help

http://www.url.here

ONLINE REFERENCE WEB SITE

Atlas   **Almanac**   **Dictionary**   **Encyclopedia**

File   Edit   View   Favorites   Tools   Help

http://w

Japan   Search

This takes you to the encyclopedia search page, where you type the search term *Japan* into the SEARCH window. A new page opens with your search results.

ENCYCLOPEDIA

Japan

Japan [jə pan′] In Japanese, Nihon or Nippon; a country (2007 est. pop. 127,433,494), 145,833 sq mi (377,835 sq km), off the coast of eastern Asia. The capital is Tokyo, which, along with neighboring Yokohama, forms the world's most populous metropolitan region.

Now you decide to find out something about California. You find these results in an encyclopedia search.

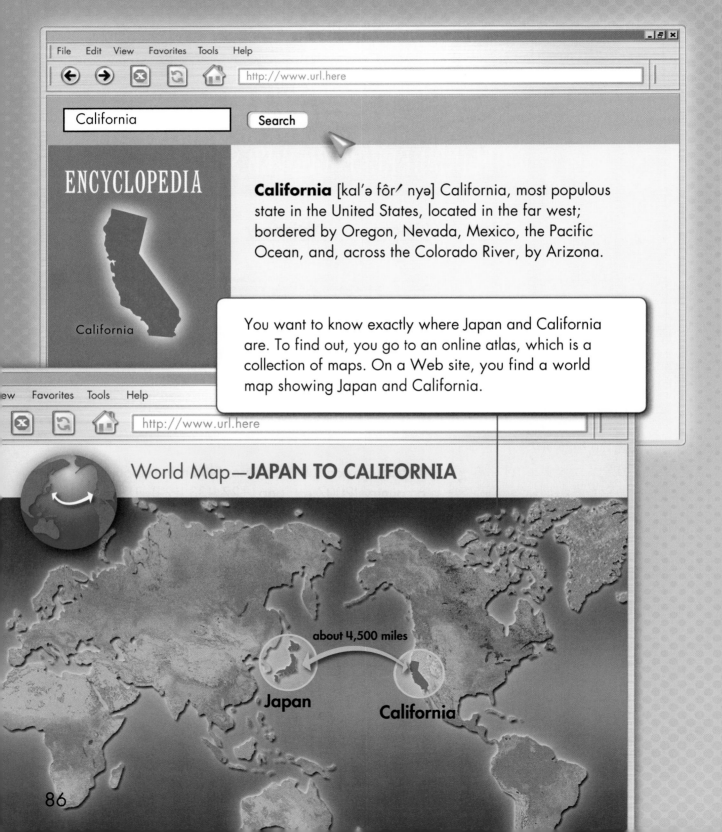

California [kal′ə fôr′ nyə] California, most populous state in the United States, located in the far west; bordered by Oregon, Nevada, Mexico, the Pacific Ocean, and, across the Colorado River, by Arizona.

You want to know exactly where Japan and California are. To find out, you go to an online atlas, which is a collection of maps. On a Web site, you find a world map showing Japan and California.

World Map—**JAPAN TO CALIFORNIA**

about 4,500 miles

Japan

California

File   Edit   View   Favorites   Tools

On another Web site, you find these photographs of Japan and California. Now you are beginning to understand why Allen Say's grandfather loved both places so much.

Scenes from
JAPAN

Scenes from
CALIFORNIA

As you have learned from your research, Japan and California are far apart. Yet both contain a beauty that can appeal to many people.

Reading Across Texts
Both Grandfather's Journey and "A Look at Two Lands" provide information about Japan and California. List the things you learned about Japan and California from the selections.

Writing Across Texts Look at the lists you made. In which place would you rather live? Write a paragraph to explain why you would want to live there.

Build Language

The Southwest

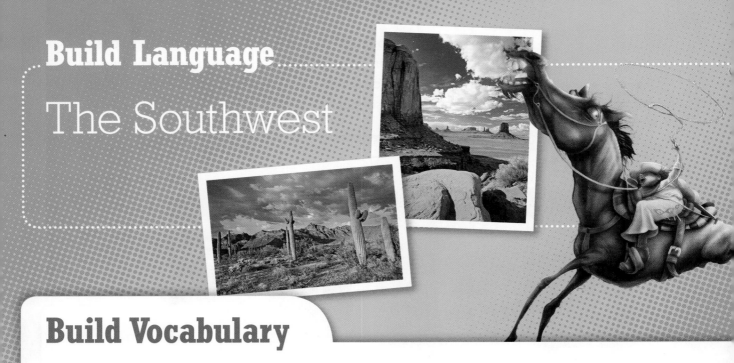

Build Vocabulary

Learn ◉ **Skill Synonyms** A synonym is a word that has almost the same meaning as another word. For example, *talk* and *chatter* are synonyms. However, a writer would use the word *chatter* to describe someone who talks constantly. Writers use synonyms to make their writing clear and interesting to readers.

Practice Use a dictionary to look up this week's Words to Know. Underline the words that you think would have a synonym. Then read "Tall Paul" on page 89.

Words to Know	prairie	bargain	offended
	lassoed	favor	shrieked
	riverbed		

On Your Own Use a thesaurus to look up the underlined words that you think have synonyms. Insert the new words in the passage. Write a short explanation about how the synonyms changed the meaning of the passage. Then read "Tall Paul" again.

R1.2 Apply knowledge of word origins, derivations, synonyms, antonyms, and idioms to determine meanings of words and phrases.

Tall Paul

Tall Paul was a cowboy who once lived on the plains. He was not just any cowboy, though. His legs were so long that he could cross a mile of prairie in only one step. He was so big and strong that he lassoed a whole herd of cattle with a single toss of his rope.

Tall Paul had a mighty big appetite too. He ate a mountain of flapjacks for breakfast. One time he got so thirsty he drank a river. The dry riverbed just lay there gasping for water.

Tall Paul felt bad about the river, so he struck a bargain with the sky. The sky would bring a flood of rain. In return, the sky asked this favor: "I will help you if you do me this service. My servant, Wind, can't blow the clouds over that mountain. I need you to flatten it a little."

Tall Paul said to the mountain, "Now don't be offended. I'll just take a little off the top." The mountain shrieked and screamed, but the deed was done. Tall Paul jumped on the mountain and turned it into a nice little mesa. Instantly the rain began to fall and soon the river was flowing again.

 Need a Review?
For additional help with synonyms, see *Words!* on p. W•3.

 Ready to Try It?
Read *The Horned Toad Prince* on pp. 92–105.

Build Comprehension

Learn   **Skill Author's Purpose**

- An author may write to persuade, to inform, to entertain, or to express ideas or feelings. Often an author has more than one purpose.

- The kinds of ideas and the way the author organizes a text can help you determine the author's purpose.

- An important reason for figuring out an author's purpose is to adjust the way you read according to what you are reading.

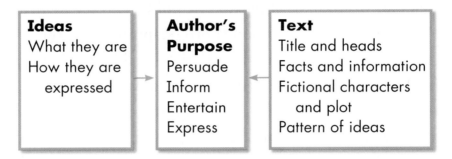

Ideas	**Author's Purpose**	**Text**
What they are	Persuade	Title and heads
How they are expressed	Inform	Facts and information
	Entertain	Fictional characters and plot
	Express	Pattern of ideas

Practice As you read "The Fox and the Grapes" on page 91, think about how there could be more than one purpose for the story.

On Your Own **Write to Read** Reread "The Fox and the Grapes." Write about an important lesson that you learned from reading the fable.

Need a Review? See the *Picture It!* lesson on p. PI•2 for additional help with author's purpose.

Ready to Try It? As you read *The Horned Toad Prince* on pp. 92–105, think about the author's purpose to help you understand the text.

 R2.2 Use appropriate strategies when reading for different purposes (e.g., full comprehension, location of information, personal enjoyment).

The Fox and the Grapes

Adapted from Aesop

Skill Look at the title, where the story comes from, and the illustrations. What do you think the author's purpose will be?

There once was a hungry fox who came upon a grapevine wound around a high trellis. Hanging from the vine was a bunch of grapes.

"What DEE-LISH-US-looking grapes," the fox said to himself. "I think I'll just step up and grab a few." So he stood up on his hind legs under the trellis, but the grapes were out of reach.

"Hmmm," said the fox. "Those DEE-licious grapes are higher up than I thought." So the fox jumped up as high as he could, but the grapes were still out of reach.

Skill Is the author's purpose what you thought it would be when you previewed the story? Why or why not?

"This is ridiculous," said the fox. "How hard can it be to grab some dee-licious grapes?" So the fox stepped back, took a running leap—and missed. The grapes were still out of reach.

"Humph!" said the fox, walking away with a little toss of his tail. "I thought at first those grapes looked delicious, but now I see they are sour."

Skill The purpose of a fable is usually to teach a lesson about life. How is the fox's behavior an example of how we sometimes act?

Turning Points

91

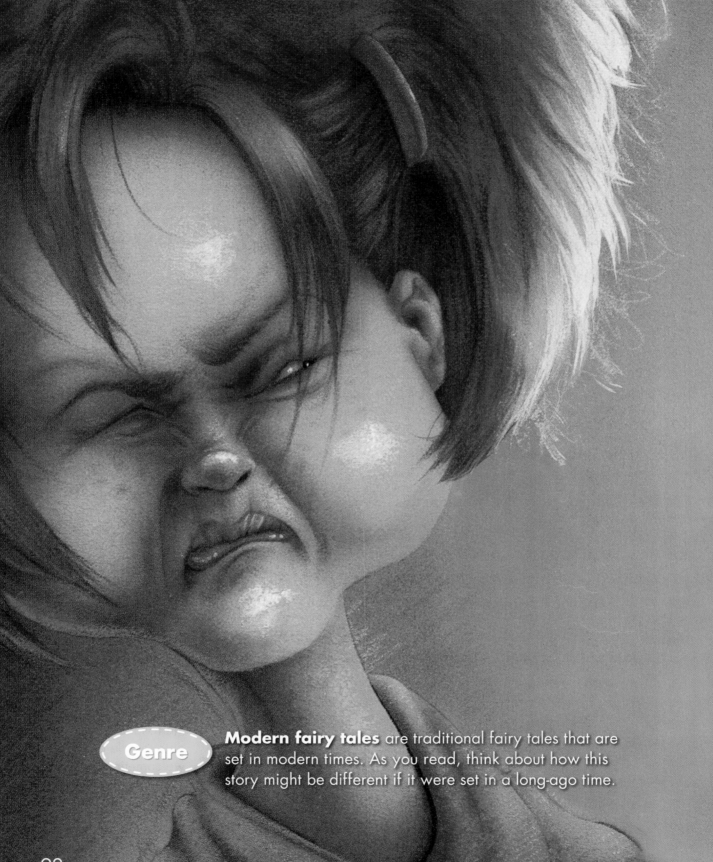

Genre

Modern fairy tales are traditional fairy tales that are set in modern times. As you read, think about how this story might be different if it were set in a long-ago time.

92

The Horned Toad Prince

by Jackie Mims Hopkins

illustrated by Michael Austin

How could a horned toad possibly be a prince?

Reba Jo loved to twang her guitar and sing while the prairie wind whistled through the thirsty sagebrush.

Singing with the wind was one of the ways Reba Jo entertained herself on the lonesome prairie. Sometimes she amused herself by racing her horse, Flash, against a tumbleweed cartwheeling across her daddy's land.

But her favorite pastime of all was roping. She lassoed cacti, water buckets, fence posts, and any unlucky critter that crossed her path.

One blustery morning, as she was riding
the range looking for something to lasso, Reba Jo came upon
a dry riverbed. Her daddy had warned her to stay away from
these *arroyos*. He'd told her that a prairie storm could blow
in quicker than a rattlesnake's strike, causing a flash flood to
rip through the riverbed. The swift water would wash away
anything or anyone in its way.

Reba Jo knew she should turn back. But right at the edge
of this gully she spied a vulture, all fat and sassy, sitting on top
of a dried-up old well, just daring her to toss her spinning rope
around his long ugly neck.

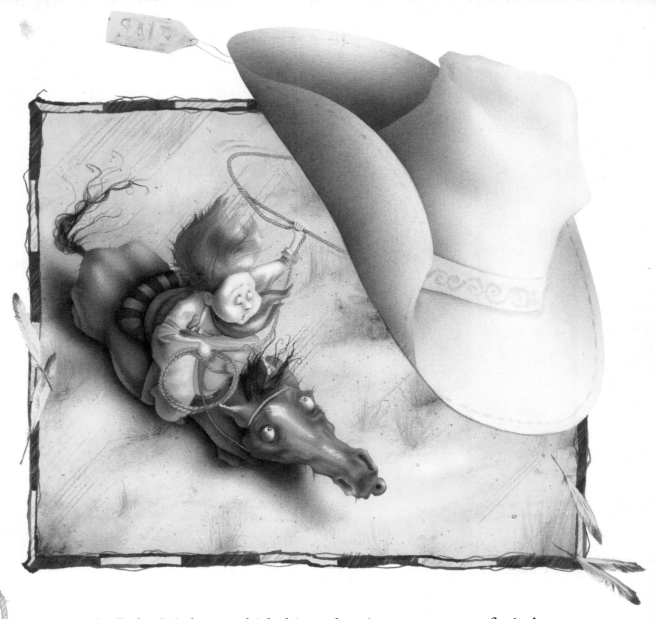

As Reba Jo's lasso whirled into the air, a great gust of wind
came whipping through the *arroyo* and blew her new cowgirl
hat right off her head and down to the bottom of the dusty
old well.

Reba Jo scrambled to the edge of the well. She peered
down into the darkness and commenced to crying. Suddenly
she heard a small voice say, *"¿Qué pasa, señorita?"*

She looked around and wondered if the wind blowing
through the *arroyo* was fooling her ears.

But then, there in the sand, she spotted a big fat horned toad looking up at her. "What's the matter, *señorita?*" he asked again.

"Oh," she cried, "the brand-new hat my daddy bought for me just blew down into this stinkin' old well. I'll never be able to get it out, and I'll be in a peck of trouble when he finds out I've been playin' down here near the *arroyo.*"

The horned toad looked at her slyly and said, "I'll fetch your *sombrero* for you if you will do *tres pequeños* favors for me."

She sniffed and asked, "Three small favors? Like what?"

"All you have to do is feed me some chili, play your *guitarra* for me, and let me take a *siesta* in your *sombrero*."

"Some chili, a song, and a nap in my hat? I don't think so, *amigo*," replied Reba Jo.

"Okay, *señorita*, but do you mind if I follow you home and listen as you explain to your *padre* where your new *sombrero* is, and how it got there?"

"Good point, toad," Reba Jo said. "You've got yourself a deal."

Reba Jo placed the little critter in a splintered wooden bucket and carefully lowered him down the dry well, where he retrieved Reba Jo's hat.

Then, without so much as a *muchas gracias*, Reba Jo snatched her hat from the horned toad and galloped home. As she rode out of sight, she ignored the horned toad's cries of "*¡Espérate!* Wait up, *señorita*, wait up!"

'Long about midday, when Reba Jo had sat down to eat, she heard a tap, tap, tapping at the ranch house door.

Reba Jo opened the door, but when she saw it was the fat horned toad, she slammed the door in his face.

His small voice called, "*Señorita, señorita, por favor.* Please let me come in."

The horned toad rapped on the door again. This time Reba Jo's father opened it and spotted the little fella on the porch.

"*Hola, señor,*" said the horned toad.

"Well howdy, mister toad. What brings you here?"

"A little deal that I made with your daughter, *señor.*"

"What's this all about, Reba Jo?" her father asked her.

Reba Jo admitted that the horned toad had done her a favor and in return she had promised to feed him some chili, play her guitar for him, and let him take a nap in her hat.

"Now, Reba Jo," said her daddy, "if you strike a bargain in these parts, a deal's a deal. Come on in, pardner, you look mighty hungry."

"I am indeed. *Yo tengo mucha hambre*," said the horned toad. "I hope that is chili I smell." He peeked at Reba Jo's meal.

"Dadburn it!" Reba Jo muttered. She pushed her bowl of chili toward him.

Soon the horned toad's belly was bulging. "Now, for a little *serenata*," he said.

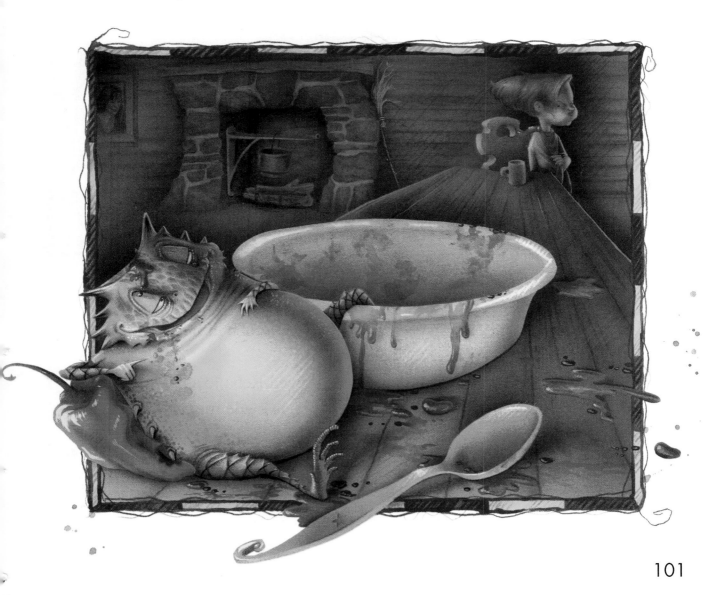

Reba Jo stomped over, grabbed her guitar, and belted out a lullaby for her guest.

Then the drowsy little horned toad eyed Reba Jo's hat and yawned, saying, "That lovely music has made me *muy soñoliento*. I'm ready for my *siesta*."

"Forget it, Bucko," Reba Jo snapped. "You're not gettin' near my hat. No lizard cooties allowed!"

"Now, señorita, remember what your wise *padre* said about striking a bargain in these parts," said the clever little horned toad.

"I know, I know," grumbled Reba Jo, "a deal's a deal." And with that, she flipped him into her hat.

"Before I take my *siesta*, I have just one more favor to ask," said the horned toad.

"Now what?" asked Reba Jo.

"Would you give me a kiss, *por favor?*" asked the horned toad.

"You've gotta be kiddin'!" shrieked Reba Jo. "You know dang well a kiss wasn't part of this deal, you low-life reptile."

"If you do this one last thing for me, we'll call it even, and I'll be on my way *pronto*," the horned toad said.

"You'll leave right away?" Reba Jo asked suspiciously. "You promise?"

"*Sí, te prometo,*" agreed the horned toad.

Reba Jo thought hard for a minute. She glared at the horned toad. "I can't believe I'm even considerin' this," she said, "but if it means you'll leave right now . . . pucker up, Lizard Lips."

103

Before Reba Jo could wipe the toad spit off her lips, a fierce dust devil spun into the yard, swept the horned toad off his feet, and whirled him around in a dizzying cloud of prairie dust.

When the dust cleared, there before Reba Jo stood a handsome young *caballero.*

"Who are you?" Reba Jo demanded, staring at the gentleman.

"I am Prince Maximillian José Diego López de España."

"Whoa, how did this happen?" Reba Jo asked in amazement.

"**Many, many years ago** when I came to this country, I offended the great spirit of the *arroyo*. The spirit put a spell on me and turned me into a horned toad. For many years I've been waiting for a cowgirl like you to break the spell. *Muchas gracias* for my freedom, *señorita*. Now I'll be leaving as I promised."

"Now hold on for just a dadburn minute," said Reba Jo, stepping in front of the nobleman. "I recollect my daddy readin' me a story where somethin' like this happened. Aren't we supposed to get hitched and ride off into the sunset?"

With a twinkle in his eye, the *caballero* replied, *"Lo siento.* So sorry, Reba Jo, when you strike a bargain in these parts, a deal's a deal. *Adiós, señorita!"*

Think, Talk and Write

Talk About It After you previewed the story, did you know what was going to happen or were you surprised? If you could ask Reba Jo three questions, what would they be?

1. This tale is perfect for storytelling. Find a part of the tale that would be especially good if read aloud by a storyteller. Why is that such a good part to read? **Think Like an Author**

2. An author's purpose can be to teach readers an important lesson. What lesson do you think the author teaches in this story? **Author's Purpose**

3. What is the most important event in the story? Why do you think so? **Story Structure**

4. List a synonym for each of the following words: *bargain, favor,* and *shrieked.* **Vocabulary**

TEST PRACTICE

Look Back and Write How does the horned toad turn into a prince? Describe this event.

Meet author Jackie Mims Hopkins on page 376.

Retell

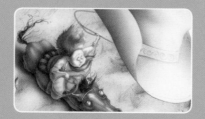  

W2.2.a Write responses to literature: Demonstrate an understanding of the literary work.

Writing

Prompt *The Horned Toad Prince* is a modern fairy tale set in the Southwest. Think about a traditional fairy tale you like. Now write a modern fairy tale based on that story.

> **Writing Trait**
>
> **Sensory details** help bring your story to life.

Student Model

Jackie and the Sunflower

On the way to the store to buy bread for her mother, Jackie met a woman dressed in yellow. The woman sold Jackie some sunflower seeds, which she said would make Jackie's life better than it was.

Jackie never imagined her mother would be so mad when she came home with sunflower seeds. "What about the bread!" her mother yelled. Jackie's mother threw the seeds out the window, and she stomped away.

Jackie hung her head out the window, and she cried buckets of tears. The tears flooded the sunflower seeds and caused them to grow. Higher and higher the sunflowers grew until they reached above the clouds. Jackie decided to climb the plant.

When she got above the clouds she found an ostrich that laid huge golden eggs. As she loaded her backpack with eggs, she heard thunderous footsteps approaching. It was a giant ostrich farmer. Jackie quickly slid down the sunflower and ran to the bank. She was rich!

Updates a traditional **fairy tale** *with a modern setting.*

Compound sentences *are correctly used.*

Sensory details help readers create a mental picture.

Use the model to help you write your own modern fairy tale.

W2.1.b Write narratives: Provide a context to enable the reader to imagine the world of the event or experience.

107

Turning Points

Story structure is the way an author arranges the events of a story.

- A **conflict,** or problem, is introduced at the beginning.
- **Rising action** builds as the problem gets more complicated.
- The **climax** is the high point of the problem.
- The **resolution,** or outcome, is what happens after the problem is resolved.

 Ready to Try It?
Read "The Fox and the Tiger." Try to identify the story's structure as you read.

Concept Link

The coyote and rattlesnake are two animals that are found in the Southwest. Make a list of other animals found in the Southwest. Which animal do you think would be the "King of the Desert"? Why?

The Fox and the Tiger

**a fable from China
retold by Susan McCloskey**

One morning, Tiger said, "I'm hungry! I'd better find something to eat!"

Tiger set out across the forest, and after a while he came across Fox.

"This is my lucky day!" Tiger said to Fox. "I'm very hungry, and you will make a fabulous breakfast!"

Fox stretched and yawned. "Oh," Fox said, "I was just thinking the same thing about you! If I weren't enjoying the sun so much, I'd gobble you up!"

"Hah!" Tiger laughed. "That's silly! I'm bigger and stronger. If I want to eat you for breakfast, I will!"

"Don't you know me?" Fox asked. "I'm King of the Forest. I will eat whomever I please. Sit beside me. You'll see that the animals are afraid to approach the waterhole when I'm here!"

"This I have to see," said Tiger, and he sat next to Fox.

Before long, Monkey came by to drink.

"I'm the King of the Forest!" cried Fox.

Monkey turned, saw Fox with Tiger, and scurried away.

The same thing happened again when Elephant approached the waterhole. Fox called out, "I'm the King of the Forest!" Elephant saw Fox with Tiger, and she thundered away.

When Tiger saw how fearful the animals were, he became afraid, too. "Oh, my," he said to Fox. "Look how late it is. I mustn't delay you from your . . ."

"Breakfast?" said Fox, gazing hungrily at Tiger.

Tiger ran, and he never went near Fox's waterhole again.

MORAL *It is possible to borrow power when you have none of your own.*

Reading Across Texts

How are the characters in *The Horned Toad Prince* and "The Fox and the Tiger" alike? How is the structure of each story similar? Make a chart to compare the characters and a chart to compare story structures.

Writing Across Texts Look at the character comparison chart. Write a paragraph explaining the ways that Reba Jo and the horned toad are like Fox and Tiger.

Build Language

The West

Build Vocabulary

Learn   ⊙ **Skill Suffixes** As you read, you may come across a word that looks familiar but has a suffix attached to it. For example, the word *biologist* has the suffix *–ist,* which means "one who is an expert in." Learning common suffixes can help you understand the meanings of many words.

Practice   Look up this week's Words to Know in a dictionary. Underline the words that have suffixes attached to them. Then read "Letter from Denali" on page 111.

Words to Know	wilderness	naturalist	glacier
	preserve	slopes	impressive
	species		

On Your Own   Make a list of words that use the same suffix as the words you underlined in this week's Words to Know. Write down a definition of the suffix and of the word. Then read "Letter from Denali" again.

G3R1.8 Use knowledge of prefixes (e.g., *un-, re-, pre-, bi-, mis-, dis-*) and suffixes (e.g., *-er, -est, -ful*) to determine meaning of words.

Letter from Denali

Dear Kevin,

Here we are in Denali National Park in Alaska. Denali is gigantic. It has more than 6 million acres of wilderness, so we certainly won't be seeing the whole park!

Denali was established to preserve the land and the plants and animals that live here. More than 650 species of flowering plants live in Denali! That's what the naturalist on the guided tour told us yesterday. She also said that to live in Denali year-round, a plant or animal species has to be able to survive long, cold winters.

Today we hiked up the lower slopes of Mt. McKinley. It is the highest mountain in North America and it is part of Denali. Farther up on the mountain, we could see a giant glacier that looked like a huge field of ice. It was a very impressive sight. Mt. McKinley has several glaciers, and some are more than 30 miles long!

I have taken a lot of pictures, but I really think this is a place you have to see for yourself!

See you soon,
Lisa

 Need a Review?
For additional help with suffixes, see *Words!* on p. W•3.

 Ready to Try It?
Read *Letters Home from Yosemite* on pp. 114–125.

Build Comprehension

Learn  **Skill Main Idea and Details**

- The topic is what a paragraph, part of an article, or a whole article is about.

- The most important thing the author has to say about the topic is the main idea.

- Supporting details are the pieces of information that tell more about the main idea.

Main Idea

Supporting Detail	Supporting Detail	Supporting Detail

Practice As you read "Send a Ranger!" on page 113, try to determine the main idea and supporting details.

On Your Own **Write to Read** Reread "Send a Ranger!" Use a main idea graphic organizer like the one above to write about a park you would like to visit.

 Need a Review? See the *Picture It!* lesson on p. PI•12 for additional help with main idea and details.

Ready to Try It? As you read *Letters Home from Yosemite* on pp. 114–125, use what you learned about main idea and details to help you understand the text.

  G5R2.3 Discern main ideas and concepts presented in texts, identifying and assessing evidence that supports those ideas.

SEND A RANGER!

The job of a park ranger is made up of a lot of different jobs. Park rangers are like police officers—they make sure people obey the rules of the park. Park rangers are like teachers—they take people on nature walks and tell them about important places. Park rangers are like scientists—they keep track of information about plants and animals. Park rangers are like firefighters—they keep close watch to help put a stop to forest fires. Park rangers are like rescue workers—they search for people who are lost or hurt.

Yes, the job of a park ranger is made up of a lot of different jobs. In fact, Stephen Mather, the first director of the National Parks Service, said: "If a trail is to be blazed, send a ranger; if an animal is stuck in the snow, send a ranger; if a bear is in a hotel, send a ranger; if there is a forest fire, send a ranger; and if someone is to be saved, send a ranger."

Do these jobs sound like fun to you? Maybe you would like to be a park ranger.

Skill The first sentence sounds like a big, overall main idea. Read on to see if it is or if there is a bigger idea.

Skill Is each example of a ranger's job a supporting detail or a new main idea?

Skill Why do you think the author restated a sentence used earlier?

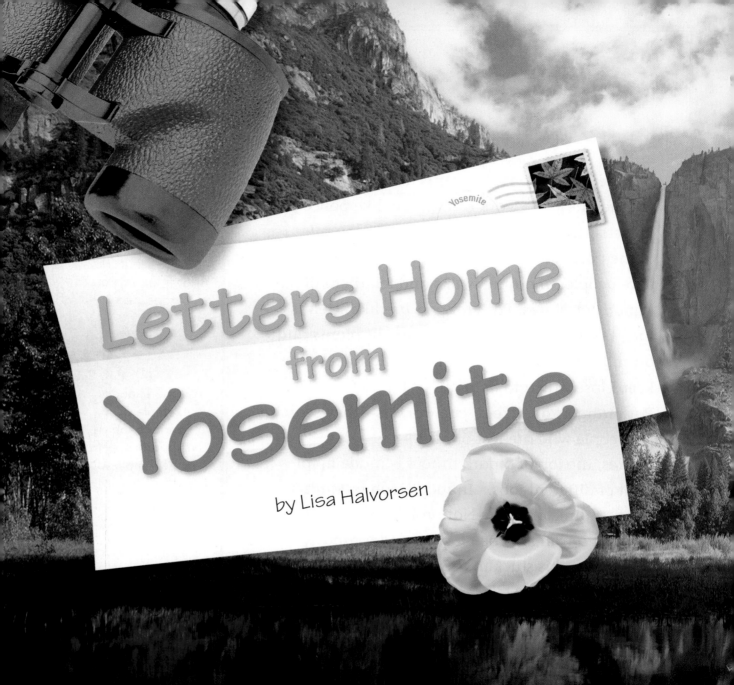

Letters Home from Yosemite

by Lisa Halvorsen

Why *do so many* people travel to
Yosemite National Park?

Arrival in...
San Francisco

As our plane touched down in San Francisco, I knew we were in for an exciting vacation. I'd been reading about Yosemite on the plane. I learned that it is America's third national park. Yosemite is known throughout the world for its amazing scenery. It has incredible waterfalls, rock formations, alpine lakes and meadows, and giant sequoia trees. It's located in the east central part of California and covers 1,170 square miles. That's an area about the size of Rhode Island!

Efforts to protect the wilderness around Yosemite began in 1864. That's when President Abraham Lincoln signed the Yosemite Grant deeding the land to California. Yosemite was finally established as a national park on Oct. 1, 1890, by an act of Congress.

Views of **Yosemite**

Yosemite Valley

Topography

Our tour guide said that one of the first people to visit this area was John Muir, a Scottish naturalist. He fought hard to convince the U.S. government to preserve Yosemite as a national park. The name supposedly comes from the Indian name "yo'hem-iteh." That means grizzly bear.

Yosemite is right in the middle of the Sierra Nevada Mountains. These mountains stretch for 430 miles along California's eastern border. The area covers 15.5 million acres, which is about the size of Vermont, New Hampshire, and Connecticut combined! This is the highest and longest single continuous range of mountains in the lower 48 states (not including Alaska and Hawaii).

Native Americans were the first people to live in Yosemite, about 7,000 to 10,000 years ago. When explorers arrived at Yosemite Valley in the 1830s and 1840s, Southern Sierra Miwok Indians were living there. They called the Yosemite Valley "Ahwahnee" (Place of the Gaping Mouth).

Sierra Nevadas from east of Tioga Pass

Merced River

Badger Pass

The first tourists arrived in 1855. They traveled on horseback. I wonder if they were as amazed as I am by the first glimpse of this scenic park.

Today, more than 3.5 million people visit the park every year. Most come in the summer months. That's a lot of visitors! And a lot of cars! But what's nice is that 94% of the park has been designated as wilderness. These areas can only be reached by foot or on horseback.

After a four-hour drive from San Francisco, we arrived at the Arch Rock entrance station. This is on the western side of the park, just north of Badger Pass. Badger is a popular ski spot. It opened in 1935 and was California's first ski area. Seven years earlier, the first ski school in the state was started in Yosemite Valley. That's where we'll begin exploring the park.

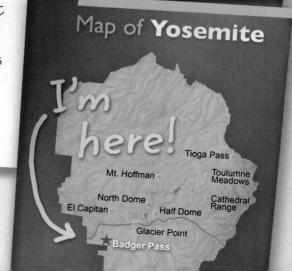

Map of **Yosemite**

I'm here!

Tioga Pass

Mt. Hoffman

Toulumne Meadows

North Dome

El Capitan

Half Dome

Cathedral Range

Glacier Point

Badger Pass

Rafting on the Merced River

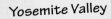
Yosemite Valley

Yosemite Valley

Yosemite Valley is only seven miles long and one mile wide, but it's where the most services are. Our campground is here, and so are many of the park's best natural attractions. It's the most heavily visited part of the park.

Today, we learned about the Miwok and Paiute people, and about the natural history of the park. Then we hopped on the shuttle bus to see famous sights like Yosemite Falls, El Capitan, and Happy Isles. One of my favorite places was Mirror Lake, where we saw Tenaya Canyon reflected in the water.

Bridalveil Creek/Fall

It seems that wherever we look, there's something bigger, higher, or more impressive than before. More than half of America's highestw waterfalls are found in Yosemite. One of the prettiest is Bridalveil Fall. It is located near the entrance to Yosemite Valley.

The Ahwahneechee called Bridalveil Fall "Pohono." It means "spirit of the puffing wind." Sometimes hard winds actually blow the falls sideways! I'm glad I brought my raincoat because we got soaked by the spray on the way up! This waterfall is 620 feet high. That's as tall as a 62-story building!

Bridalveil Fall

Giant Sequoias

I saw a Grizzly Giant! No, it's not a huge person. It's an enormous sequoia tree! It's the largest species of tree in the world and it is found only on the western slopes of the Sierra Nevada Mountains. A sequoia tree can grow to over 300 feet tall and 40 feet around, and can live more than 3,000 years!

At about 2,700 years old, the Grizzly Giant is the oldest tree in the park and the fifth oldest in the world. Many of the sequoias have nicknames, like the Clothespin Tree, Siamese Twins, and the Dead Giant. You can even walk through some of them!

Mariposa Grove of sequoia trees

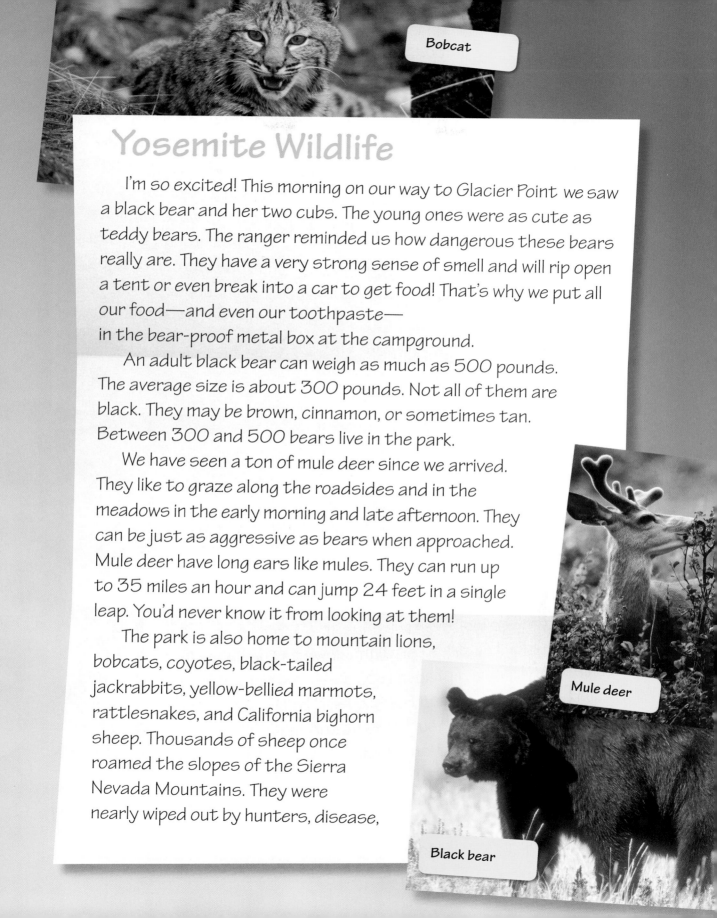

Bobcat

Yosemite Wildlife

I'm so excited! This morning on our way to Glacier Point we saw a black bear and her two cubs. The young ones were as cute as teddy bears. The ranger reminded us how dangerous these bears really are. They have a very strong sense of smell and will rip open a tent or even break into a car to get food! That's why we put all our food—and even our toothpaste—
in the bear-proof metal box at the campground.

An adult black bear can weigh as much as 500 pounds. The average size is about 300 pounds. Not all of them are black. They may be brown, cinnamon, or sometimes tan. Between 300 and 500 bears live in the park.

We have seen a ton of mule deer since we arrived. They like to graze along the roadsides and in the meadows in the early morning and late afternoon. They can be just as aggressive as bears when approached. Mule deer have long ears like mules. They can run up to 35 miles an hour and can jump 24 feet in a single leap. You'd never know it from looking at them!

The park is also home to mountain lions, bobcats, coyotes, black-tailed jackrabbits, yellow-bellied marmots, rattlesnakes, and California bighorn sheep. Thousands of sheep once roamed the slopes of the Sierra Nevada Mountains. They were nearly wiped out by hunters, disease,

Mule deer

Black bear

Steller's jay

and lack of food. A ranger said they were successfully reintroduced to the park in 1986.

More than 240 species of birds have been spotted in Yosemite. Some of them are endangered, like the willow flycatcher and the great gray owl. Some—like the bald eagle—just spend the winter in the park. My favorite is the Steller's jay, a noisy blue bird with a black crest. It will steal food off your plate if you don't watch out!

I also like to watch bats swooping through the air to catch insects. Did you know that one bat can eat up to 600 mosquito-sized insects in an hour? Yosemite has 15 species of bats. These include the rare spotted bat, which has big ears and three white spots on its back.

Glacier Point

The view from Glacier Point was totally awesome. It made me dizzy to look over the edge. It's 3,200 feet—a little more than a 1/2 mile—straight down to the floor of Yosemite Valley! In the distance I could see Yosemite Falls. I could also see El Capitan and Half Dome. I like the way light reflected off the bare rock surfaces at sunrise and sunset, "painting" them pink, purple, and gold.

The ranger told us that this is a good place to see peregrine falcons in flight. They can dive at speeds up to 200 miles per hour and catch their prey in mid-air. They nest in high places on very narrow rock ledges.

El Capitan

El Capitan is Spanish for "the Captain." This is the biggest single block of granite on Earth. It is more than 3,600 feet from its base to its top. It's a favorite climbing spot for visitors from all over the world. It can take anywhere from several hours to several days to scale this rock. So it's not unusual to see people camped out on the rock ledges.

The highest single waterfall on the North American continent is Ribbon Fall. It plunges 1,612 feet off a cliff on the west side of El Capitan.

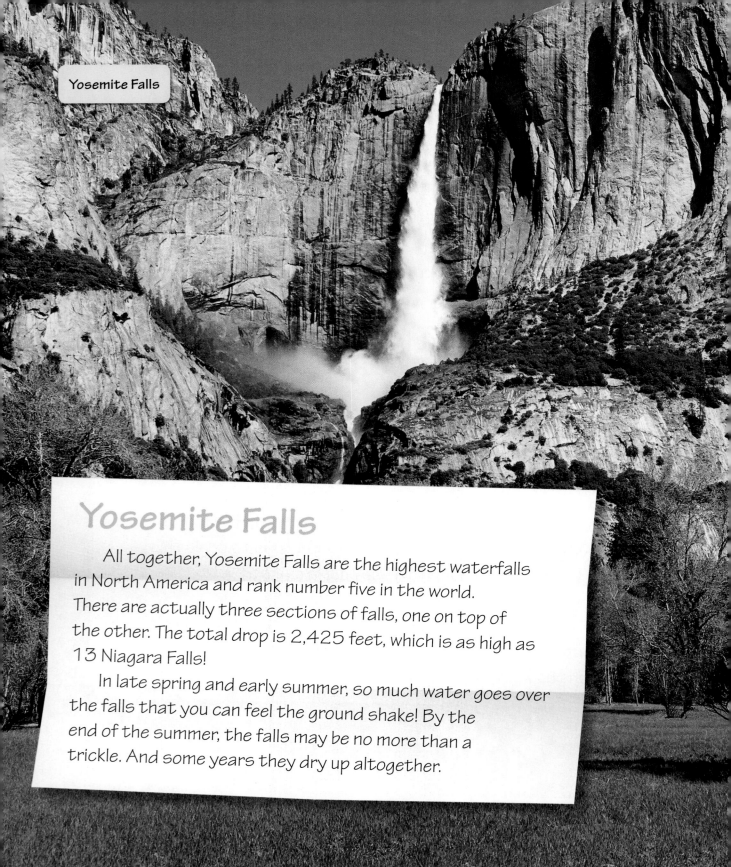

Yosemite Falls

Yosemite Falls

All together, Yosemite Falls are the highest waterfalls in North America and rank number five in the world. There are actually three sections of falls, one on top of the other. The total drop is 2,425 feet, which is as high as 13 Niagara Falls!

In late spring and early summer, so much water goes over the falls that you can feel the ground shake! By the end of the summer, the falls may be no more than a trickle. And some years they dry up altogether.

Lyell

The first person to climb Mt. Lyell was John Tileston in 1871. At 13,114 feet, Mt. Lyell is the park's highest mountain. It also has the largest active glacier, the Lyell Glacier, which clings to the northwest side of the peak. It is about 1/4 mile square. Melting snow from the glacier feeds the Tuolumne River. The river, in turn, provides water to San Francisco by way of a reservoir.

Today the rivers and streams of Yosemite provide places to fish, wade, or raft. But in the past, people flocked to the water to pan for gold! While some gold was found, the area did not yield as much of this precious metal as the foothills to the west of the park did.

Lyell Fork

Tioga Pass

On our last day we drove over Tioga Pass. It's 9,945 feet above sea level. It's the highest highway pass in the Sierra Nevada range and in all of California.

Because it's so high, many flowers and plants that grow here differ from those in lower elevations such as the Yosemite Valley. The trees are also small and stunted, because it's difficult for them to grow at such high altitudes.

Wherever you go—high in the mountains, or low in the valleys—Yosemite is truly one of the most awesome places on Earth!

Tioga Pass

125

Think, Talk and Write

Talk About It Make a list of things you would like to do on a trip to Yosemite. Share your favorite activity with a friend and tell why it is your favorite.

1. Why do you think the author chose to use letters and photographs to tell about Yosemite? **Think Like an Author**

2. Reread the letter from Glacier Point on page 122. Which sentence states the main idea of the passage? Which details support the main idea? **Main Idea and Details**

3. Make a main idea and details graphic organizer for the selection. At the top of your graphic organizer, record the passage's main idea. In the boxes below the main idea, record details that support it. **Graphic Organizers**

4. The author uses the word *impressive* to describe many wonders in Yosemite. Tell about some of these wonders, and explain how they would be impressive. Use words from the Words to Know list in your response. **Vocabulary**

TEST PRACTICE

Look Back and Write Why do you think so many people travel to Yosemite National Park? Use examples from the passage to support your opinion.

Meet author **Lisa Halvorsen on page 376.**

Summarize

Yosemite Valley

Merced River

Mariposa Grove of sequoia trees

W2.2.a Write responses to literature: Demonstrate an understanding of the literary work.

Writing

Prompt In *Letters Home from Yosemite,* the author tells the true story of a trip to the West. Think about an experience you have had while visiting a special place in the West. Now write a narrative account about what you learned.

> **Writing Trait**
>
> **Voice** engages readers and speaks directly to them.

Student Model

A Trip to the Grand Canyon

On our family vacation, we visited the Grand Canyon in Arizona. I had never seen such magnificent rock formations before. It is no wonder that nearly five million people visit Grand Canyon National Park each year.

Our guide said, "The park is spread out over 1,218,375 acres. **The canyon is 6,000 feet at the deepest point, and it is 15 miles at its widest point."**

One day, we hiked down to the bottom of the canyon. **It took us more than five hours.** We were hot and exhausted, but we saw some unusual plants and animals. I took a lot of pictures. It was an amazing experience.

As we walked along the Colorado River, we saw a beaver. We also saw antelope squirrels and pocket mice, which are common to the area.

If you're planning a vacation, the Grand Canyon is a fun place to explore and learn about its amazing features.

Narrative nonfiction can include quotes from people involved.

The voice is friendly and informative.

Clauses and complex sentences are used correctly.

Turning Points

Use the model to help you write your own narrative account.

 W2.1.a Write narratives: Relate ideas, observations, or recollections of an event or experience.

127

Proposition and support is a text structure writers use to present ideas on a topic.

- A **proposition** is an idea that a writer is presenting. Propositions can appear at the beginning, middle, or end of a text.

- The **support** for an idea can be presented in statements of fact and opinion. Writers will also use description to support their ideas.

Good readers analyze texts to determine whether a writer's proposition is valid.

 Ready to Try It?
Read "Four Days in Yosemite." Look for the writer's proposition as you read.

Concept Link

Yosemite National Park is one of many beautiful regions in California. Research a region in California and describe the plants, animals, and geography of the area. Share the information with your class.

FOUR DAYS IN YOSEMITE
by William Jones

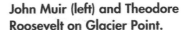

May 1903—Night was falling across Yosemite National Park in California. The last rays of the sun were already gone. The park was a land of tall shadows. Five campers settled in for the night. They were camping beside a spring in one of Yosemite's most beautiful spots, Mariposa Grove. Two of the men worked for the national park, and one man was a cook. The other two were famous men with important roles in history.

John Muir (left) and Theodore Roosevelt on Glacier Point.

One of the famous men was John Muir, the conservationist. He had taken on a role to protect America's wilderness areas. The other famous man was President Theodore Roosevelt, the twenty-sixth President of the United States. Ever since he was a young boy, Mr. Roosevelt had loved the outdoors. He considered it a presidential duty to protect nature.

This camping trip in Yosemite in 1903 brought together Theodore Roosevelt and John Muir for the first time. Their friendship began when Mr. Roosevelt wrote to John Muir. In the letter, the President told Mr. Muir of his plans to tour the West. He asked Mr. Muir to be his guide through Yosemite. President Roosevelt wrote, "I do not want anyone with me but you, and I want to drop politics absolutely for four days and just be out in the open with you." Out in the open, under wide blue skies and starry nights, in this wild and beautiful setting, the two men formed a solid friendship.

During the day, the campers rode horses for several miles north to Glacier Point. From this sky-high cliff they had a spectacular view of the park. They could see Nevada Falls, Vernal Falls, and Yosemite Falls. At this time of year, the waterfalls were wild and rushing. Water pounded down the cliffs carrying the icy-cold runoff of melting snow.

President Roosevelt and John Muir (fourth and fifth from left) with group in front of Grizzly Giant.

President Roosevelt gazed across the wide forests and canyons and understood how John Muir felt about the wilderness. Here was a landscape of unending natural beauty. The President wanted more than ever to help protect places like this.

The men also camped near some of Yosemite's meadowlands. The meadows in May were washed in bright colors. Red, yellow, pink, purple, and blue wildflowers carpeted the land. In the evening, Mr. Muir showed the President how to make a forest bed from ferns, flowers, and sweet-smelling cedar branches. In the morning, they found themselves covered in four inches of snow! It was said that Roosevelt shouted, "I wouldn't miss this for anything! This is bully!"

On the final evening of their trip, Mr. Muir and President Roosevelt returned to the valley. A fancy banquet dinner had been planned to honor the President, but he skipped this event. He wanted to spend his last night as he had the other nights—in nature with only a few people. He slept under the stars in Bridalveil Meadow.

President Roosevelt's trip to Yosemite made him even more determined to protect America's natural places. He understood his friend John Muir's love of Yosemite. He said that camping there was like "lying in a great solemn cathedral, far vaster and more beautiful than any built by the hand of man."

Because of the great passion of President Roosevelt and John Muir for the American wilderness, people today are able to enjoy thousands of miles of unspoiled nature.

Reading Across Texts

Preserving national parks is important. John Muir, Abraham Lincoln, and Theodore Roosevelt worked to preserve Yosemite National Park. How did their work make it possible for people to enjoy the park today?

Writing Across Texts Write a short paragraph summarizing how visitors to Yosemite National Park today can have some of the same experiences as visitors many years ago.

We're All in the Telephone Book

by Langston Hughes

We're all in the telephone book,
Folks from everywhere on earth—
Anderson to Zabowski,
It's a record of America's worth.

We're all in the telephone book.
There's no priority—
A millionaire like Rockefeller
Is likely to be behind me.

For generations men have dreamed
Of nations united as one.
Just look in your telephone book
To see where that dream's begun.

When Washington crossed the Delaware
And the pillars of tyranny shook,
He started the list of democracy
That's America's telephone book.

Speak Up

by Janet S. Wong

You're Korean, aren't you?

Why don't you speak Korean?

Say something Korean.

C'mon. Say something.

Say some other stuff.
Sounds funny.
Sounds strange.

Listen to me?

But I'm American,
can't you see?

But I was born here.

Yes.

Just don't, I guess.

I don't speak it.
I can't.

Halmoni. Grandmother.
Haraboji. Grandfather.
Imo. Aunt.

Hey, let's listen to you
for a change.

Say some foreign words.

Your family came from
somewhere else.
Sometime.

So was I.

CITY I LOVE

by Lee Bennett Hopkins

In the city
I live in—
city I love—
mornings wake
to
swishes, swashes,
sputters
of sweepers
swooshing litter
from gutters.

In the city
I live in—
city I love—
afternoons pulse
with
people hurrying,
scurrying—
races of faces
pacing to
must-get-there
places.

In the city
I live in—
city I love—
nights shimmer
with lights
competing
with stars
above
unknown heights.

In the city
I live in—
city I love—
as dreams
start to creep
my city
of senses
lulls
me
to
sleep.

Midwest Town

by Ruth De Long Peterson

Farther east it wouldn't be on the map—
Too small—but here it rates a dot and a name.
In Europe it would wear a castle cap
Or have a cathedral rising like a flame.

But here it stands where the section roadways meet.
Its houses dignified with trees and lawn;
The stores hold *tête-à-tête* across Main Street;
The red brick school, a church—the town is gone.

America is not all traffic lights,
And beehive homes and shops and factories;
No, there are wide green days and starry nights,
And a great pulse beating strong in towns like these.

Teamwork

What is the value of teamwork?

Teamwork

Build Language

Developing New Understandings

Build Vocabulary

Learn ◉ **Skill** **Prefixes and Suffixes** When a prefix or a suffix is added to a root word, it changes the meaning of the word. For example, the prefix *un-* means "the opposite of," as in *unfriendly*. The suffix *-less* means "without," as in *careless*. Learning prefixes and suffixes can help you figure out the meanings of words.

Practice Use a dictionary and what you know about prefixes and suffixes to write definitions for this week's Words to Know. Then read "At the Game" on page 139.

Words to Know	unbelievable	swatted	fouled
	marveled	rim	hoop
	jersey	speechless	

On Your Own Read "At the Game" again. Imagine that you have to write a newspaper headline for the game between the Tigers and the Lions. Come up with three newspaper headlines about the game, using at least three words from this week's Words to Know.

G3R1.8 Use knowledge of prefixes (e.g., *un-, re-, pre-, bi-, mis-, dis-*) and suffixes (e.g., *-er, -est, -ful*) to determine the meanings of words.

At the Game

"Hello, sports fans! This is Bud Sherman, coming to you live from the Grandview Center, where it's the Tigers 84 and the Lions 82 with only two minutes left to play. Tigers forward Matt Roberts has been flawless, scoring 28 points and 10 rebounds. However, Lions' center Darren Jones has been unbelievable under the basket with seven blocked shots.

"The Tigers move the ball down court. Roberts is looking for another three pointer. The ball is in his hands. He shoots, and the ball hits off the rim. Maxwell rebounds and tries a second shot, but it's swatted away by Jones. The Lions have the ball and quickly move to the hoop. Oh no, Maxwell has fouled Jones! He grabbed Jones by the jersey. The Tigers' coach is furious! That's Maxwell's fourth foul. Jones, a reliable free-throw shooter, makes both shots to tie the game. Only 20 seconds left to play. Taylor passes to Roberts. You know, I have always marveled at the way Roberts moves around the court, but his performance tonight just leaves me speechless. Roberts shoots from three-point range—and he scores! The Tigers win, 87 to 84!"

 Need a Review?
For additional help with prefixes and suffixes, see *Words!* on pp. W•5–W•6.

 Ready to Try It?
Read "What Jo Did" on pp. 142–151.

Teamwork

Build Comprehension

Learn **◉ Skill Cause and Effect**

- An effect is *what* happens. A cause is *why* it happens.

- Clue words such as *because, so,* and *since* can help you figure out *what* happens and *why* it happens.

- Using a graphic organizer such as the one below can help you understand cause and effect.

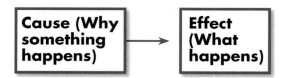

| Cause (Why something happens) | → | Effect (What happens) |

Practice   As you read "Up, Up, and Down" on page 141, try to determine *what* happens and *why* it happens.

On Your Own   **Write to Read** Reread "Up, Up, and Down." Use both the text and a graphic organizer to show how you use energy to help you play.

 Need a Review? See the *Picture It!* lesson on p. PI•4 for additional help with cause and effect.

 Ready to Try It? As you read "What Jo Did" on pp. 142–151, use what you learned about cause and effect to help you understand the text.

R2.6 Distinguish between cause and effect and between fact and opinion in expository text.

Up, Up, and Down

Have you ever seen basketball players leap high into the air to shoot a ball into a basket? Or even higher still to block a shot? How do they jump so high?

The trick is to beat Earth's gravity, since gravity is the force that pulls people to the ground. To move away from this force, people need energy.

Think of a spring, or better yet, think of a trampoline. Your weight on the trampoline presses the surface down. That stores energy in the springs. When that energy is released, it is enough to lift you high into the air.

In a similar way, you can build up energy in your legs. If you stand straight and then try to jump up, you can't. You may be able to lift off the ground an inch or so, but that's all. That's why you bend at the knees before jumping up. When you bend, it's as if you are putting springs in your legs. Release those springs, and up you go.

Of course, the energy is not nearly enough to overcome Earth's gravity. That's why Earth will always pull you back down again.

Skill What clue word helps you figure out *what* happened and *why?*

Skill What causes energy to be stored in a trampoline?

Skill What would you write as the *cause* for this paragraph? What would you write as the *effect?*

Teamwork

141

What Jo Did

text and images by Charles R. Smith Jr.

What can **Jo do** that others cannot?

ittle Joanna Marie loved to play basketball. She especially loved the sound the ball made as it fell through the net. She would practice every day, touching the backboard as often as she could. Since Joanna's parents had no idea how high a basketball rim should be, they hung it on the side of their roof, which was a whopping sixteen feet high.

Joanna saw rims on TV and figured they looked about the same height as her own—**she had no idea they were only ten feet high.**

Joanna also didn't realize that most people couldn't jump up and touch the backboard because she hadn't ever played with anyone else. But her parents marveled at how high she jumped, and how she could run up to the backboard with the ball and lay it up and in. Her father was especially proud because he couldn't even touch the bottom of the net. Not even with the help of a broom.

One day Joanna, her hair bundled up under her baseball cap, was dribbling her basketball on the way to the store to get some sugar for her mother. Her mother said that she didn't have to hurry home, as long as she was in by dark. As Joanna moved down the street, a basketball came rolling out of nowhere and bumped her high-tops.

"I'm sorry, man, I didn't mean to hit you with the ball like that," said a young boy dressed in sneakers, shorts, and a Bulls tank top as he picked up the ball.

"Oh, that's okay. I wasn't even paying attention," Joanna said.

"Hey, we need one more to play a game. You in?" he asked her.

"Sure, why not?" she responded.

As Joanna approached the other boys, she remembered that she had her hat on.

They probably think I'm a boy, she thought. Might as well enjoy the ride.

The boys picked teams, and since Joanna was smaller than everyone else, she got picked last. It didn't bother her, though, because she had never played with anyone before and was just happy to be there.

"Hey, kid, what's your name?" asked a freckle-faced kid with red hair.

"Ahhh . . . Jo. My name is Jo," Joanna said nervously.

"All right, Joe, you pick up T.J. over there, see. Make sure he doesn't score a basket. He can jump pretty high, ya know!"

Jo moved around, not really touching the ball at first, just trying to get a feel for playing with other people. She had never even passed the ball or received a pass herself. Playing with others took getting used to, but in no time she was passing the ball. The only thing that puzzled her was why the hoop was so low.

Even though the boys passed the ball around a lot, T.J. didn't really touch it much, and when he did, he didn't take a shot. Finally, he was wide open for a jump shot when Jo came out of nowhere, jumped high into the air, **and swatted his shot into the next court.**

"Wow, did you see that?

Did you see how high he jumped?" the freckle-faced kid said, his mouth wide open.

"I've never seen anybody jump that high. Not even Michael Jordan," said the kid with the Bulls jersey on.

"Unbelievable."

"Where'd you learn to do that?"

"Oh, my goodness!!!"

"Poor T.J."

"Hey—I got fouled, and besides, it wasn't that high," said T.J., but his face was so red that he couldn't hide his embarrassment.

"Uh, uh . . . it's just something I picked up. I practice a lot with my dad," Jo added, surprised at how big a deal the boys made of her block.

"Man! You must have some dad," one of the boys said.

The game continued, and Jo was passed the ball more often. Her teammates encouraged her to shoot more, and when she did, they were amazed how the ball arced in the air like a rainbow before falling straight through the hoop, without touching the rim. As the game progressed, Jo felt hot, but she knew she couldn't take her hat off, or else she'd be found out.

Whenever a boy got the ball and Jo came over to play defense, he quickly passed the ball away. Jo blocked a few more shots, which created more *ooooohs* and *aaaaaaahs,* and one of the boys on her team asked her if she could dunk the ball.

"Dunk? What's that?" Jo asked. This was a word she had never heard before.

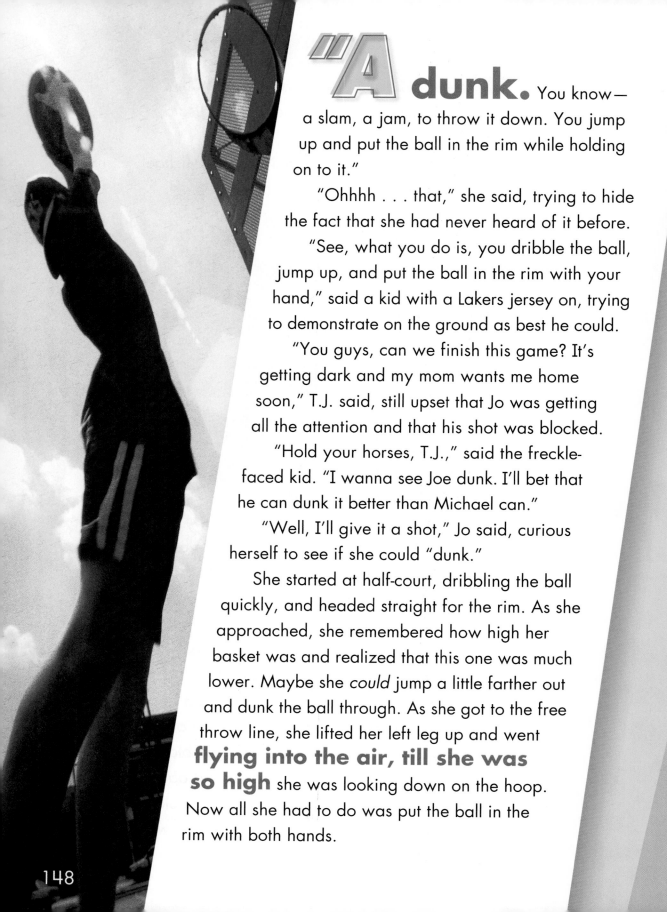

"A dunk. You know—
a slam, a jam, to throw it down. You jump
up and put the ball in the rim while holding
on to it."

"Ohhhh . . . that," she said, trying to hide
the fact that she had never heard of it before.

"See, what you do is, you dribble the ball,
jump up, and put the ball in the rim with your
hand," said a kid with a Lakers jersey on, trying
to demonstrate on the ground as best he could.

"You guys, can we finish this game? It's
getting dark and my mom wants me home
soon," T.J. said, still upset that Jo was getting
all the attention and that his shot was blocked.

"Hold your horses, T.J.," said the freckle-
faced kid. "I wanna see Joe dunk. I'll bet that
he can dunk it better than Michael can."

"Well, I'll give it a shot," Jo said, curious
herself to see if she could "dunk."

She started at half-court, dribbling the ball
quickly, and headed straight for the rim. As she
approached, she remembered how high her
basket was and realized that this one was much
lower. Maybe she *could* jump a little farther out
and dunk the ball through. As she got to the free
throw line, she lifted her left leg up and went
**flying into the air, till she was
so high** she was looking down on the hoop.
Now all she had to do was put the ball in the
rim with both hands.

She was up there for a while before she felt her hands on the rim, the ball going through, and her feet touching the ground.

When she landed, all of the boys' mouths were hanging open, and for a moment they were speechless.

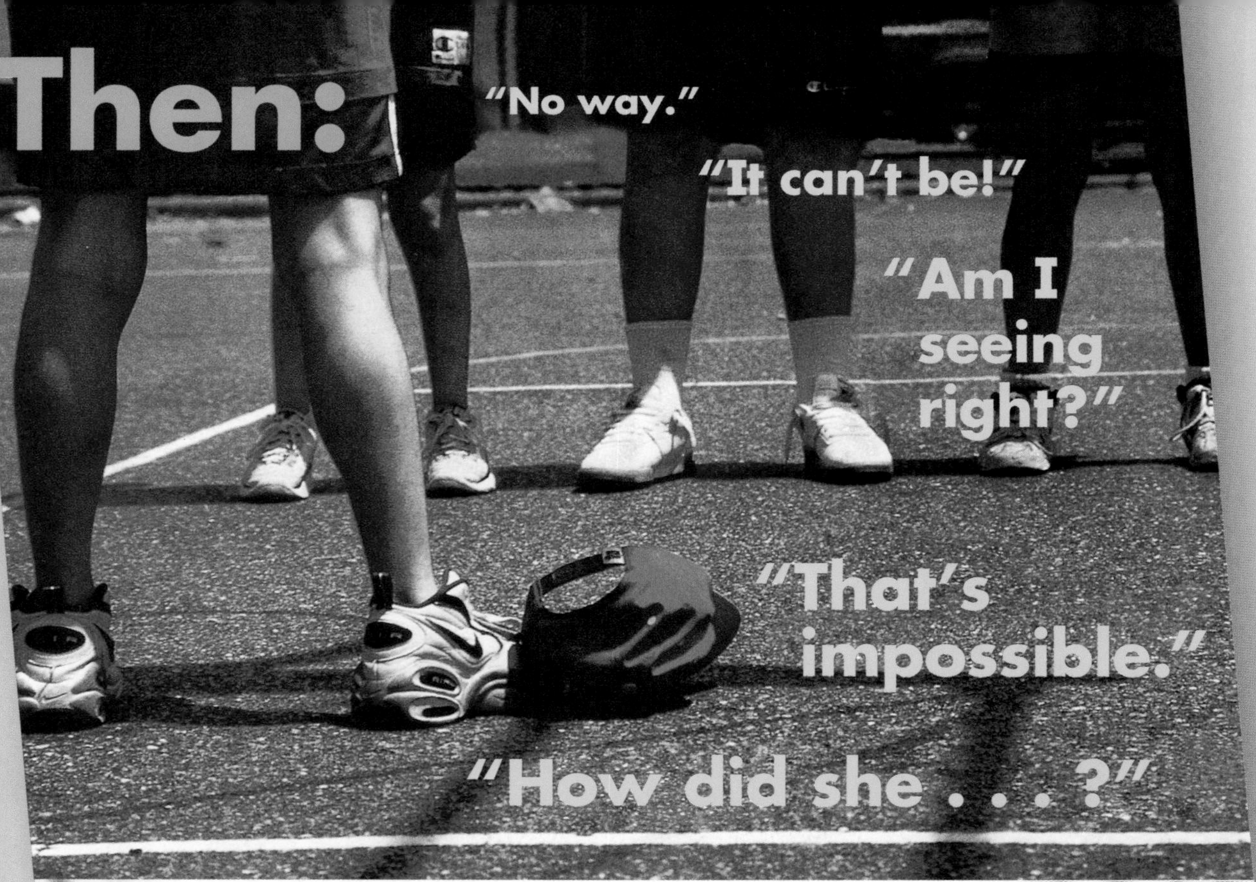

Then:

"No way."

"It can't be!"

"Am I seeing right?"

"That's impossible."

"How did she . . . ?"

As the boys stared at her, Jo looked down at the ground and saw her hat lying there.

She froze.

"So, like . . . you're a girl?" said the kid with the Lakers jersey.

"Ahhhh . . . yeah . . . you could say that," Jo answered slowly.

"I can't believe it, you guys, we've been playing basketball with a girl," T.J. said with disgust.

"Hey, she may be a girl, but I'd play on her team anytime." The kid with the Bulls jersey approached Jo and gave her a high five.

After that, they congratulated Jo and introduced themselves. They even came up with a nickname for her: Jumpin' Jo. In the end, T.J. walked up to her and apologized.

"Sorry, Jo," he whispered. "I just never played against a girl before. Especially a girl as good as you. I've never seen anyone who can jump like that! You should come and play with us again sometime.

But next time, leave the hat at home."

Think, Talk and Write

Talk About It Suppose Joanna went home and told her parents about the game. What do you think she would say?

1. The author uses basketball terms such as *dunk.* Why? Identify five more basketball terms in the story and tell why they are there. **Think Like an Author**

2. What does Joanna do to T.J.'s jump shot? Why does he react the way he does? **Cause and Effect**

3. Have you ever surprised someone with a skill or talent the person didn't know you had? What was that person's reaction? **Prior Knowledge**

4. Write three words from the Words to Know list that describe people's reactions to Joanna's basketball talent. What other words from the story describe what other people said when they saw her play? **Vocabulary**

TEST PRACTICE ★ **Look Back and Write** What was Jo able to do that others couldn't do? Review the story and write about Jo's special talent.

Meet author and photographer Charles R. Smith Jr. on p. 378.

Retell

W2.2.a Write responses to literature: Demonstrate an understanding of the literary work.

Writing

Fiction

Prompt The characters in "What Jo Did" develop new understandings about each other. Think about a fictional situation in which people develop new understandings about one another. Now write a story about them.

Writing Trait

Strong Verbs add impact to your story.

Student Model

The New Girl

As **Liz** lugged her backpack into writing class, she noticed a girl she hadn't seen before. The girl shyly glanced in Liz's direction before taking a seat near the window.

The **teacher** directed the students to write a poem about a personal experience. Liz immediately began writing a poem in her **notebook**. When she looked up, she noticed that the new girl was staring out the window.

"She'll never make it in this class," thought Liz.

The teacher called an end to the writing time. She asked the new girl to read her poem first. Liz was amazed that the girl had finished the **assignment**. Her beautiful poem clearly expressed how hard it was to leave your home and move to a new school.

A little embarrassed by her earlier thoughts, Liz walked over to the girl after class and introduced herself. Liz learned that both she and the girl, **Kayla**, had a lot in common.

Introduces characters and real-life events.

Strong verbs clearly relate characters' actions.

Common and proper nouns are used correctly.

Use the model to help you write your own story.

W2.1.d Write narratives: Provide insight into why the selected event or experience is memorable.

Skill Talk

Cause and effect is used to show how one thing happens because of something else. Writers often use clue words such as *since, because, if, then,* and *as a result* to signal causes and effects. If you find a clue word, ask yourself, "What happened?" and "Why did it happen?"

 Ready to Try It?
Read "Learning to Fly." Look for clue words that show cause and effect.

Concept Link

In 2005, the average height of NBA basketball players was 6 feet 7 inches tall. Use the library or Internet to find other interesting facts about NBA athletes. Make a list of the different players' accomplishments.

154

to Fly

by Alex Rivera

Spud Webb was 5 feet 7 inches tall, and Dominque Wilkins, his Atlanta Hawks teammate, was 6 feet 8 inches tall. If these two NBA players had a slam-dunk contest, which player do you think would win?

You would probably pick Dominique Wilkins. After all, he was more than a foot taller. Webb was a guard and one of the shortest players in NBA history. Plus, Dominique Wilkins was famous for his slam-dunking skills. How could Webb possibly beat him?

Well, the two NBA stars actually did compete in a slam-dunk contest. The year was 1986. There are several kinds of slam-dunks. Webb did some of the most difficult.

Many people were shocked to see Spud Webb dunk a basketball.

Year	Slam-Dunk Winners
1985	**Dominique Wilkins** Atlanta Hawks
1986	**Anthony "Spud" Webb** Atlanta Hawks
1987	**Michael Jordan** Chicago Bulls
1988	**Michael Jordan** Chicago Bulls
1989	**Kenny Walker** New York Knicks
1990	**Dominique Wilkins** Atlanta Hawks
1991	**Dee Brown** Boston Celtics
1992	**Cedric Ceballos** Phoenix Suns
1993	**Harold Miner** Miami Heat
1994	**Isaiah Rider** Minnesota Timberwolves
1995	**Harold Miner** Miami Heat

155

Spud standing next to his teammate Dominique Wilkins.

He did the elevator two-handed double pump, the one-handed off the backboard one-handed jam, a full circle helicopter one-handed, a half circle reverse double-pump slam, and more.

Now the judges rarely awarded a player a perfect score on any attempt, but Webb received two perfect scores in his victory. Afterwards, Wilkins talked about how amazed he was. He had never seen his teammate make a slam-dunk before—not in a game and not even in practice. How in the world did a man of his small stature learn to fly so high?

Anthony Jerome Webb was born in 1963 in Dallas, Texas. His grandmother nicknamed him "Spud" when he was a baby. Spud Webb had always dreamed of playing big-time basketball. In junior high, he talked the coach into letting him play even though he was so short. In his first game, Spud scored 20 points. Then in high school Spud had to do the same thing and talk the coach into letting him play. During his high school career, Spud Webb averaged 26 points a game and was named Player of the Year.

Spud learned to dunk the summer before his last year in high school, when he was just 4 feet 11 inches tall. Spud had amazing spring

Spud →

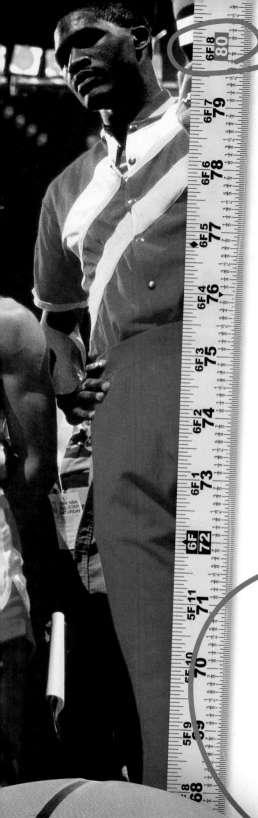

← Wilkins

and strength in his legs that allowed him to outleap much taller players. He proved that how tall you were didn't mean everything.

Then he moved on to play college basketball at North Carolina State. By then he was 5 feet 7 inches tall. At North Carolina State, he averaged 10 points a game. But could he possibly move on to the NBA, where the average player was 12 inches taller?

The answer was a very definite Yes. Spud Webb played in the NBA from 1985 to 1998. During those thirteen seasons he averaged nearly 10 points a game.

"I don't play small," Spud said. "You have to go out and play with what you have. I admit I used to want to be tall. But I made it in high school, college, and now the pros. So it doesn't matter."

With those words, Spud Webb told the world that height was not all that mattered. What mattered most was that you played hard and never gave up.

Reading Across Texts

"What Jo Did" and "Learning to Fly" are about people who surprise others with their abilities. Make a compare-and-contrast chart to show how Jo and Spud Webb are alike and how they are different.

Writing Across Texts Look at the chart you made. Then write two paragraphs comparing Jo and Spud Webb.

Build Language

Working Together

Build Vocabulary

Learn ◉ **Skill Unfamiliar Words** As you read, you may come across unfamiliar words. Sometimes learning an unfamiliar word's origin can help you understand the word's meaning. For example, the word *saddle* comes from a word that means "to sit." You can learn word origins by using a dictionary.

Practice Read "At a Guest Ranch" on page 159. Then use a dictionary to help you figure out the meanings of this week's Words to Know. See if you can find information about each word's origin.

Words to Know	dudes roundup	spurs bawling	coyote

On Your Own Read "At a Guest Ranch" again. Think about what it would be like to stay at a dude ranch. Write a journal entry about a day at the ranch, using words from the Words to Know list.

R1.2 Apply knowledge of word origins, derivations, synonyms, antonyms, and idioms to determine the meanings of words and phrases.

AT A GUEST RANCH

Howdy, partner! That may sound corny, but it's appropriate because my family and I have paid to stay at a ranch. This gives visitors a chance to see what ranch life is really like. Guests are called dudes. That's what the cowhands in the Old West called people from back East. Some dude ranches are only for entertaining visitors—excuse me—dudes. Some are real cattle or sheep ranches that take in a few dudes on the side.

Our ranch, the Double K near Bozeman, Montana, is a working cattle ranch. We went with the cowhands on a roundup. It was exciting to watch. With just a touch of their spurs, cowhands move their horses into the herd to cut out one cow. It was hot, dusty, and noisy too. The cattle were mooing and the calves were bawling.

We also rode out on a trail and camped under the stars. Dinner from a chuck wagon, a bedroll by the campfire, and a coyote howling in the distance—I felt as if I were in a Western movie!

 **Need a Review?**
For additional help with word origins to determine the meanings of unfamiliar words, see *Words!* on p. W•9.

 Ready to Try It?
Read *Coyote School News* on pp. 162–179.

Teamwork

Build Comprehension

Learn   ◉ **Skill Draw Conclusions**

- A conclusion is a decision you reach that makes sense after you think about the details and facts in what you read.

- As you read, use information from the text and your own prior knowledge to help you draw conclusions.

- Using a graphic organizer such as the one below can help you check to see if your conclusion makes sense.

Practice   As you read "Home, Home on the Range" on page 161, think about what conclusions you can draw about life on a ranch.

On Your Own   **Write to Read** Reread "Home, Home on the Range." Would you like to live on a ranch? Use the text to draw a conclusion about the types of transportation that ranchers use. Write a paragraph that explains how you came to this conclusion.

 Need a Review? See the *Picture It!* lesson on p. PI•6 for additional help with drawing conclusions.

 Ready to Try It? As you read *Coyote School News* on pp. 162–179, draw conclusions to help you understand the text.

   G3R2.2 Ask questions and support answers by connecting prior knowledge with literal information found in, and inferred from, the text.

HOME, HOME ON THE RANGE

A ranch is a particular kind of farm where cattle or sheep are raised. Most ranches in the United States are located in the West, in wide-open country called the range. Most ranches are enormous, consisting of several thousand acres.

Skill What conclusion can you draw as to why ranches must be so large? Think about what you know about cattle and sheep to draw a conclusion.

Cattle and sheep need a lot of room to roam and graze. In addition, they must be able to get to streams and ponds for fresh drinking water.

Ranchers today still use horses to get around, just as cowhands did in the days of the Old West. But they also use vehicles, such as trucks, jeeps, and even helicopters. This is especially important in the winter. When snow covers the ground, the livestock can't graze, so ranchers must bring hay to them.

Skill Think back to what you know about cattle and how they eat. What conclusion can you draw about how they get food in winter?

The children of ranchers have to get around too. Because ranches are so large and far apart, most ranchers' children must ride a bus a long way to school.

What do you think of life on a ranch?

Skill What detail about ranchers' children could you write on your graphic organizer?

Teamwork

161

Historical fiction is a story that is made up around real events in history. Decide what those real events might have been as you read about children in a southern Arizona country school in 1938–1939.

COYOTE SCHOOL NEWS

by Joan Sandin

What stories make the news at Coyote School?

Rancho San Isidro

My name is Ramón Ernesto Ramírez, but everybody calls me Monchi. I live on a ranch that my great-grandfather built a long time ago when this land was part of Mexico. That was before the United States bought it and moved the line in 1854. My father has a joke about that. He says my great-grandfather was an *americano,* not because he crossed the line, but because the line crossed him.

In my family we are six kids: me, my big brother Junior, my big sister Natalia, my little tattletale brother Victor, my little sister Loli, and the baby Pili. My *tío* Chaco lives with us too. He is the youngest brother of my father.

The real name of our ranch is Rancho San Isidro, after the patron saint of my great-grandfather, but most of the time everybody calls it the Ramírez Ranch.

On our ranch we have chickens and pigs and cattle and horses. The boys in the Ramírez family know

164

how to ride and rope. We are a family of *vaqueros.* In the fall and spring we have roundup on our ranch. Many people come to help with the cattle and the horses. Those are the most exciting days of the year, even more exciting than Christmas.

The things I don't like about our ranch are always having to get the wood for the fire, and the long and bumpy ride to school.

My tío Chaco drives the school bus.

"It's not fair," I tell him. "We have to get up earlier than all the other kids at Coyote School, and we get home the latest too."

"Don't forget," says my tío, "you get first choice of seats."

Ha, ha. By the time the last kid gets in we are all squeezed together like sardines in a can. And the bus is shaking and bumping like it has a flat tire.

"I wish President Roosevelt would do something about these roads," I tell my tío.

"Hey, you know how to write English," he says. "Write him a letter."

"Maybe I will," I say.

americano (*AH-mair-ee-CAHN-oh*)—
    American
tío (TEE-oh)—uncle
rancho (RAHN-choe)—ranch
san (sahn)—saint
vaqueros (bah-CARE-rose)—cowboys

165

Coyote School

"Mira, mira, Monchi," Natalia says, pinching my cheek. "There's your little *novia."*

She means Rosie. I like Rosie, but I hate it when Natalia teases me. Rosie lives at Coyote Ranch, close enough to school that she can walk. Always she waits by the road so she can race the bus.

"¡Ándale! ¡Ándale! Hurry up!" we yell at my tío Chaco, but every time he lets her win.

Rosie wasn't first today anyway. Lalo and Frankie were. Their horses are standing in the shade of the big mesquite tree.

Yap! Yap! Yap! Always Chipito barks when he sees us, and Miss Byers says, "Hush, Chipito!" Then she smiles and waves at us.

Miss Byers is new this year. Her ranch is a hundred miles from here, in Rattlesnake Canyon, so five days of the week she and Chipito live in the little room behind the school. All of us like Miss Byers, even the big kids, because she is young and nice and fair. We like that she lives on a ranch, and we like her swell ideas:

1. Baseball at recess,
2. The Perfect Attendance Award,
3. *Coyote News.*

mira (MEER-ah)—look
novia (NOVE-ee-ah)—girlfriend
ándale (AHN-dah-lay)—come on; hurry up

Coyote News

All week we have been working on our first *Coyote News*. Natalia made up the name, and Joey drew the coyote. First we looked at some other newspapers: the *Arizona Daily Star*, *Western Livestock Journal*, and *Little Cowpuncher*. That one we liked best because all the stories and pictures were done by kids.

"Monchi," said Loli, "put me cute."

"What?" I said. Sometimes it's not easy to understand my little sister's English.

"Miss Byers says you have to help me put words to my story," she said.

"Okay," I told her. "But I have my own story to do, so hurry up and learn to write."

Loli's story was *muy tonta*, but one thing was good. She remembered how to write all the words I spelled for her.

Even if Victor is my brother I have to say he is a big tattletale—*chismoso.* When Gilbert was writing his story for *Coyote News,* Victor told on him for writing in Spanish. But Miss Byers did not get mad at Gilbert. She smiled at him! And then she said Spanish is a beautiful language that people around here have been speaking for hundreds of years, and that we should be proud we can speak it too!

Ha ha, Victor, you big chismoso!

When we finished our stories and pictures, Miss Byers cut a stencil for the mimeograph. Then she printed copies of *Coyote News* for us to take home, and we hung them up on the ceiling to dry the ink. My tío Chaco said it looked like laundry day at Coyote School.

muy (MOO-ee)—very
tonta (TONE-tah)—silly
chismoso (cheese-MOE-soe)—tattletale
señor (sin-YORE)—Mr.
grandote (grahn-DOE-tay)—great big, huge

Issue Number One September 15, 1938

COYOTE NEWS
I am new!

Stories and Pictures by the Students of Coyote School, Pima County, Arizona

Something New at Coyote School

Coyote News was the idea of our teacher, but we write the stories and draw the pictures. The big kids help the little kids...Rosie Garcia, Grade 3

About Coyote School

This year we have 12 kids and all the grades except Grade 5...Billy Mills, Grade 3

We Ride Our Horses to School

The road to Rancho del Cerro is a very big problem for the bus of Mr. Ramirez. For that reason Lalo and I ride our horses to school--16 miles all the days. The year past it was 2,352 miles. We had to put new shoes on the horses 5 times...Frankie Lopez, Grade 6

Ándale Ándale We want to go home

by Lalo Lopez

The Perfect Attendance

Miss Byers will give a prize to anybody who comes to school all the days, no matter what. The prize is called The Perfect Attendance Award and it is a silver dollar! For me perfect attendance is not easy, but oh boy, I would like to win that silver dollar............Monchi Ramirez, Grade 4

Yap! Yap!

by Cynthia

Chipito

The dog of the teacher is called Chipito. He is very cute. He likes Loli best.....story by Loli Ramirez, Grade 1 with help by Monchi Ramirez, Grade 4

Señor Grandote

Our bus driver ran over a big rattlesnake. We took the skin and gave it to our teacher. She measured him with the yardstick. He was 5 feet and 7 inches! She hung him on the wall next to President Roosevelt. We kids call him Señor Grandote because in Spanish it means Mr. Huge...............Gilbert Perez, Grade 6

Señor Grandote

by Joey Brown

169

Chiles

Every day I am asking my father when we will have roundup. He says I am making him *loco* with my nagging and that first we have to pick *todos los chiles*.

All of us kids are tired of picking the chiles. It doesn't matter that we get home late from school, we still have to do it. And then, before the chiles dry out, we have to string them to make the *sartas*.

Last night we were taking about 600 pounds of the chiles to my tío Enrique's ranch. I was in the back of the truck when it hit a big rock.

All the heavy sacks fell on me. Oh boy, it hurt so much! But I did not tell my father. He had told me not to ride in the back of the truck, and I was afraid he would be mad.

My hand was still hurting this morning when Miss Byers did Fingernail Inspection.

"Monchi," she said, "what happened to your wrist? It's all black-and-blue and swollen."

"The chiles fell on him," Victor told her. "My father told him not to ride in the back."

"¡Chismoso!" I hissed at him.

Miss Byers called my tío Chaco over, and they had a long talk.

"Back in the bus, *mi'jo*," my tío said. "I have to take you to Tucson."

"Tucson!" I said. "Why?"

"You got to see the doctor," he said. So we drove all the way to Tucson to my *tía* Lena's house. At first my aunt was surprised and happy to see us, but then my tío told her why we were there.

"Monchi!" my tía said. "*¡Pobrecito!*" Then she told my tío Chaco to go back with the bus and she would take care of me.

My tía took me to a doctor. He moved my hand around. It hurt when he did that.

"I'm afraid the wrist is broken," he told my tía. "I need to set it and put it in a cast."

So I got a cast of plaster on my arm, and I had to stay in Tucson. But for me that was no problem! My tía felt very sorry for me. She cooked my favorite foods, and I got to pick the stations on her radio. That night Miss Byers called on the telephone to ask about me. She said she would come early Monday morning to drive me to school.

On Sunday my tía took me to the Tarzan picture show at the Fox Theater. It was swell! After the show we got ice cream and walked around downtown to look in the windows of the stores. I saw many things I liked. The best was a silver buckle with a hole to put a silver dollar. *¡Ay caramba!* I wish I had a buckle like that.

loco (LOW-coe)—crazy
todos (TOE-dose)—all
los (lohs)—the
chiles (CHEE-less)—chile peppers
sartas (SAR-tahs)—strings of chile peppers
mi'jo (MEE-hoe)—my son, sonny
tía (TEE-ah)—aunt
pobrecito (pobe-ray-SEE-toe)—
    poor little thing
¡ay caramba! (EYE car-RAHM-bah)—
    oh boy!

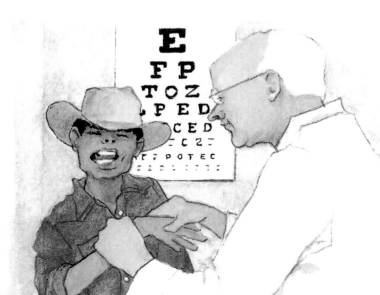

171

Nochebuena

For *Nochebuena* we are many people. Some are family I see only at Christmas and roundup and weddings and funerals. The day before Nochebuena my cousins from Sonora arrived. Now we could make the *piñata!*

First we cut the strips of red, white, and green paper. Then we paste them on a big *olla*. When the piñata is ready, we give it to my mother to fill with the *dulces* she hides in her secret places.

On Nochebuena, Junior and my tío Chaco hung the piñata between two big mesquite trees and we kids lined up to hit it, the littlest ones first. My mother tied a *mascada* over my little brother Pili's eyes and my tía Lena turned him around and around. She gave him the stick and pointed him toward the piñata. My tío Chaco and Junior made it easy for him. They did not jerk on the rope when he swung.

"*¡Dale! ¡Dale!*" we were yelling, but Pili never came close. None of the little kids could hit it. Then it was Loli's turn.

BAM.

Some peanuts fell out. Gilbert and I dived to get them. One by one, the other kids tried and missed. Then it was Natalia's turn. She took a good swing and—*BAM*.

The piñata broke open, and all the kids were in the dirt, screaming and laughing and picking up gum and nuts and oranges and candies.

Just before midnight we got into my tío Chaco's bus and my father's pickup to go to the Mass at Amado. When we got home my mother and my tías put out *tamales* and *menudo* and *tortillas* and cakes and coffee and other drinks. We had music and dancing. Nobody told us we had to go to bed.

Sometime in the night Santa Claus came and gave us our presents. Junior got a pair of spurs, Victor got a big red top, and Loli got a little toy dog that looks like Chipito. But I got the best present. It was a silver-dollar buckle, the one I had seen with my tía Lena in Tucson. It doesn't have a dollar yet, only a hole, but when I win the Perfect Attendance I will put my silver dollar in that hole.

Nochebuena (NO-chay-BUAY-nah)—
    Christmas Eve
piñata (peen-YAH-tah)—clay pot *(olla)*
    filled with treats
olla (OY-yah)—clay pot
dulces (DOOL-sehss)—sweets, candy
mascada (mas-KAH-dah)—scarf
¡dale! (DAH-lay)—hit it!
tamales (tah-MAH-less)—steamed
    filled dough
menudo (men-OO-doe)—tripe soup
tortillas (tor-TEE-yahs)—flat Mexican bread

COYOTE NEWS

Happy New Year!

Stories and Pictures by the Students of Coyote School, Pima County, Arizona

Miss Byers' Radio

Miss Byers brought her new radio to school. It has a big battery, so it doesn't matter that Coyote School has no electricity. We got to hear President Roosevelt's speech to the Congress. He told them to be prepared for war. Then he said, "Happy New Year."........Monchi Ramirez, Grade 4

Our President's Voice

None of us kids had heard the President's voice before. When he said "war" it sounded like "waw." We were all laughing because we never heard anybody who talked like that, but Billy said some of the dudes do.............Rosie Garcia, Grade 3

Our President

waw

by Joey Brown

Some Noisy Children

When the President was talking, Loli was noisy. Miss Byers gave her peanuts to make her quiet. I was quiet without the peanuts...Victor, Grade 2

Yap!

By Frankie Lopez

Music on the Radio

We got to listen to the music on Miss Byers' radio. She has many stations, but I liked best to hear the one with the rancheras..........Gilbert Perez, Grade 6

No Earrings for Christmas

Santa Claus didn't bring me any earrings. Loli says it's because he knows that I don't have any holes in my ears like she does......Cynthia Brown, Grade 2

The Perfect Attendance Report

Miss Byers says Santa Claus must have given some of our kids the flu and chicken pox for Christmas. The only kids who still have perfect attendance are Natalia, Monchi, Victor, and me.........Billy Mills, Grade 3

La Fiesta de los Vaqueros Rodeo Parade

We are so excited because Miss Byers just told us something wonderful. Our school gets to be in the Tucson Rodeo Parade!...Natalia Ramirez, Grade 8

Roundup!

The vaqueros were hollering, "¡Ándale! ¡Ándale!" They were cutting through the cattle on their horses, swinging their lassoes in the air to rope out the steers. My tío Chaco threw his saddle up on his horse, Canelo, and joined them. We kids clapped and whistled. Sometimes we helped my father or my tíos. We brought them rope or a fresh horse or something to drink.

That night we boys got to eat with the vaqueros and sit by the fire and listen to them play their guitars and sing their *rancheras*. We got to hear their exciting stories and their bragging and their bad words. When my father came over to Junior and me I thought he was going to tell us to go in to bed, but instead he said, "Tomorrow I want you boys to help with the branding." Junior had helped since he was eleven, but it was the first time my father had ever asked me.

"Tomorrow I have school," I said.

"School!" said Junior. "Monchi, don't you understand? You get to help with the branding!"

"He doesn't want to lose the Perfect Attendance," said Victor.

"The Perfect Attendance!" said Junior. "Monchi, you are crazier than a goat. You are a Ramírez. We are a family of vaqueros. Roundup is more important than the Perfect Attendance."

I knew Junior was right, but I touched the empty hole of my silver-dollar buckle and I sighed. *Adiós,* Perfect Attendance.

rancheras (rahn-CHAIR-ahs)—Mexican folk songs
fiesta (fee-ESS-tah)—party, celebration
de (day)—of
adiós (ah-DYOHSS)—good-bye

For two exciting days Junior and I helped with the roundup. First the vaqueros lassoed the calves and wrestled them down to the ground. Then Junior and I held them while my father and my tío Enrique branded them and cut the ears and gave them the shot.

¡Qué barullo! The red-hot irons were smoking, and the burned hair was stinking. The calves were fighting and bawling like giant babies. They were much heavier than Junior and me. It was hard work and dangerous to hold them down. I got dust in my eyes and in my nose, but I didn't care.

After the work of the roundup was over, we made the fiesta! First was a race for the kids. We had to ride as fast as we could to the chuck wagon, take an orange, and ride back again. Junior won on Pinto. He got a big jar of candies and gave some to all of us. Last came Victor and his little *burro.* All that day we had races and roping contests.

That night we had a big *barbacoa.* The kids got cold soda pops. When the music started, all the vaqueros wanted to dance with Natalia. The one they call Chapo asked her to be his novia, but Natalia told him she doesn't want to get married. She wants to go to high school.

Monday morning when we left for school, the vaqueros were packing their bedrolls. We waved and hollered from our bus, *"¡Adiós! ¡Adiós! ¡Hasta la vista!"*

qué (kaye)—what, how
barullo (bah-ROO-yoe)—noise, racket
burro (BOOR-row)—donkey
barbacoa (bar-bah-KOH-ah)—barbecue
hasta la vista (AH-stah lah VEE-stah)—
    see you

COYOTE ¡Hasta la vista! NEWS

Stories and Pictures by the Students of Coyote School, Pima County, Arizona

Adiós Coyote School! Lalo Natalia *Good-bye, everybody! Thank you, Miss Byers!*

by Lalo Lopez

Eduardo (Lalo) and Natalia Graduate!

Lalo and I have passed the Eighth Grade Standard Achievement Test! I am happy to graduate and I am excited about high school, but I will miss my teacher and all the kids at my dear Coyote School...Natalia Ramirez, Grade 8

I Lose the Perfect Attendance

I was absent from school to help with the roundup. It was very exciting, but now it is over and I am feeling sad. The vaqueros are gone and I will not get a silver dollar for my buckle....Monchi Ramirez, Grade 4

The Perfect Attendance Report

The only one who still has perfect attendance is Victor. Even Miss Byers has been absent, because when it was roundup on her ranch a big calf stepped on her foot. We had Miss Elias for 3 days. Miss Byers had to pay her 5 dollars a day to take her place.....Gilbert Perez, Grade 6

Please forgive me, Miss Byers — 300 pounds

BY Rosie Garcia

A Visit to the Boston Beans

Mr. and Mrs. Bean invited my family to visit them this summer in Boston. Boston is Back East. It is even bigger than Tucson. No other kid at Coyote School has ever gone that far away!.............Billy Mills, Grade 3

Earrings

My daddy is getting married. Joey and I will get a new mother and 4 new brothers. Laura is nice and she can cook, but the best part is she has pierced ears and now I will get to have them too!....Cynthia Brown, Grade 2

Last Issue for the School Year

This is the last issue before the summer vacation. I am saving all my Coyote News newspapers so that someday I can show my children all the swell and exciting things we did at Coyote School..........Rosie Garcia, Grade 3

The Last Day of School

On the last day of school Miss Byers gave us a fiesta with cupcakes and candies and Cracker Jacks and soda pops. We got to listen to Mexican music on her radio. I didn't have to dance with Natalia. I got to dance with Rosie.

Then Miss Byers turned off the radio and stood in the front of the room between President Roosevelt and Señor Grandote. She called Natalia and Lalo up to the front and told them how proud we were that they were graduates of Coyote School, and how much we would miss them. We all clapped and whistled.

Next, Miss Byers gave Edelia a paper and said, "Please read what it says, Edelia."

Edelia read: "Edelia Ortiz has been promoted to Grade Two." Miss Byers had to help her to read "promoted," but we all clapped and cheered anyway. Edelia looked very happy and proud.

Then Miss Byers asked Victor to come to the front of the room, and I knew what that meant. I didn't want to listen when she said how good it was that he had not missed a day of school, and I didn't want to look when she gave him the silver dollar. I knew I should be

happy that Victor won the Perfect Attendance, but I was not.

"And now, boys and girls," Miss Byers said, "it's time for the next award."

"What next award?" we asked.

"The *Coyote News* Writing Award for the student who has contributed most to *Coyote News* by writing his own stories and by helping others write theirs. The winner of the *Coyote News* Writing Award is Ramón Ernesto Ramírez."

"Me?" I said.

All the kids were clapping and whistling. I just sat there.

"Go up to the front," Natalia said and gave me a push.

Miss Byers smiled and shook my hand. "Congratulations, Monchi," she said, and then she gave me the award.

¡Ay caramba! The *Coyote News* Writing Award was a shiny silver dollar!

"Oh thank you, Miss Byers!" I said. *"¡Gracias!"* I was so surprised and happy. I pushed the silver dollar into the round hole on my buckle. It fit perfectly!

"¡Muy hermosa!" Miss Byers said.

She was right. It was very beautiful.

gracias (GRAHS-see-ahs)—thank you
hermosa (air-MOE-sah)—beautiful

179

Think, Talk and Write

Talk About It The children of Coyote School really enjoyed writing the *Coyote News*. What would you want to write about at the Ramirez Ranch and Coyote School?

1. The author helps you get to know Monchi through his words and actions. Find examples of how Monchi's words and actions help you get to know him. **Think Like an Author**

2. How do the members of Monchi's family feel about one another? How do they feel about being a family? Support your answer with details from the story. **Draw Conclusions**

3. How is Coyote School different from your school? Give some examples. **Prior Knowledge**

4. Write about life on the Ramirez Ranch. Use at least three words from the Words to Know list to describe what it would be like to live there. **Vocabulary**

Look Back and Write Look back at the *Coyote News*. What are some of the stories you enjoyed reading that made the news at Coyote School?

Meet author **Joan Sandin on p. 377.**

Retell

W2.2.a Write responses to literature: Demonstrate an understanding of the literary work.

Writing

Prompt *Coyote School News* tells a story about people working together that is based on real events in history. Think about a historical time in which people worked together. Now write a story about the people in this historical setting.

Writing Trait

Vivid adjectives add impact to your writing.

Student Model

On the Trail

My name is Abigail Brandt. My family and I are traveling west by wagon train. We are going to start our own farm when we get to Oregon.

We have been on the trail for more than a week now. Travel is extremely slow. Four strong oxen pull our wagon. My determined father walks along beside the **animals**, encouraging them to move faster.

The people in the wagon **trains** wake before the bright light of day. We all gather the animals together and make breakfast. Soon, we are ready to travel. The dusty, bumpy **trails** await us.

By evening, everyone is grimy and exhausted. My **brothers** and I are sent to get cool, refreshing water from a nearby stream. My father tends to the animals, and my mother prepares our food. After supper, we gather around the blazing campfire to sing **songs** and dream about a hopeful future.

Historical fiction tells about fictional characters in real settings.

Vivid adjectives help readers picture events.

Regular plural nouns are correctly used.

Use the model to help you write your own historical fiction story.

Teamwork

W2.1.b Write narratives: Provide a context to enable the reader to imagine the world of the event or experience.

181

Skill Talk

Steps in a process give detailed directions about how to make or do something.

- Picture the steps in your mind to help you visualize the process.
- Authors often use numbered steps and clue words, such as *first, next,* and *finally* to show the order.
- Look for text features, such as boldface type, check marks, and graphic sources to help you pick out important information.

 Ready to Try It?
Read "How to Start a School Newspaper." Look for text features to help you follow the directions.

Concept Link

Most major newspapers have an online edition for people to read on their computers. Find an online newspaper. Make a list of other team members that you would need to publish an online edition of a newspaper.

Starting your own school paper can be fun! You get to share news and say what you think about it. But starting a paper takes planning and teamwork. Here's how to do it.

First, pick your team. You'll need to fill these jobs:

✓ The **editor** decides what stories writers will work on. Everybody comes up with ideas, but the editor has the final say.

✓ The **writers** write the stories. They talk to people and dig up facts.

✓ The **copyeditor** checks the writers' work. He or she fixes spelling and other mistakes.

✓ The **photo editor** chooses pictures to go with the stories.

✓ The **designer** decides where the stories and pictures will go on the page. The final result is called a layout.

✓ The **staff adviser** is the adult who guides you. The adviser answers your questions and steers your paper in the right direction.

How to Start a School Newspaper

by Lisa Klobuchar

Next, figure out what to write about. Find out what your classmates want to read about. Ask around, or place an idea box outside your classroom. Here are just a few kinds of writing to put in your paper:

✓ **News** stories tell about what is going on in your school, your town, or even around the world. They must be factual, or true.

✓ In **sports** stories, you can tell when games will be played at your school. You can describe the sports action and list scores, or you can profile a player.

✓ **Arts and entertainment** stories may tell about special school events or introduce readers to a poem, short story, piece of artwork, or movie.

✓ In an **advice column**, students can ask questions about anything, and "Dear So-and-So" will answer them.

Finally, start writing! It feels wonderful to share your ideas and stories with your classmates. And there's no better way to do that than to start a school newspaper.

Reading Across Texts

This selection identifies several kinds of writing that can go into a school newspaper. Compare and contrast the list from this selection to the kind of writing in *Coyote News*.

Writing Across Texts Choose one kind of newspaper writing and write an article that might appear in your own school's newspaper.

Build Language

Team Accomplishments

Build Vocabulary

Learn ◉ **Skill Prefixes** Prefixes are word parts added to the beginning of a word that change its meaning. For example, the prefix *dis-* means "not." If you *disagree,* you do not agree with someone or something. Learning prefixes can help you figure out the meanings of unknown words as you read.

Practice Read "Writing a Play About History" on page 185. Use what you learned about prefixes to help you figure out the meanings of this week's Words to Know. If you need more help use a dictionary.

Words to Know	arrangements	descendants	advice
	argument	snag	script
	dishonest		

On Your Own Reread "Writing a Play About History." Write a journal entry describing a play you would like to write about a historical event. Use words from the Words to Know list.

G3R1.8 Use knowledge of prefixes (e.g., *un-, re-, pre-, bi-, mis-, dis-*) and suffixes (e.g., *-er, -est, -ful*) to determine meanings of words.

Writing a Play About *History*

If you decide to write a play about history, make arrangements to spend a lot of time on careful research. Sometimes there is some argument about which facts are true. Although few writers mean to be dishonest, they may not always check their facts carefully.

It might be interesting to write about the descendants of the people who sailed on the *Mayflower*. Some of our Presidents, including Presidents John Adams, John Quincy Adams, and Franklin Roosevelt had ancestors on the *Mayflower*.

Astronaut Alan Shepard Jr. is also part of this special group. I'm sure you'll be able to find many more names to add to this list!

Your work can hit a snag if you don't make your information interesting. Take this advice and make sure your script tells a good story. You'll learn a lot while writing your play. You'll want to work hard to make sure your audience enjoys every minute of it!

 Need a Review?
For additional help with prefixes, see *Words!* on p. W•5.

 Ready to Try It?
Read *Scene Two* on pp. 188–201.

Teamwork

Build Comprehension

Learn   ◉ **Skill** **Draw Conclusions**

- When you draw a conclusion about a topic, you think about the facts and details that an author provides.

- Prior knowledge, what you already know about a topic, is often used to draw a conclusion.

- Using a graphic organizer like the one below can help you draw conclusions that make sense.

Practice   Use what you learned about drawing conclusions as you read "Visiting a California Ghost Town" on page 187.

On Your Own   **Write to Read** Reread "Visiting a California Ghost Town." Would you like to visit a ghost town? Write a letter to a friend telling why you should both take a trip to a ghost town.

 Need a Review? See the *Picture It!* lesson on p. PI•6 for additional help with drawing conclusions.

 Ready to Try It? As you read *Scene Two* on pp. 188–201, use what you've learned about drawing conclusions to help you understand the text.

G5R2.4 Draw inferences, conclusions, or generalizations about text and support them with textual evidence and prior knowledge.

Visiting a California Ghost Town

You can visit a town called Bodie if you would like to see a real ghost town. A ghost town is a town that has been abandoned. In 1859, gold was discovered in Bodie. By 1880, the town grew to about 10,000 people. By 1882, the boom was over and people started moving away.

Skill Why is Bodie called a ghost town?

In 1962, Bodie became a California State Historic Park. The park service keeps Bodie in a state of "arrested decay." This means that things are kept just as they were found. About 170 buildings are still standing. They are almost all kept locked to keep things inside the same as they once were. If you look inside some of the buildings, it may appear that the people just left. You may even see books left open on desks or a store filled with goods.

Skill What are three facts you learned about Bodie?

Bodie is a wonderful place to go if you like learning about the past. Walk around this town. See if you can imagine what it was like living in the Old West.

Skill What conclusion can you draw about visiting a ghost town?

Teamwork

187

Genre

Plays are stories performed in front of an audience. As you read, think about how one character can play two parts.

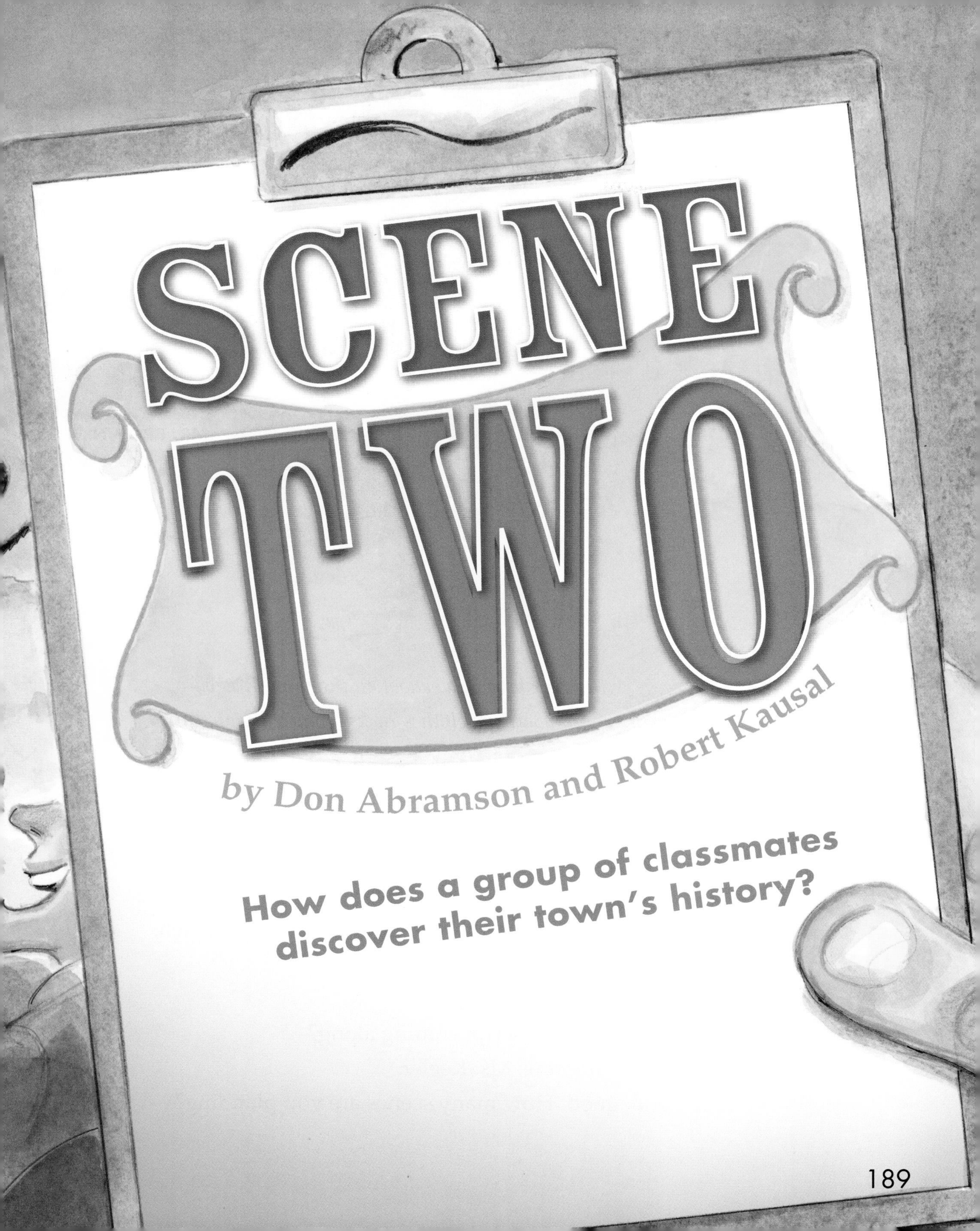

SCENE TWO

by Don Abramson and Robert Kausal

How does a group of classmates discover their town's history?

CHARACTERS

JASMINE DELORES KERRY ANGIE

MITCH HAP MS. KEELER
a teacher MR. BROWN
a teacher

SETTING: *A room next to the stage in a school auditorium. It is bare, except for a table and chairs, perhaps clothes racks, a makeup table and mirror, some boxes, etc.*

AT RISE: *MR. BROWN enters, carrying a clipboard. He shows in MITCH, JASMINE, HAP, ANGIE, KERRY, and DELORES, all carrying books, backpacks, etc. MS. KEELER follows.*

MR. BROWN: All right, kids, you can work on your script in here while the others rehearse on the stage.

JASMINE: Thank you, Mr. Brown.

MS. KEELER: And how's that script coming along?

ANGIE: Oh, we're doing fine, Ms. Keeler.

MS. KEELER: Good, good. How many scenes are you planning?

KERRY: We were going to do a scene for each year of Riverside's history, but we thought a hundred thirty-four would run long.

MR. BROWN: You think? Just keep in mind it's a skit in our Founders' Day talent show. You're sharing the stage with—*(He consults his clipboard.)* Betty and Beverly Tanner singing "If I Ain't Got You"—

MS. KEELER: "Don't Have." Sorry! Force of habit.

MR. BROWN *(still reading)*: Milton the Miraculous Magician—oh, by the way, if you see an escaped rabbit come by here, try to corner him or something—Gloria Newman and her Hula Hoop™ Extravaganza—well, you get my point. It's a talent show. Nobody's going to win an acting award.

MS. KEELER: We'll let you work now.

KERRY: Right, thanks. *(Mr. Brown and Ms. Keeler leave.)* Okay, so where are we?

ANGIE: We finished scene one.

DELORES: Who's got scene two?

MITCH AND JASMINE *(together)*: I do. *(They look at each other.)*

MITCH: I was supposed to write it.

JASMINE: I told you I was going to write it.

MITCH: Two too?

JASMINE: Yes.

DELORES: Two twos?

JASMINE: I guess.

KERRY *(like a train)*: Too-too-too-*tooo!* *(They all look at him; he grins and shrugs.)*

ANGIE: Cool it, Kerry.

HAP: I wrote a scene too. No, I mean it's *also* a scene, not two a scene—I mean—

DELORES: Don't get Kerry started again.

JASMINE: We'll see, Hap. Let's get this scene two business straightened out first.

KERRY: You guys could arm-wrestle for who goes first.

DELORES: Kerry!

JASMINE: I'll go first. Here, I made copies of the script. *(She distributes the scripts.)* Kerry, you play Joshua Wilkins; Angie, you read Becky Isaacs; and Hap, play Gunther Isaacs for now. *(They all take their scripts and move down center.)* This is scene two, now. After Gunther Isaacs and his wife and two daughters have moved to Riverside—except it isn't Riverside yet—and they've built their cabin and planted their crops. Lights up.

KERRY: Huh?

JASMINE: Begin.

KERRY *(JOSHUA):* Becky, I must tell you I truly appreciate your family's hospitality this week.

ANGIE *(BECKY):* Joshua, in truth, my mother bade you stay because she is so eager to hear news from the East.

MITCH *(interrupting):* Hold up. What does that mean, "bade you stay"?

JASMINE: It's a past tense of "bid."

MITCH: Like an auction?

JASMINE: No, no! Like in "invite." Go on.

MITCH *(to the others):* She reads too many books.

KERRY *(JOSHUA):* You know, Becky, I came west looking for land. If I could find the right spot, I might be of a mind—

MITCH *(interrupting):* Now, what does *that* mean—"of a mind"?

JASMINE: It means "to think; to have an opinion." Stop interrupting, Mitch.

MITCH: Well, why can't they talk regular English?

JASMINE: Because it's history, that's why. They're speaking—*(She searches for a word but can't find it.)*—historical. *(to the actors)* Please!

ANGIE (*BECKY*): My father owns all this land, Joshua. If you but talked to him—

HAP (*GUNTHER, enters*): If you talked to me about what?

ANGIE (*BECKY*): Hello, Papa!

KERRY (*JOSHUA*): About your land, Gunther. What if a young fellow desired to stay here?

HAP (*GUNTHER*): Why then, Joshua, I'm sure some sort of arrangements could be made. I can see more and more settlers moving into the area. Soon we'll have a town, and that town will become a city. And someday in the future—

MITCH (*interrupting*): You know what? I'm "of a mind" about this scene, Jasmine. It's bo-o-oring!

JASMINE: Well, that's too bad—it's *his-tor-y*.

KERRY: This skit should *be* history.

BO-O-ORING!

193

MITCH: Yeah, but you've got to read *my* scene about Gunther Isaacs. *(handing out scripts)* Here, Hap, you're still Gunther—Delores, you're Gunther's wife, Amity Isaacs, and Kerry, you're Peter Marlon. *(They all move to their places.)* Scene Two. And—action!

KERRY (PETER): Gunther, it's been awesome doing business with you.

HAP (GUNTHER): You made my day, Peter. High five. *(Following the script, he raises his hand, but unsurely. Kerry high-fives him.)*

JASMINE *(interrupting):* Now, wait a minute! The Founders did *not* high-five each other.

MITCH: How do you know? *(He holds up his hand; Kerry high-fives him. Then quickly, before Jasmine can think of an answer he continues)* Action, action!

HAP (GUNTHER): So, Pete, when are you going to start clearing your land?

KERRY (PETER): First, I think I'll get my wife and son in Philly.

DELORES (AMITY, *enters):* Take my advice, Peter, build first. Your family'll thank you for it.

HAP (GUNTHER): Yo, Amity, you never complained before.

DELORES (AMITY): About sleeping outdoors while you built a barn for the horses? What good would that do me?

HAP (GUNTHER): Good point. You know how much those horses are worth? *(to* PETER) Anyway, if you head east now, it'll be winter before you get back.

KERRY (PETER): Cool, I'll go give them a call now.

DELORES *(dropping character):* Give them a call? Mitch, even I know they didn't have telephones back then.

MITCH: Um—I guess you're right. We'll make it a telegraph. Action, action, action!

KERRY: How did we ever get scene one written? *(as* PETER): Well, I'll go start my cabin. And I'm sure looking forward to fishing in that river.

HAP (GUNTHER): Me too. Later, dude. (PETER, *exits)*

DELORES (AMITY): What's this about fish? You know there are no fish in that river!

HAP (GUNTHER): I made that mighty river by damming that sorry-looking creek.

DELORES (AMITY): True, but what about the fish?

HAP *(GUNTHER):* I thought—you know—if you dam it, they will come.

DELORES *(AMITY):* The fish? They'll have to crawl through the forest to get here.

HAP *(GUNTHER):* But you've got to admit, the dam helped.

DELORES *(AMITY):* Oh, that pathetic creek looks like a real river now. But Gunther, what if the settlers find out?

HAP *(GUNTHER, shrugs):* Good point.

JASMINE: Mitch, you can't put that on stage!

MITCH: Why not?

JASMINE: Because it's not true, that's why not! *(holding up a book she has dug out of her backpack)* I've read all the way through *The History of Riverside,* and I know it's not in here. Besides, Gunther Isaacs was a Founding Father. He would never—

MITCH: I got it off the Internet. Look, I got a printout— *(He digs in his backpack and finds several pages of printout. He hands them to Jasmine.)*

JASMINE *(scanning the article quickly):* ". . . another tale told of Gunther Isaacs, but probably an apocryphal one. . . ." Don't you know what that means?

MITCH: I thought it meant—like, "secret."

JASMINE: No—it means—it means—oh, wait a minute. *(She digs in her backpack to find her electronic dictionary. She punches in the word and reads the screen.)* It means "of doubtful authorship or authenticity." See, it's made up!

MITCH: Well, so?

DELORES: I think what Jasmine is getting at, Mitch, is that it's a lie.

KERRY: It *is* a good story, though.

HAP: But this is a play about history!

KERRY: Do you think anybody'll know the difference?

DELORES: I think a lot of the audience will know about the town's history.

JASMINE *(waving her book):* Some of them might even have read *The History of Riverside.*

MITCH: But face it, Gunther Isaacs was a shady character.

DELORES: You're saying he was dishonest?

MITCH: If he was, at least he wasn't dull!

JASMINE: The scene's out, and that's final!

MITCH: If the scene's out, I'm out. And you can't use scene one either.

HAP: Come on, Mitch. We all worked on that scene together.

MITCH: Well then, I'll just take back the lines I wrote.

DELORES: That's silly. You can't just take back some lines!

MITCH: Sure I can. They're my lines. So—who's with me?

HAP: Mitch, don't do this.

MITCH: Whose side are you on, Hap? Come on.

DELORES: This isn't about sides.

MITCH: Sure it is.

ANGIE *(in a surprisingly sharp voice):* Will you all stop this! *(They all fall silent and look at her.)* I'm sorry. But my mom's a family counselor, and if there's one thing I learned, it's how to settle arguments.

MITCH: That's a lot of hooey!

ANGIE: No, it isn't!

DELORES: Be quiet, Mitch.

KERRY: Me, I enjoy a good argument.

DELORES: We can tell.

ANGIE: You can talk about what you really want. But then you really have to listen. Jasmine, Mitch, why do you want to put on this skit?

JASMINE: Well, I guess I want to bring history alive.

MITCH: I want people to be entertained.

ANGIE: Does the skit have to have this scene to be entertaining?

MITCH: I was just trying to add a little humor.

ANGIE: Well then, can't we all work together—?

MITCH: Look, we don't need another lecture on teamwork.

KERRY: Yeah, when I hear the word *teamwork*, I just want to punch somebody.

DELORES: Look, I've got an idea. If this story about damming up the creek is apoc—uh—made up, why does the Web site even run it?

ANGIE: Well, they do *say* the story probably isn't true.

DELORES: So why can't we do the same thing? Then we could keep Mitch's scene.

MITCH: Yeah—we could have the narrator say—um— "There's another story about Gunther Isaacs—"

JASMINE: "Some say it's true, and some say it's untrue—"

MITCH: "But we say—it's a good story."

HAP: Yes!

KERRY: Write that down. (*Mitch does so.*)

ANGIE: Can we move on now?

DELORES: Yes!

HAP: Would you like to hear *my* scene?

MITCH: I suppose we've got to.

JASMINE: If we're really cooperating now—

MS. KEELER (*enters*): Teamwork, yes.

(KERRY *quickly and secretly punches* MITCH'S *arm.*)

MITCH: Hey!

(KERRY *grins and shrugs as if to say: "I couldn't help myself."*)

MS. KEELER (*not noticing*): That's so important when you're doing this sort of thing. How're things going?

ANGIE: We—uh—hit a snag, but we solved it.

MS. KEELER: Good. We're going to have a great show. Dixie's tap dancing to the "Star-Spangled Banner" is going to bring down the house. Now tell me, I hope you're all contributing to this script.

DELORES: Yes, we've all been working together.

199

HAP: Now we're going to read my scene.

MS. KEELER: Hap, did you write about your ancestor, Cornelius Hapgood?

HAP: Yes, I did.

MS. KEELER: I'm so glad. Kids, I don't know if you know this, but Hap's family are descendants of Riverside's earliest settlers.

KERRY: The buffalo?

HAP: No, my great, great, great, great—I don't know how many greats—grandfather was Cornelius Hapgood.

ANGIE: Wow, that's *great*, Hap.

DELORES: Who's Cornelius Hapgood?

HAP: He opened Riverside's first shoe store—for people *and* horses.

DELORES: Okay. So what's your scene about, Hap?

HAP: Picture this: the curtain rises. Sunset. Cornelius Hapgood is talking to his faithful horse Bucketmouth—

ANGIE: Bucketmouth?

JASMINE: Wait a minute! Where are we going to get a horse?

HAP: Good point. Okay—picture this: the curtain rises. Sunset. Cornelius Hapgood walks on stage, talking to himself—
(reads, as CORNELIUS*):* Oh, my dogs are tired—

KERRY: Dogs? I thought he had a horse.

HAP: They're his *feet*. Okay—picture this: the curtain rises—

KERRY: I know! Sunset, dogs, feet. Get on with it!

HAP (CORNELIUS)*:* I plum wore out these boots down to my socks. Where can a person buy full-grain leather shoes that are rugged, yet stylish?

MITCH: Ms. Keeler, I think we're going to need another hour. Or two.

HAP (CORNELIUS)*:* I'm talkin' comfortable, yet affordable. Maybe a waterproof moccasin with fringes. . . .
(As he talks, the lights fade out.)

Think, Talk and Write

Talk About It A play can help you learn about the past. *Scene Two* is a play about different ways to tell about a town's history. Explain how that happens in this play.

1. Why do you think the authors have Jasmine always checking everyone's facts? **Think Like an Author**

2. What conclusions can you come to about the way history can be told? **Draw Conclusions**

3. What does working on scene two of the play allow the students to do? What do you think they learned while doing it? **Answer Questions**

4. When Angie says that they "hit a snag" she means that the students had some problems. What were some of them? **Vocabulary**

Look Back and Write Why do you think people might want to know about the history of their town? Write some of the reasons people would want to learn more about their town's past.

Meet authors Don Abramson on page 375 and Robert Kausal on page 376.

Retell

W2.2.a Write responses to literature: Demonstrate an understanding of the literary work.

Writing Play

Prompt The characters in *Scene Two* must overcome obstacles in order to accomplish their team's goal. Think about what you might accomplish working with a team. Now write a short play about how the team accomplishes its goal.

Student Model

The Sweat Shirt

Characters: Grace, Ava, Curtis, James

Setting: A school art room

Grace: Okay, **people** let's get our act together. (The students look angry about what Grace is saying.) I'm sure our team can come up with the winning design for this year's new school sweat shirts.

James: Listen, Grace, don't treat us like **children**.

Curtis: Okay, let's start talk about our ideas.

Grace: Well, since our school colors are green and gold, I say that we should have green sweat shirts with gold writing.

Ava: Sounds good. Does everyone agree?

Curtis and James (together): Yes!

James: The wolf is our mascot, so I could draw a picture of one.

Grace: We should design some fancy letters ourselves that say The **Wolves**.

A play takes place in a specific seting.

Dialogue helps us know what each character is like.

Irregular plural nouns are used correctly.

Use this beginning to help you write your own play.

 W2.1.a Write narratives: Relate ideas, observations, or recollections of an event or experience.

Teamwork

203

Poetry Talk

Imagery is a technique authors use to help readers experience the way things look, sound, smell, taste, and feel. Imagery, or sensory words, makes characters and settings seem real by appealing to the reader's senses. It can also help create a mood or dramatize an action. When reading poetry, look for words that help you see, smell, hear, taste, or feel what is happening.

 Ready to Try It?
Read the poem "Front Porch." Look for images that help you see and experience these places.

Concept Link

Think about a community project you would like to work on and the team you would need to do it. Make a list of the things you would need to accomplish this project.

FRONT PORCH

BY LESLIE NELSON JENNINGS

People who live in cities never know
   The creak of hickory rockers and the hum
Of talk about what happened years ago.
   Just sitting on the sunny side of some
Old house can bring us closer to events
   Than counting seconds, though the world says not.
If looking backward doesn't make good sense
   Tomorrow, then, may be as well forgot.

Those who planned farmsteads hereabouts took time
   Enough to square a beam and see it placed.
A man of sixty wasn't past his prime
   And nothing worth a penny went to waste.
We can remember many things with pride,
Who built front porches neighborly and wide.

Reading Across Texts

This poem makes readers think about the past. Draw a picture of something in the past to illustrate the poem.

Writing Across Texts

Take a look at the drawing you made. Write a new poem based on your drawing.

Build Language
Animals

Build Vocabulary

Learn ◉ **Skill Unfamiliar words** are words that you do not know. You can use context clues, reading the words and sentences around the unfamiliar word, to figure out the meaning. If context clues don't help, you can look the word up in a dictionary or glossary.

Practice Read "Racing Dreams" on page 207. Use context clues or a dictionary to help you figure out the meanings of this week's Words to Know. Write a sentence for each word in your journal.

Words to Know	vast	ambition	roamed	rickety
	quicksand	resistance	infested	landslide

On Your Own Reread "Racing Dreams." Imagine that you're a reporter at a horse race. Write a news article on the race. Use words from the Words to Know list in your article.

🐻 **G3R1.7** Use a dictionary to learn the meanings and other features of unknown words.

RACING Dreams

One summer my parents sent me to camp in Wisconsin. I spent a lot of time taking horseback riding lessons. It was my ambition to become a great rider. As we roamed down the trails, I dreamed about being a famous rider.

First, my imaginary horse and I would gallop over the vast plains. We would leap over rickety gates and pass untouched through fields infested with locusts. My horse would amaze everyone with his bravery. He would leap over quicksand without the slightest resistance. My horse would be so fast that it could outrun a landslide. Nothing would scare him!

Everyone would want us to run in a great race. My horse and I would train for long hours. We would work hard. The day would come and all the fastest horses and their riders would be there to see who was the best. My horse and I would fly around the track. We would pass all the other horses.

 Need a Review?
For additional help with using context clues to determine the meanings of unfamiliar words, see *Words!* on p. W•7.

Ready to Try It?
Read *Horse Heroes* on pp. 210–221.

Teamwork

Build Comprehension

Learn ◉ **Skill Fact and Opinion**

- A statement of fact can be proved true or false by looking in a reference book, asking an expert, or using your own knowledge or experience.

- A statement of opinion cannot be proved true or false. It is a belief or judgment. It often contains a word of judgment, such as *best, greatest,* or *beautiful.* Opinions may begin with the words *in my opinion* or *I believe.*

- Using a graphic organizer like the one below can help you check for statements of fact and statements of opinion.

Statement	Fact? How Can It Be Checked?	Opinion? What Are Clue Words?

Practice   Use what you learned about statements of fact and opinion as you read "Bug Boys" on page 209.

On Your Own   **Write to Read** Reread "Bug Boys." Use both the text and a graphic organizer like the one above to write a short paragraph about jockeys.

 Need a Review? See the *Picture It!* lesson on p. PI•7 for additional help with fact and opinion.

 Ready to Try It? As you read *Horse Heroes* on pp. 210–221, use what you've learned about fact and opinion to understand the text.

  R2.6 Distinguish between cause and effect and between fact and opinion in expository text.

Bug * Boys

In the sport of horse racing, a jockey is the one who rides the horses. Jockeys start out when they are young. An apprentice jockey is called a "bug boy" because a mark called an asterisk appears after their name in the race program. Some people think that the mark looks like a bug!

Willie Shoemaker was one of the most well-known jockeys in racing. He won his first horse race at the age of seventeen. He was small in size, weighing under one hundred pounds. Many people believe he was the greatest jockey of all time. He won the Kentucky Derby four times. Another jockey, Pat Day, started out as a rodeo cowboy. Because he was 4 feet 11 inches tall, people thought he would do well as a jockey. In 1989, he set a record when he won eight of nine races in a single day!

Chris McCarron was called the best jockey of the year in 1974. After a career as a jockey, Chris McCarron worked on the 2003 film *Seabiscuit*. The movie was about a real horse and the people who worked with him.

Skill What three facts did you learn about jockeys?

Skill What opinion did people have about Willie Shoemaker?

Skill This sentence contains a statement of fact and a statement of opinion about Pat Day. What is the fact? What is the opinion?

Teamwork

209

HORSE HEROES

True Stories of Amazing Horses

Written by Kate Petty

*How are horses
useful to humans?*

Expository nonfiction recounts a true event
or series of events. As you read, think about the
roles horses have played in history.

Horses and humans have worked together for thousands of years. From the vast wilderness to the Hollywood movie set, horses have served us faithfully while playing an important role in history. Horses can be found in our history, art, religion, and mythology. Let's look at some of history's most famous horse heroes.

Long Journey
Pony Express riders took the mail 2,000 miles from Missouri to California.

Pony Express

When the little mustang came into view, the crowd began to cheer.

Her rider, Johnny Fry, led her into the packed town square of St. Joseph, Missouri, that warm April evening in 1860. Johnny checked the mail pouch on the mustang's back for the last time as she snorted excitedly.

A cannon boomed. They were away! The mustang raced off into the evening twilight,

This poster for the Pony Express service dates from 1861.

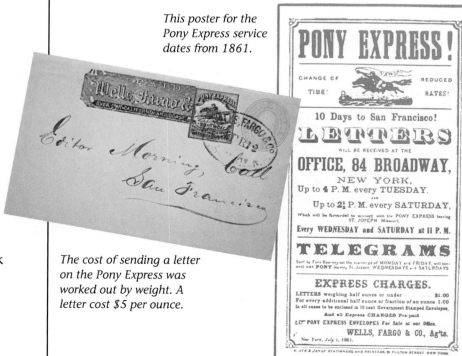

First Delivery
Johnny Fry's mail sack held 49 letters and three newspapers.

The cost of sending a letter on the Pony Express was worked out by weight. A letter cost $5 per ounce.

leaving the cheering crowds far behind.

Horse and rider had entered history as the first ever Pony Express team.

In 1860, there were no such things as telephones and fax machines. If you lived on the West Coast of the United States, keeping up to date with the latest news on the East Coast was almost impossible. It could take more than a month for mail to travel across the continent by wagon.

Mustang
This hardy breed is descended from the horses brought to America by Spanish explorers.

The Pony Express was a horse relay designed to keep the mail moving day and night. It cut down the time taken for mail to reach California to just eight days.

Each horse and rider galloped at top speed to the next station. The rider leaped off the exhausted horse shouting, "Pony rider coming!" The mail was transferred to a fresh horse, and the rider galloped off again on his new mount.

There were 157 relay stations, and riders changed horses about six to eight times.

The teams risked death together on a daily basis.

Much of the route lay through the homelands of American Indians, some of whom declared war on the white invaders of their territory.

Express Riders
Pony Express riders had to be under 18 years old and weigh less than 126 pounds, so as not to slow down their horses.

Transfer
It took a rider two minutes to transfer between horses.

Saddle Up
Mail pouches were sometimes sewn into the rider's saddle.

One of the bravest riders was "Pony Bob" Haslam. In May 1860, he arrived at a station in Nevada to find the keeper dead and all the horses gone. He set out for the next station, which was 40 miles away.

"I knew I had to carry on. As I rode through the night, I kept watching my pony's ears. I knew he'd hear any ambush before I did."

At the next station he persuaded the keeper to leave with them. Bob and his tireless horse saved the man's life—the next night that station was attacked.

Express riders carried rifles in case of trouble.

The Pony Express teams rode across rocky mountain passes and wide, empty plains in scorching sun, pouring rain, and freezing blizzards. If their rider fell off, some brave horses carried on alone to the next station.

The final stop was Sacramento, California. Crowds of eager people would gather to watch the arrival of the last rider on the route bringing them their mail and newspapers.

The success of the Pony Express teams proved that it was possible for the East and West coasts to keep in touch. It was a milestone on the way to modern America. The horses and riders that ran the Pony Express were real pioneers.

The Pony Express is remembered today by horse lovers who ride the Express's desert tracks for pleasure. Their journeys pay tribute to the riders of 1860, who insisted that "the mail must get through."

The Pony Express closed down when the transcontinental telegraph system opened in 1861. Stagecoach operators Wells, Fargo & Company took over the route.

Lincoln
In 1860, Abraham Lincoln's first speech as U.S. President was carried by the Pony Express.

Aimé Tschiffely

Aimé Tschiffely
was a Swiss teacher
living in Argentina.

Americas

Tschiffely wanted to ride
from South to North
America across the
Panama Canal.

Tale of Two Horses

When Aimé Tschiffely (Ay-may Shiff-ell-ee) told people about his idea early in 1925, they thought he had gone mad.

"Impossible! It can't be done!"

Tschiffely wanted to be the first man ever to ride from Buenos Aires in Argentina all the way to Washington, D.C.

He realized that the 10,000-mile journey would be full of difficulties, but it had been his secret ambition for years.

Tschiffely knew that he needed two tough and resourceful horses if he was to succeed. He chose Gato and Mancha, Criollo horses aged 15 and 16. They had belonged to an Argentinian Indian chief and roamed free on the plains.

They were not handsome and they were headstrong, but they knew how to survive in the wild.

Tschiffely and the horses set off in April 1925. After four months, the travelers crossed over into Bolivia.

In that time the trio had learned to trust each other and to work together as a team.

One day, as they rode along the shore of a lake in Peru they reached a shallow strip of water. Gato reared up and refused to go on.

A man rushed toward them, shouting that the water hid dangerous quicksand. He led them to a safe trail. Tschiffely was amazed. The horse had saved their lives!

As they rode on through Peru, they began to climb the Andes—a huge range of snow-capped mountains.

One morning, they came to a sight that made Tschiffely's blood run cold. The way forward was along a rickety old rope bridge that stretched over a deep gorge. One slip would prove fatal.

When they reached the middle, the bridge swayed violently. If Mancha panicked and turned back, they would both fall to their deaths. But Mancha waited calmly for the bridge to stop moving, and then went on. When Gato saw his companions safe on the other side, he crossed the bridge as steadily as if he were walking on solid ground.

Criollo
These horses are very tough and can carry heavy weights over long distances.

Horse Sense
People believe that horses have a sixth sense that warns them about danger.

217

Herd Instincts

Wild horses stay in groups, or herds. Mancha and Gato would instinctively follow each other, whatever the dangers.

From Peru, Tschiffely headed into Ecuador and followed a series of tracks through lush forests over high mountains and down into valleys. At night, Tschiffely never tied up the horses. He knew they would not run. The three travelers were sharing a great adventure, each showing the others the way.

Zigzagging up a narrow trail one day, Tschiffely saw that the path ahead had been swept away by a landslide, leaving a sheer drop. There was no choice but to turn back and find another route. Tschiffely tightened Gato's packs to get ready for a long detour.

But Mancha had other ideas, Tschiffely saw with horror that Mancha was preparing to jump the gap. His heart rose in his mouth as Mancha sailed through the air and landed on the other side.

The horse turned and neighed to his companions not to be afraid. Tschiffely and Gato soon followed. As their adventure stretched on, the three travelers reached the Panama Canal and crossed into Costa Rica and then Mexico.

Moving through dense jungle, the trio had to cope with mosquito bites and attacks by vampire bats and poisonous snakes.

Once Mancha slipped into a crocodile-infested river. He only just managed to find a foothold and pull himself up the bank as Tschiffely clung on for dear life.

Two and a half years after setting out from Buenos Aires, Tschiffely reached Washington, D.C. He had achieved his lifelong ambition.

"I could never have done it," he said, "without Mancha and Gato. My two pals have shown powers of resistance to every hardship."

Tschiffely was given a hero's welcome, even meeting President Coolidge in the White House. Admirers suggested that the horses should live in a city park. But Tschiffely took Mancha and Gato back to Argentina and set them free.

Dense Jungle
The jungles of Central and South America are home to some of the world's most dangerous snakes, such as the 30-foot (10 meter) anaconda.

Born Free
Horses who grow up in the country can become sad and listless if confined in a city.

Horses seem to remember that their ancestors were hunted by crocodiles and know to be afraid of them.

Movie Town

The 1930s was the golden age of filmmaking in Hollywood, California.

Perfect Partners

Roy Rogers was called the King of Cowboys, and Trigger soon became known as the Smartest Horse in the Movies.

Hollywood Hero

In 1932, a star was born. He was a beautiful golden color with a white, flowing mane and tail. Son of a palomino mare and a racehorse, Golden Cloud was to become the most famous horse of his day.

Golden Cloud made his big-screen debut in 1938. His owners, Hudkin Stables, lent him out to play a part in the Hollywood film *The Adventures of Robin Hood.*

Later that year, Republic Studios decided to make a series of Westerns featuring the singing cowboy actor, Roy Rogers. They brought several horses round for Roy to audition. He fell for Golden Cloud the moment he climbed on the horse's back.

While they were making their first film, *Under Western Stars,* Golden Cloud was renamed "Trigger" because he was so quick.

Roy loved Trigger so much that after their third film, he bought Trigger for $2,500. From then on, they became full-time partners.

Trigger loved the camera. He often stole the show from Roy Rogers with a well-timed yawn or a graceful dance step.

He knew more than 60 tricks. He could walk 150 steps on his hind legs, stamp his hoof to count, and draw a gun from a holster.

Trigger became one of the most popular characters in show business. He starred in 887 films and 101 TV shows, and once even had a party in the Grand Ballroom of the Astor Hotel in New York City.

Like a true star, Trigger made special personal appearances. He always traveled in style, carried his own horse-sized passport, and signed his name with an X in hotel registers.

Trigger finally retired in 1957, and died in 1965, age 33. Roy Rogers was heartbroken. He said he had lost "the greatest horse who ever came along."

Trigger's fan club produced hundreds of books and toys for its members.

Today, we may be less dependent on the horse for transportation and work, but we continue to be amazed by stories of its strength, speed, and intelligence. Humans and horses will always make a great team.

Think, Talk and Write

Talk About It *Horse Heroes* tells about some great adventures with horses. Would you like to go on an adventure with a horse? Why or why not?

1. On page 219, the author quotes what Tschiffely said about Mancha and Gato: "My two pals have shown powers of resistance to every hardship." Why do you think the author included this quote? **Think Like an Author**

2. The statement "He was a beautiful golden color with a white, flowing mane and tail" contains both statements of fact and opinion. Which part of the sentence is a statement of fact? Which part is a statement of opinion? **Fact and Opinion**

3. "Pony Bob" Haslam kept watching his pony's ears. What did he think his horse might hear? **Monitor and Clarify**

4. The Pony Express delivered mail across the country. Write someone a letter using words from the Words to Know list. **Vocabulary**

TEST PRACTICE

Look Back and Write *Horse Heroes* tells about how horses were used to deliver mail, travel across the continent, and perform in motion pictures. What made these horses so amazing?

Meet author **Kate Petty on page 377.**

Summarize

W2.2.a Write responses to literature: Demonstrate an understanding of the literary work.

Writing

Prompt *Horse Heroes* introduces readers to courageous animals. Think about an animal that has done something remarkable. Now write an expository composition about it.

> **Writing Trait**
>
> An **introductory paragraph** helps readers focus on the topic.

Student Model

Hero of Brookfield Zoo

Binti Jua is a lowland gorilla that lives at Brookfield Zoo near Chicago, Illinois. She became a hero on August 16, 1996. She rescued a 3-year-old boy who had tumbled over the railing and fallen more than 18 feet into the gorilla exhibit below.

The introductory paragraph sets up the composition.

Binti Jua walked over to the unconscious boy. The spectators screamed, fearing that she would hurt the child. She lifted the **boy's** arms as if checking for signs of life. Other gorillas came close, but Binti Jua grunted until they went away.

Tells about real people and events.

Taking the boy in her strong arms, Binti Jua carried him to the **zookeeper's** entrance. She waited with the child until the paramedics came to take him to the hospital. Binti Jua's 17-month-old baby, Koola, clutched her back during the entire time.

Singular possessive nouns are correctly used.

The boy spent four days in the hospital. He was treated for a concussion and was released. He recovered fully. Binti Jua's gentleness made her a hero.

Use the model to help you write your own expository composition.

 W1.2.a Create multiple-paragraph compositions: Provide an introductory paragraph.

223

Teamwork

E-mail, or "electronic mail," is a message sent through the Internet. You can e-mail Web sites for information to help you with projects or just to answer questions you may have.

Text Features

- The "To:" box shows to whom the message is going. The "Subject:" box tells what the topic of the message is.

- The message itself looks like the body of a letter.

 Ready to Try It?
Read "Riding the Pony Express." Look for text features that will help you write your own e-mail.

Concept Link

With the help of horses, the Pony Express allowed mail to cross the continent in just eight days instead of a month. Make a list of other ways in which animals help us accomplish our work.

224

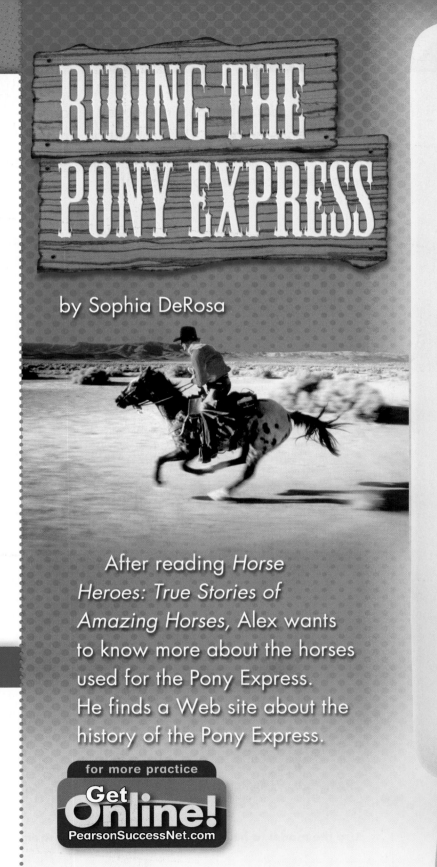

RIDING THE PONY EXPRESS

by Sophia DeRosa

After reading *Horse Heroes: True Stories of Amazing Horses*, Alex wants to know more about the horses used for the Pony Express. He finds a Web site about the history of the Pony Express.

for more practice

Get Online!
PearsonSuccessNet.com

The site gives an e-mail address to contact for more information. Alex decides to e-mail the Web site.

File   Edit   View   Favorites   Tools   Help

http://www.url.here

THE PONY EXPRESS

Send   Attach   Address

To: Receiver's e-mail address goes here

Cc:

Subject: Pony Express Horses

The e-mail address of the person to whom you are writing goes here.

If you do not know to whom to address your e-mail, use "Dear Sir or Madam."

Dear Sir or Madam:

I just read about how the Pony Express got started. Now I want to know more about the different types of horses used by the Pony Express. I have to give an oral report for class. Can you tell me where I might find more information about the horses? Thank you.

Alex Gonzales

The next day Alex receives this reply

Write   Reply   Send   Forward   Delete   Address   Print

From: Davis, Julia <Julia.Davis@EmailAddress.edu>
To: Gonzales, Alex <Alex.Gonzales@EmailAddress.com>
Date: Tuesday, November 1, 20__, 11:15 AM
Subject: Information About Pony Express

Hi Alex,

Our Web site has several links that can help you learn about the Pony Express. For information about the horses and where and how far they ran, follow the Pony Riders link.

Thanks for visiting us. Let us know if we can be of further help.

Julia Davis, Pony Express Archivist

Alex returns to the Pony Express History site and follows a series of links to the Pony Riders link.

vorites   Tools   Help

    http://www.url.here

Home   **Visitor Center**   **Museums**   **Pony Riders**

MUSEUMS

PONY RIDERS

226

When Alex clicks on the link, he finds this description.

Home   Visitor Center   Museums   Pony Riders

PONY RIDERS

The trail that the Pony Express followed was not the same in every place. Riders rode different kinds of horses for different parts of the trip. While riders changed every 75 to 100 miles, horses changed every ten to fifteen miles.

From the eastern starting point in Missouri, the trail went through flat plains. Fast, active horses were needed. Morgans and Thoroughbred horses were used.

The Pinto was used for crossing rivers, canyons, and hot deserts. It was small, strong, and fast.

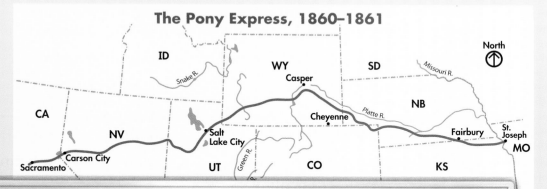

The Pony Express, 1860–1861

Reading Across Texts

Look at the information in this selection and in *Horse Heroes* for details about the horses used by the Pony Express riders. List some of these details.

Writing Across Texts Choose an area in the West and use your information about horses to help you plan a ride on the Pony Express.

Build Language

U.S. Government

Build Vocabulary

Learn ◉ **Skill Unfamiliar Words** As you read, you may come across an unfamiliar word. Identifying a word's root can sometimes help you figure out the word's meaning. For example, the root of the word *uncontrollable* is *control*.

Practice Use a dictionary and what you know about root words to write definitions of this week's Word to Know. Then read "Class Election" on page 229.

Words to Know	vain	humble	howling
	responsibility	politics	solemnly
	Constitution		

On Your Own As you reread "Class Election," think about who is the best candidate. Write a short paragraph explaining why you think that person would make a good class president.

🐻 **R1.3** Use knowledge of root words to determine the meanings of unknown words within a passage.

Class Election

The students in Grade 4 are electing class officers. Four students are running for president.

Steven is vain about his looks. He puts only his name and his face on his signs. He says politics is dull, but winning is fun. Suzanne acts humble about how well she plays sports. Yet all her signs show her making the winning goal in last year's soccer championship. Omar solemnly promised that he would run a clean campaign, but he makes fun of the other candidates. Still, his speeches are a howling success. Maya says that unlike the President of the United States, the president of Grade 4 does not have to "protect and defend the Constitution of the United States." However, she says the Grade 4 president does have a responsibility to all the fourth-grade students, not just the ones who vote for him or her. Maya was the Grade 3 president and is captain of the softball team. If you were a student in this school, whom would you vote for?

 Need a Review?
For additional help with using root words to determine the meanings of unfamiliar words, see *Words!* on p. W•4.

 Ready to Try It?
Read *So You Want to Be President?* on pp. 232–243.

Teamwork

Build Comprehension

Learn   **Skill** **Main Idea and Details**

- The focus of a text is the topic.

- The main idea is the most important idea about the topic.

- Supporting details are pieces of information that tell more about the main idea.

- Using a graphic organizer like the one below can help show how details support the main idea.

Main Idea		
Supporting Detail	Supporting Detail	Supporting Detail

Practice   As you read "A White House History" on page 231, look for main ideas and supporting details.

On Your Own   **Write to Read** Reread "A White House History." Use both the text and a graphic organizer like the one above to write a summary of the passage.

 Need a Review? See the *Picture It!* lesson on p. PI•12 for additional help with main idea and details.

▶ **Ready to Try It?** As you read *So You Want to Be President?* on pp. 232–243, look for main ideas and supporting details.

G5R2.3 Discern main ideas and concepts presented in texts, identifying and assessing evidence that supports those ideas.

A WHITE HOUSE HISTORY

The White House is where the U.S. President lives and works in Washington, D.C. However, our first President, George Washington, never even lived there! The building wasn't finished while he was in office. Construction of the White House was not begun until 1792.

Skill What is the topic of this article?

Our second President, John Adams, moved into the White House in 1800. Even then, the building wasn't completely finished. As a result, it was somewhat uncomfortable for daily life. The President's wife, Abigail, had nowhere to hang the family's laundry, so she used the East Room. Today that room is the biggest and grandest room in the White House.

In 1814, while our fourth President, James Madison, was in office, disaster hit the White House. The United States was again at war with England, and the British burned the White House. It had to be rebuilt.

Skill What is the main idea of the third paragraph?
(a) While President James Madison was in office, disaster hit the White House.
(b) The United States was again at war with England.
(c) The White House had to be rebuilt.

Almost every President has made changes to the White House. The building does not belong to any one President, though. It belongs to the American people.

Skill What is the main idea of this paragraph?

Teamwork

231

 **Expository nonfiction** gives information about real people and events. As you read, note new or surprising information about our country's Presidents.

232

So You Want to Be President?

by Judith St. George

illustrated by David Small

What does it take to be President of the United States?

There are good things about being President, and there are bad things about being President. One of the good things is that the President lives in a big white house called the White House.

Another good thing about being President is that the President has a swimming pool, bowling alley, and movie theater.

The President never has to take out the garbage.

The President doesn't have to eat yucky vegetables. As a boy, George H. W. Bush had to eat broccoli. When George H. W. Bush grew up, he became President. That was the end of the broccoli!

One of the bad things about being President is that the President always has to be dressed up. William McKinley wore a frock coat, vest, pin-striped trousers, stiff white shirt, black satin tie, gloves, a top hat, and a red carnation in his buttonhole every day!

The President has to be polite to everyone. The President can't go anywhere alone. The President has lots of homework.

People get mad at the President. Someone once threw a cabbage at William Howard Taft. That didn't bother Taft. He quipped, "I see that one of my adversaries has lost his head."

Lots of people want to be President. If you want to be President, it might help if your name is James. Six Presidents were named James. (President Carter liked to be called Jimmy.) Four Johns, four Williams (President Clinton liked to be called Bill), three Georges, two Andrews, and two Franklins—all became President.

If you want to be President, your size doesn't matter. Presidents have come in all shapes and sizes. Abraham Lincoln was the tallest—six feet four inches. (His stovepipe hat made him look even taller.)

James Madison was the smallest—five feet four inches and only one hundred pounds. William Howard Taft was the biggest—more than three hundred pounds. He was so big that he had a special tub built for his White House bathroom. (Four men could fit in the tub!)

Though the Constitution says you'll have to wait until you're thirty-five, young, old, and in between have become President. Theodore (Teddy) Roosevelt at forty-two was the youngest. He had pillow fights with his children and played football on the White House lawn. "You must always remember that the President is about six," a friend said. Ronald Reagan was the oldest. When he first ran for President, he was sixty-nine. He joked that it was the thirtieth anniversary of his thirty-ninth birthday.

Do you have pesky brothers and sisters? Every one of our Presidents did. Benjamin Harrison takes the prize—he had eleven! (It's lucky he grew up on a six-hundred-acre farm.) James Polk and James Buchanan both had nine. George Washington, Thomas Jefferson, James Madison, and John Kennedy each had eight. (Two Presidents were orphans, Andrew Jackson and Herbert Hoover.)

A President in your family tree is a plus. John Quincy Adams was John Adams's son. George W. Bush was the son of George H. W. Bush. Theodore Roosevelt and Franklin Roosevelt were fifth cousins. Benjamin Harrison was William Harrison's grandson. James Madison and Zachary Taylor were second cousins.

Do you have a pet? All kinds of pets have lived in the White House, mostly dogs. Herbert Hoover had three dogs: Piney, Snowflake, and Tut. (Tut must have been a Democrat. He and his Republican master never got along.) Franklin Roosevelt's dog, Fala, was almost as famous as his owner.

George H. W. Bush's dog wrote MILLIE'S BOOK: ADVENTURES OF A WHITE HOUSE DOG (as reported to Mrs. Bush!). Ulysses Grant had horses, Benjamin Harrison's goat pulled his grandchildren around in a cart, the Coolidges had a pet raccoon, Jimmy Carter and Bill Clinton preferred cats.

Theodore Roosevelt's children didn't just have pets, they ran a zoo. They had dogs, cats, guinea pigs, mice, rats, badgers, raccoons, parrots, and a Shetland pony called Algonquin. To cheer up his sick brother, young Quentin once took Algonquin upstairs in the White House elevator!

Though most Presidents went to college, nine didn't: George Washington, Andrew Jackson, Martin Van Buren, Zachary Taylor, Millard Fillmore, Abraham Lincoln, Andrew Johnson, Grover Cleveland, and Harry Truman. (Andrew Johnson couldn't read until he was fourteen! He didn't learn to write until after he was married!)

Thomas Jefferson was top-notch in the brains department—he was an expert on agriculture, law, politics, music, geography, surveying, philosophy, and botany. In his spare time he designed his own house (a mansion), founded the University of Virginia, and whipped up the Declaration of Independence.

Almost any job can lead to the White House. Presidents have been lawyers, teachers, farmers, sailors, engineers, surveyors, mayors, governors, congressmen, senators, and ambassadors. (Harry Truman owned a men's shop. Andrew Johnson was a tailor. Ronald Reagan was a movie actor!)

There they are, a mixed bag of Presidents! What did they think of being head man? George Washington, who became our very first President in 1789, worried about his new line of work. "I greatly fear that my countrymen will expect too much from me," he wrote to a friend. (He was a howling success.) Some loved the job. "No President has ever enjoyed himself as much as I," Theodore Roosevelt said. Others hated it. "The four most miserable years of my life," John Quincy Adams complained.

Every President was different from every other and yet no woman has been President. No person of color has been President. No person who wasn't a Protestant or a Roman Catholic has been President. But if you care enough, anything is possible. Thirty-four Presidents came and went before a Roman Catholic—John Kennedy—was elected. Almost two hundred years passed before a woman—Geraldine Ferraro—ran for Vice President.

It's said that people who run for President have swelled heads. It's said that people who run for President are greedy. They want power. They want fame.

But being President can be wanting to serve your country—like George Washington, who left the Virginia plantation he loved three times to lead the country he loved even more.

It can be looking toward the future like Thomas Jefferson, who bought the Louisiana Territory and then sent Lewis and Clark west to find a route to the Pacific. (They did!)

It can be wanting to turn lives around like Franklin Roosevelt, who provided soup and bread for the hungry, jobs for the jobless, and funds for the elderly to live on.

It can be wanting to make the world a better place like John Kennedy, who sent Peace Corps volunteers around the globe to teach and help others.

Every single President has taken this oath: "I do solemnly swear (or affirm) that I will faithfully execute the office of President of the United States, and will to the best of my ability, preserve, protect and defend the Constitution of the United States."

Only thirty-five words! But it's a big order when you're President of this country. Abraham Lincoln was tops at filling that order. "I know very well that many others might in this matter as in others, do better than I can," he said. "But . . . I am here. I must do the best I can, and bear the responsibility of taking the course which I feel I ought to take."

That's the bottom line. Tall, short, fat, thin, talkative, quiet, vain, humble, lawyer, teacher, or soldier—this is what most of our Presidents have tried to do, each in his own way. Some succeeded. Some failed. If you want to be President—a good President—pattern yourself after the best. Our best have asked more of themselves than they thought they could give. They have had the courage, spirit, and will to do what they knew was right. Most of all, their first priority has always been the people and the country they served.

Think, Talk and Write

Talk About It *So You Want to Be President?* tells about our past Presidents. What did you enjoy most about the selection? What made you sad?

1. An author's tone, or attitude, shows how the author feels about a topic. What is the author's tone in *So You Want to Be President?* Find parts of the selection that support your answer. **Think Like an Author**

2. Reread page 238. What sentence states the main idea of this page? What supporting details can you find? **Main Idea and Details**

3. Suppose a friend announces plans to run for President. What will you say to encorage him or her? **Summarize**

4. *Solemnly* and *howling* both have root words. What are they? How can you use what you know about root words to determine the meaning of the words? **Vocabulary**

Look Back and Write Look back at *So You Want to Be President?* What did you learn about what it takes to be President of the United States?

Meet author **Judith St. George on page 379 and** illustrator **David Small on page 378.**

Summarize

W2.2.a Write responses to literature: Demonstrate an understanding of the literary work.

Writing

Prompt *So You Want to Be President?* explains what it is like to be President of the United States. Think about two U.S. Presidents. Now write an expository composition that explains their similarities and differences.

> **Writing Trait**
>
> A good **body paragraph** has facts and details.

Student Model

Two Popular Presidents

Andrew Jackson, the 7th President, and Theodore Roosevelt, the 26th President, were two of our most popular leaders. President Jackson stood for ordinary Americans' rights to better themselves. Roosevelt believed that he should represent all the people.

These Presidents' war experiences made them famous. Jackson fought in the Revolutionary War and the War of 1812. He was a prisoner of war in the Revolutionary War at the age of 14! Later he became a hero in the War of 1812. Roosevelt helped create the first volunteer United States cavalry regiment. He led his soldiers up San Juan Hill in Cuba during the Spanish-American War.

Both these leaders' lives were interesting and adventurous. Jackson was born in a log cabin. He was the first President to ride on a railroad train. Roosevelt was a writer and a sportsman. The teddy bear was named for him after he refused to shoot a bear when he was on a hunting trip! Teddy is a nickname for Theodore.

Expository nonfiction tells about real people and events.

The body paragraph contains facts and details.

Plural possessive nouns are correctly used.

Use the beginning of this model to help you write your own expository composition.

W1.2.c Create multiple-paragraph compositions: Include supporting paragraphs with simple facts, details, and explanations.

Teamwork

OUR NATIONAL PARKS

by Susan Gavin

Did you know that the President of the United States has the power to set aside land for national parks? Ulysses S. Grant helped create the world's first national park, Yellowstone National Park, in 1872. In 1864, Abraham Lincoln set aside land that became Yosemite National Park in 1890.

Visit one of the 55 parks in the U.S. national park system. (A sampling is on page 247.) Walk through caves, climb mountains, and see wildlife, rain forests, and glaciers. As you enjoy these natural areas, remember that U.S. Presidents helped protect them.

Sequoia
CALIFORNIA

Established: 1890
Size: 456,552 acres
Highlights: giant sequoia trees; Mt. Whitney (14,491 feet)

Mammoth Cave
KENTUCKY

Established: 1941
Size: 52,830 acres
Highlight: world's longest known network of caves

Everglades
FLORIDA

Established: 1947
Size: 1,399,078 acres
Highlight: largest subtropical wilderness in the United States

Death Valley
CALIFORNIA, NEVADA

Established: 1994
Size: 3,367,628 acres
Highlights: largest national park outside of Alaska; desert, dunes, gorges

Big Bend
TEXAS

Established: 1944
Size: 801,163 acres
Highlights: desert land; on the Rio Grande; dinosaur fossils

Reading Across Texts
"Our National Parks" and *So You Want to Be President?* tell about things Presidents have done. List some other things Presidents have done.

Writing Across Texts Make a list of three or four Presidents and tell something they each did that was good for the country.

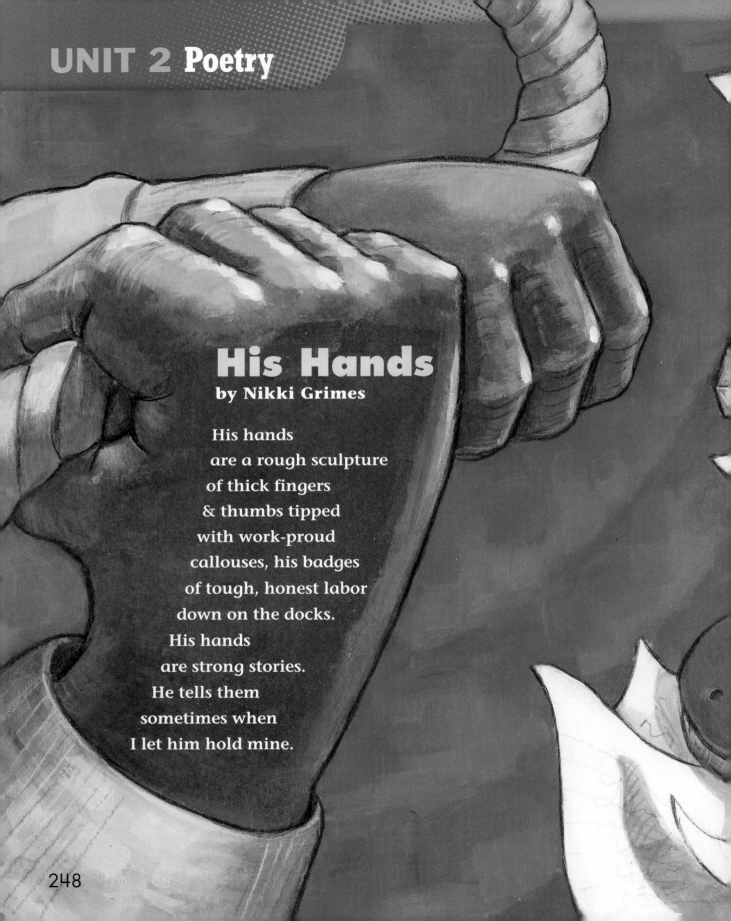

His Hands
by Nikki Grimes

His hands
are a rough sculpture
of thick fingers
& thumbs tipped
with work-proud
callouses, his badges
of tough, honest labor
down on the docks.
His hands
are strong stories.
He tells them
sometimes when
I let him hold mine.

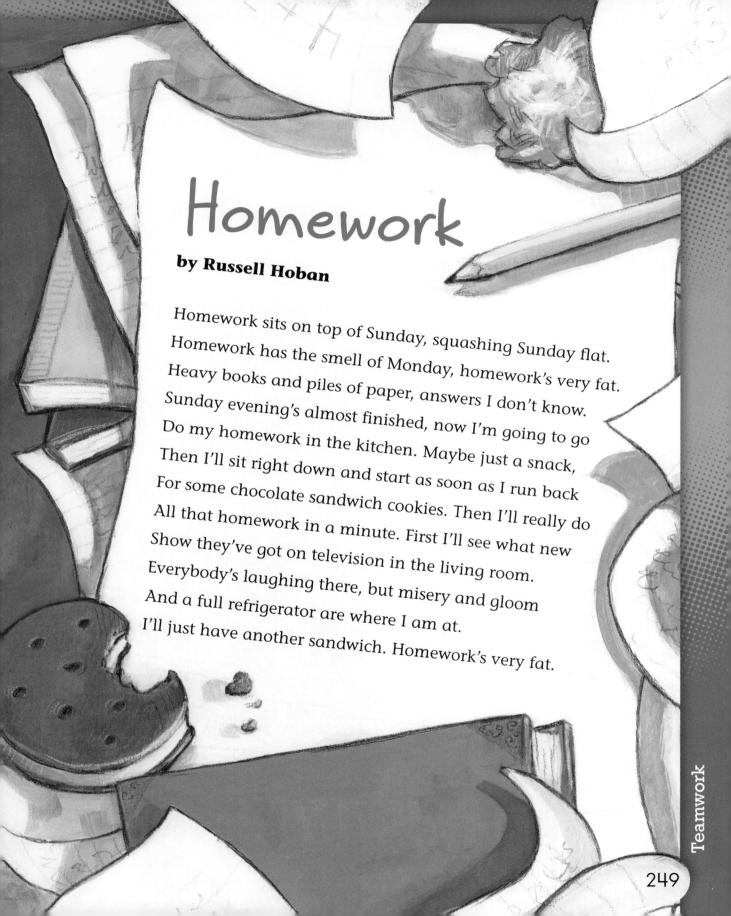

Homework

by Russell Hoban

Homework sits on top of Sunday, squashing Sunday flat.
Homework has the smell of Monday, homework's very fat.
Heavy books and piles of paper, answers I don't know.
Sunday evening's almost finished, now I'm going to go
Do my homework in the kitchen. Maybe just a snack,
Then I'll sit right down and start as soon as I run back
For some chocolate sandwich cookies. Then I'll really do
All that homework in a minute. First I'll see what new
Show they've got on television in the living room.
Everybody's laughing there, but misery and gloom
And a full refrigerator are where I am at.
I'll just have another sandwich. Homework's very fat.

Lem Lonnigan's Leaf Machine

by Andrea Perry

Lem Lonnigan's Leaf Machine cleans lawns with ease
by vacuuming all that falls down from the trees.
And as you might guess, he's quite busy in autumn.
Just look in a yard full of trees and you'll spot 'im!

He uses a special attachment to get
those few stubborn leaves that have not fallen yet,
extending its claws to reach sky-scraping heights
for snatching up stragglers and sometimes stray kites.

But if by mistake
his machine gets a nest
or a squirrel or bird
in its yard-cleaning zest,
then Lem hits the switch
to discharge it post haste
and carefully sees
that the tenant's replaced.

He's fast and efficient.
He's clean and he's neat
as he rides his machine
tree to tree down the street.
So don't waste time raking
and bagging this fall!
Lem's Leaf Machine's ready,
so give him a call!

Patterns in Nature

THE BIG ?
What are some patterns in nature?

Get Online!

PearsonSuccessNet.com

See It!
- Concept Talk Video
- Background Building Audio Slide Show
- Comprehension Think Aloud Video
- *Picture It!* Animation
- e-Books

Hear It!
- Selection Snapshot and Response
- Paired Selection e-Text
- Grammar Jammer
- e-Books

Do It!
- Online Journal
- Reading Street Pursuit Online Game
- Story Sort
- New Literacies Activity
- Success Tracker

Patterns in Nature

Build Language

The Seasons

Build Vocabulary

Learn   ◉ **Skill** **Multiple-Meaning Words** Sometimes when you are reading, you may see a word whose meaning you know, but that meaning does not make sense in the sentence. For example, the word *trip* can mean "a journey or voyage" or "to stumble or fall." You can use context clues to decide which meaning the author is using.

Practice   Write down the definitions of this week's Words to Know in your journal. If necessary, use a dictionary to see which of these words has more than one meaning. Then read "The Old House on Dwyer Road" on page 255.

Words to Know	fascinated	draft	terror
	timid	etched	
	parlor	frost	

On Your Own   Read "The Old House on Dwyer Road" again. As you read, see if you can find other multiple-meaning words. How can context clues help you choose the correct meaning?

🐻 **R1.6** Distinguish and interpret words with multiple meanings.

THE OLD HOUSE ON DWYER ROAD

Alec was fascinated by old houses. He heard that there was a very interesting old house on Dwyer Road. People said that strange things happened in the house at night—thumps, howls, and groans. They said that it was not a place for the timid. Alec was intrigued. He got permission to stay overnight in the house.

The house had a parlor, dining room, kitchen, and storeroom on the first floor. Alec decided to stay in the parlor. He settled into a comfortable armchair and began to read a book. Suddenly Alec felt a cold draft, even though no door or window was open. Then he thought he heard footsteps in the hall. He got up and walked toward the parlor doors.

The doors had designs etched into the glass that made them look as though they had frost on them. Shadowy forms seemed to flit past the doors. Alec reached for the door handles. Then terror seized him. He could not make himself open the doors.

 Need a Review?
For additional help with multiple-meaning words, see *Words!* on p. W•10.

 **Ready to Try It?**
Read *The Stranger* on pp. 258–271.

Build Comprehension

Learn   ⊙ **Skill Cause and Effect**

- An effect is *what* happens. A cause is *why* it happens.

- Sometimes clue words, such as *because, so,* and *since,* signal causes and effects.

- Sometimes a cause has more than one effect. Sometimes an effect has more than one cause.

- Look at the photo and caption below. How can it help you understand cause and effect?

A combine cuts the stalks and separates the grain from them as it moves across a field.

Practice   Use what you learned about cause and effect as you read "Fall Harvest" on page 257.

On Your Own   **Write to Read** Reread "Fall Harvest." If the combine is a cause, write down or chart the effects of this machine.

 Need a Review? See the *Picture It!* lesson on p. PI•4 for additional help with cause and effect.

▶ **Ready to Try It?** As you read *The Stranger* on pp. 258–271, use what you learned about cause and effect to help you understand the text.

🐻 **R2.6** Distinguish between cause and effect and between fact and opinion in expository text.

Fall Harvest

What do you think of when you hear the word autumn? Changing leaves and cooler weather? To a farmer, autumn means harvest time. After growing all summer, crops are ripe and ready to be harvested in the fall.

Grains, such as wheat, are harvested with huge machines called combines. A combine cuts plant stalks and separates the grain from the straw and other plant waste. It collects the grain and returns straw to the ground.

Some machines used by farmers mow grasses, such as alfalfa and clover. Farmers let the mowed grasses lie in the fields to dry out. These dried grasses are called hay. Then a machine called a hay baler gathers the hay and binds it into bales.

Most apples are harvested in the fall. Because ripe apples are easily bruised, they must be carefully picked by hand. Apples can keep for up to a year if they are stored properly, so you can buy apples all year long.

Pumpkins, too, are harvested by hand. Below-freezing temperatures will kill a vine and damage the pumpkins. That's why farmers usually harvest their pumpkins in October, just in time for Halloween.

Skill What is the effect of letting mowed grass lie in a field?

Skill Being able to buy apples year-round is an effect. What is the cause?

Skill Sometimes a cause has more than one effect. What are the effects of below-freezing temperatures?

The Stranger

text and art
by Chris Van Allsburg

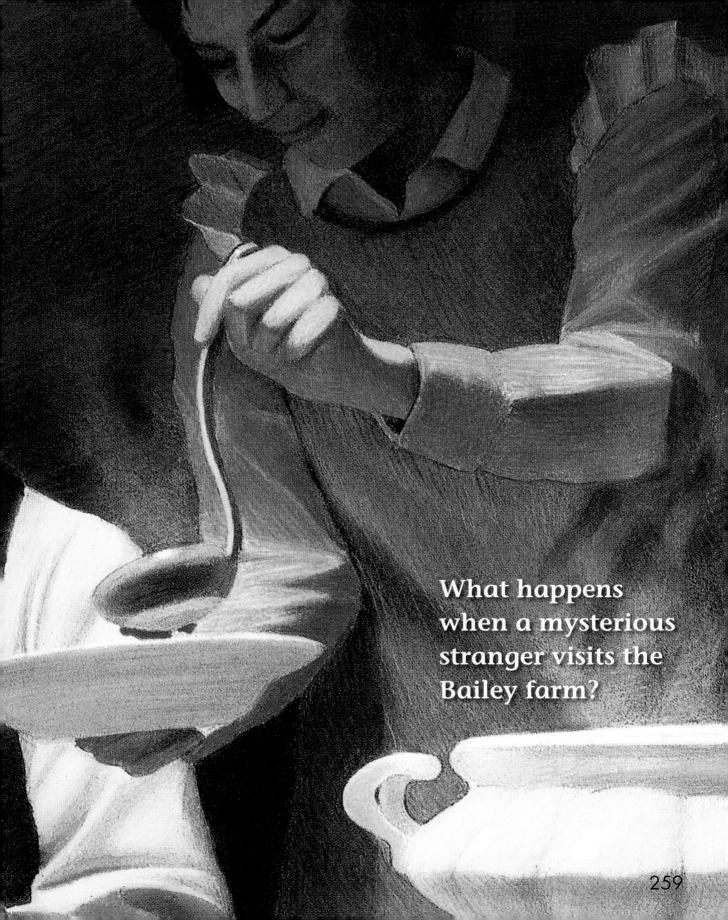

What happens
when a mysterious
stranger visits the
Bailey farm?

It was the time of year Farmer Bailey liked best, when summer turned to fall. He whistled as he drove along. A cool breeze blew across his face through the truck's open window. Then it happened. There was a loud "thump." Mr. Bailey jammed on his brakes. "Oh no!" he thought. "I've hit a deer."

But it wasn't a deer the farmer found lying in the road, it was a man. Mr. Bailey knelt down beside the still figure, fearing the worst. Then, suddenly, the man opened his eyes. He looked up with terror and jumped to his feet. He tried to run off, lost his balance, and fell down. He got up again, but this time the farmer took his arm and helped him to the truck.

Mr. Bailey drove home. He helped the stranger inside, where Mrs. Bailey made him comfortable on the parlor sofa. Katy, their daughter, peeked into the room. The man on the sofa was dressed in odd rough leather clothing. She heard her father whisper ". . . must be some kind of hermit . . . sort of fellow who lives alone in the woods." The stranger didn't seem to understand the questions Mr. Bailey asked him. "I don't think," whispered Mrs. Bailey, "he knows how to talk."

Mr. Bailey called the doctor, who came and listened to the stranger's heart, felt his bones, looked in his eyes, and took his temperature. He decided the man had lost his memory. There was a bump on the back of his head. "In a few days," the doctor said, "he should remember who he is and where he's from." Mrs. Bailey stopped the doctor as he left the house. He'd forgotten his thermometer. "Oh, you can throw that out," he answered. "It's broken, the mercury is stuck at the bottom."

Mr. Bailey lent the stranger some clean clothes. The fellow seemed confused about buttonholes and buttons. In the evening he joined the Baileys for dinner. The steam that rose from the hot food fascinated him. He watched Katy take a spoonful of soup and blow gently across it. Then he did exactly the same. Mrs. Bailey shivered. "Brrr," she said. "There's a draft in here tonight."

The next morning Katy watched the stranger from her bedroom window. He walked across the yard, toward two rabbits. Instead of running into the woods, the rabbits took a hop in his direction. He picked one of them up and stroked its ears, then set it down. The rabbits hopped away, then stopped and looked back, as if they expected the stranger to follow.

When Katy's father went into the fields that day, the
stranger shyly tagged along. Mr. Bailey gave him a pitchfork
and, with a little practice, he learned to use it well. They
worked hard. Occasionally Mr. Bailey would have to stop
and rest. But the stranger never tired. He didn't even sweat.

That evening Katy sat with the stranger, watching the
setting sun. High above them a flock of geese, in perfect V
formation, flew south on the trip that they made every fall.
The stranger could not take his eyes off the birds. He stared
at them like a man who'd been hypnotized.

Two weeks passed and the stranger still could not remember who he was. But the Baileys didn't mind. They liked having the stranger around. He had become one of the family. Day by day he'd grown less timid. "He seems so happy to be around us," Mr. Bailey said to his wife. "It's hard to believe he's a hermit."

Another week passed. Farmer Bailey could not help noticing how peculiar the weather had been. Not long ago it seemed that autumn was just around the corner. But now it still felt like summer, as if the seasons couldn't change. The warm days made the pumpkins grow larger than ever. The leaves on the trees were as green as they'd been three weeks before.

One day the stranger climbed the highest hill on the Bailey farm. He looked to the north and saw a puzzling sight. The trees in the distance were bright red and orange. But the trees to the south, like those round the Baileys', were nothing but shades of green. They seemed so drab and ugly to the stranger. It would be much better, he thought, if all trees could be red and orange.

The stranger's feelings grew stronger the next day. He couldn't look at a tree's green leaves without sensing that something was terribly wrong. The more he thought about it, the more upset he became, until finally he could think of nothing else. He ran to a tree and pulled off a leaf. He held it in a trembling hand and, without thinking, blew on it with all his might.

At dinner that evening the stranger appeared dressed in his old leather clothes. By the tears in his eyes the Baileys could tell that their friend had decided to leave. He hugged them all once, then dashed out the door. The Baileys hurried outside to wave good-bye, but the stranger had disappeared. The air had turned cold, and the leaves on the trees were no longer green.

Every autumn since the stranger's visit, the same thing happens at the Bailey farm. The trees that surround it stay green for a week after the trees to the north have turned. Then overnight they change their color to the brightest of any tree around. And etched in frost on the farmhouse windows are words that say simply, "See you next fall."

Think, Talk and Write

Talk About It As you read this tale, what questions did you ask yourself? Which questions did you answer, and how?

1. The author gives clues about the stranger, such as the broken thermometer on page 262. What other clues does the author give? What clue would you have included? Explain.
Think Like an Author

2. Mr. Bailey brings the stranger home after he hits the stranger with his truck. What happens at the farm while the stranger is there? What happens after he leaves? **Cause and Effect**

3. What questions about the setting—where and when the story takes place—did you have? How did you answer your questions? **Ask Questions**

4. How are the words *terror* and *timid* related? Which one describes a more extreme condition? What other words are related to them? Explain. **Vocabulary**

TEST PRACTICE

Look Back and Write Reread the question on page 259. What happens when the stranger visits the Bailey farm? Which of these events could not have happened in real life?

Meet author and illustrator Chris Van Allsburg on page 379.

Retell

W2.2.a Write responses to literature: Demonstrate an understanding of the literary work.

Writing Fantasy

Prompt *The Stranger* is a fantasy about a change of season on a farm. Think about a fantastical story in which a seasonal change takes place. Now write a fantasy based on your ideas.

Writing Trait

Vary the structure with **simple and compound sentences.**

Student Model

Our Unusual Winters

Every December 21 at midnight, people from Burr Town **abandon** their homes. They don't just leave for the day, but for the whole winter!

They have to leave because on December 22 winter starts. It doesn't just get gradually cold. At midnight, the season **transforms** from fall to winter instantly. In the time it takes to snap your fingers, the air temperature goes from chilly to very-far-below freezing. The wind blows at more than seventy miles per hour.

During the winter so much snow falls that you can't see more than a few feet in front of you. The ground **freezes,** and the roads **become** coated with thick ice. Water in streams, rivers, and lakes turns to ice. It **is** crazy!

That's why we spend the winter at my grandmother's house. There, winter happens gradually, and as spring gets closer, the weather starts to get warmer every day. We can finally go home in the spring.

Fantasy has impossible things happening.

Action verbs and **linking verbs** are used correctly.

Both **simple and compound sentences are used.**

Use the model to help you write your own fantasy.

W2.1.b Write narratives: Provide a context to enable the reader to imagine the world of the event or experience.

Patterns in Nature

273

Cause and Effect We see examples of cause and effect every day of our lives. Think about something that happened and ask yourself why it happened. Sometimes authors use clue words such as *because, so,* and *since,* to help readers see causes and effects. Other times, good readers must ask themselves, *what happened?* (effect) and then ask, *why did it happen?* (cause).

 Ready to Try It?
Look for causes and effects as you read "Time for a Change."

Concept Link

Seasons in the Southern and Northern Hemisphere are opposite. When it is summer in the Northern Hemisphere, it is winter in the Southern Hemisphere. Write a short paragraph that explains why this happens.

TIME FOR A CHANGE

by Helen Strahinich

FROM FROSTY DAWNS TO FALLING LEAVES TO FLYING GEESE, AUTUMN IS A BUSY TIME OF YEAR.

WHY DO WE HAVE SEASONS?

The seasons are caused by the way the Earth moves around the sun. Imagine a line that runs from the top of the North Pole, through the center of the Earth, and out through the bottom of the South Pole. This line is called the Earth's axis. In some pictures of the Earth, its axis runs straight up and down. But as the Earth moves around the sun, its axis is really tilted.

For half of the year, the Earth's northern half, or Northern Hemisphere, is tilted toward the sun. This is when countries in the Northern Hemisphere, including most of the United States, have spring and summer. The days are long, sunny, and warm. But when the Northern Hemisphere is tilted away from the sun, these countries have autumn and winter.

The autumn equinox marks the first day of fall in the Northern Hemisphere, September 21, 22, or 23. On that day, the Earth gets 12 hours of daylight and 12 hours of darkness. From then on, the days grow shorter, and the weather gets cooler. Autumn ends on December 21 or 22. That day is known as the winter solstice. It is the start of winter and the shortest day of the year. Then it is time to brace for the snowstorms of winter.

THE REASON FOR SEASONS

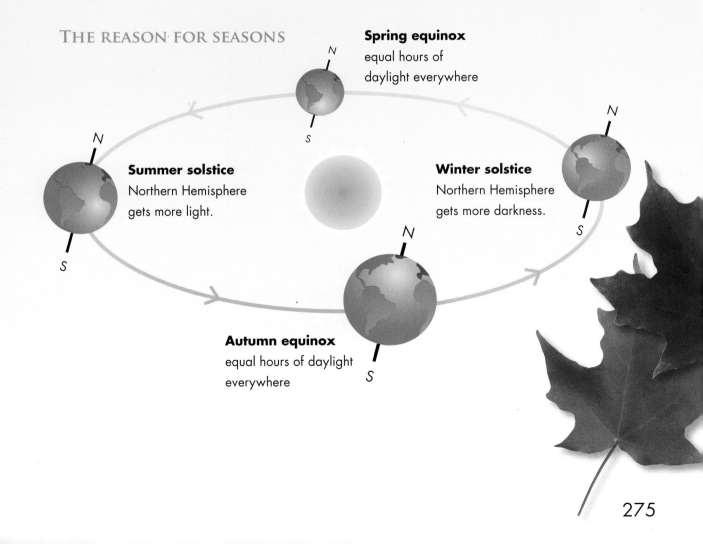

Spring equinox
equal hours of
daylight everywhere

Summer solstice
Northern Hemisphere
gets more light.

Winter solstice
Northern Hemisphere
gets more darkness.

Autumn equinox
equal hours of daylight
everywhere

275

WHY DO LEAVES CHANGE COLOR IN THE FALL?

Leaves are like tiny factories. They make food that allows trees to grow. The energy that powers these tiny factories is sunlight.

Leaves contain a green substance called chlorophyll. This material gives leaves their green color during spring and summer. Leaves also have yellow- and orange-colored pigments, but in much smaller amounts. So you can't see them.

In the fall, the tree's food factories start to shut down for winter. As chlorophyll breaks down, the green color of the leaves fades. Now the yellow and orange colors burst through. In some trees, food trapped in the leaves turns the leaves red.

Seen from afar, these trees seem to put on a fireworks display each autumn. The best places to view these fireworks are in the eastern United States and southeastern Canada. These regions are thick with forests of leaf-bearing trees.

WHY DO CANADA GEESE MIGRATE SOUTH EACH AUTUMN?

Nobody knows for sure. It may be the cold or it may be instinct. Whatever the reason, these geese seem to have a kind of inner clock. It tells them to fly south before their ponds, lakes, and other nesting areas freeze over and snow covers their food.

Have you ever spotted Canada geese flying in their trademark V formation? It's a sight to see. The strongest geese take turns leading the flock. Each goose creates an airstream that makes it easier for those behind it to fly.

Most winters, Canada geese will move to regions like central Missouri, southern Illinois, and Tennessee.

In mild winters, many Canada geese will stay in places like Wisconsin. But harsh winters will drive Canada geese as far south as Mexico.

Don't worry, though. They always return home in the spring. Just like clockwork.

Reading Across Texts
Reread page 275 in "Time for a Change." Use the information given to determine which dates the stranger most likely visited the Baileys. Tell why you think so.

Writing Across Texts
What do you think would be the consequences if we didn't have seasons? Make a list of your ideas.

277

Build Language

Animal Migration

Build Vocabulary

Learn ◉ **Skill** **Multiple-Meaning Words** When reading, you may come across a word whose meaning you know, but that meaning does not make sense in the sentence. For example, *bank* can mean "a place where money is kept" or "the ground beside a river." You can use context clues to figure out which meaning is being used.

Practice Read "Paradise Island" on page 279. Then use context clues to figure out the meanings of this week's Words to Know. See if you can find which of these words has more than one meaning.

Words to Know	lagoon	bluff	rumbling
	biologist	massive	tropical

On Your Own Read "Paradise Island" again. As you read, see if you can find other words that have multiple meanings. Use a dictionary to write down the meanings.

🐻 **R1.6** Distinguish and interpret words with multiple meanings.

PARADISE ISLAND

Welcome to Paradise Island! To find out more about what you can do on our island, check out these exciting activities.

• Walk or run on the gorgeous white sand beaches that ring the whole island. They were voted the Best Beaches in the World last year by *Touring* magazine!

• Swim in the beautiful blue-green waters of our lagoon. Protected from the ocean by a reef, the lagoon is also perfect for canoeing and kayaking.

• Take a walk with our staff biologist. You can learn about the many strange and colorful birds and other animals that live on the island.

• Climb the bluff for wonderful views of the island and the ocean. We offer climbs for beginners and experts.

• Take a day trip to the volcano. You can ride or hike to the top and look down into the massive crater. It has always been quiet (except for a rumbling noise every once in a while).

Paradise Island is a tropical paradise. Come see it for yourself and have the best vacation of your life!

 Need a Review?
For additional help with multiple-meaning words, see *Words!* on p. W•10.

 Ready to Try It?
Read *Adelina's Whales* on pp. 282–291.

Build Comprehension

Learn ◉ **Skill Fact and Opinion**

- A statement of fact tells something that can be proved true or false. You can prove it true or false by reading about the topic, observing, or asking an expert.

- A statement of opinion tells a person's ideas or feelings.

- Sometimes statements of opinion begin with clue words such as *I believe* or *In my opinion*.

- Use the graphic organizer below to help you separate statements of fact from statements of opinion.

Statement	Support	True or False/ Valid or Faulty
Statement of fact	Other facts	True
Statement of opinion	Logic or known facts	Valid
Statement of opinion	Weak opinion or incorrect facts	Faulty

Practice   As you read "Something Must Be Done" on page 281, think about where each piece of information would fit on the graphic organizer above.

On Your Own   **Write to Read** Reread "Something Must Be Done." Write down a statement of fact from the passage. Then form two statements of opinion about this fact.

 Need a Review? See the *Picture It!* lesson on p. PI•7 for additional help with fact and opinion.

 Ready to Try It? As you read *Adelina's Whales* on pp. 282–291, use what you know about statements of fact and statements of opinion.

  R2.6 Distinguish between cause and effect and between fact and opinion in expository text.

SOMETHING MUST BE DONE

What is the largest animal that ever lived? Is it an elephant? That's not even close. This animal can be as big as four elephants. Is it a dinosaur? Guess again.

The largest animal in the world is the blue whale. This beautiful animal can grow as big as 100 feet long! You might think that an animal so big could live through anything. This is not so.

Skill Some sentences contain both facts and opinions. What is the statement of fact in this sentence? What is the statement of opinion?

In the 1800s and early 1900s, whaling was big business. People killed whales to make things such as oil and candles. Whales were hunted almost to extinction. In time, people developed other ways of lighting houses and workplaces. They understood that the whaling business was harming the whales. Today most countries ban whaling, but even so, many types of whales are still endangered.

Skill How could you prove that this statement of fact is true?

Whales face other challenges too. They can get caught in fishing nets and drown. (Remember, whales are mammals; they need to breathe air.) They can get sick from pollution in the ocean. Sometimes they run into ships. Governments can make more laws to protect whales and their habitats. For example, some shipping lanes were changed to make ships go around an area where mother whales bring their young.

Skill Is this a statement of fact or an opinion? Which clue word(s) can help you find the answer?

Many people believe that we should tell our governments that saving whales is important. We can make a difference!

Adelina's Whales

text and photographs by Richard Sobol

What is so unusual about the whales that visit Adelina?

La Laguna is the name of a quiet, dusty fishing village on the sandy shore of Laguna San Ignacio, in Baja California, Mexico. A few dozen homesites are scattered along the water's edge. These little houses are simple one- or two-room boxes patched together with plywood and sheet metal. Drinking water is stored outside in fifty-gallon plastic barrels, and electricity is turned on for only a few hours each day.

Adelina Mayoral has lived her whole life in La Laguna. She is a bright ten-year-old girl. She loves the ocean and the feeling of the ever-present wind that blows her long, dark hair into wild tangles. She knows what time of day it is by looking at the way the light reflects off the water. Adelina can tell what month it is by watching the kind of birds that nest in the mangroves behind her home. She can even recognize when it is low tide. Simply by taking a deep breath through her nose, she can smell the clams and seaweed that bake in the hot sun on the shoreline as the water level goes down.

California

Arizona

Baja California

Mexico

Gulf of California

Laguna San Ignacio

In late January, every afternoon after school, Adelina walks to the beach to see if her friends—the gray whales—have returned. At this same time every year the whales come, traveling from as far away as Alaska and Russia. They slowly and steadily swim south, covering more than five thousand miles along the Pacific Coast during November, December, and January.

One night Adelina is awakened by a loud, low, rumbling noise. It is the sound of a forty-ton gray whale exhaling a room-size blast of hot wet air. As she has always known they would, the gray whales have come again to visit. Adelina smiles and returns to her sleep, comforted by the sounds of whales breathing and snoring outside her window. At daybreak she runs to the lagoon and sees two clouds of mist out over the water, the milky trails of breath left by a mother gray whale and her newborn calf.

The waters of the protected lagoon are warm and shallow. The scientists who have come to visit and study the whales have explained that Laguna San Ignacio is the perfect place for the mother whales to have their babies and then teach them how to swim. But Adelina knows why they really come—to visit her!

Adelina's family lives far away from big cities with highways and shopping malls. Her little village does not have any movie theaters or traffic lights, but she knows that her hometown is a special place. This is the only place on Earth where these giant gray whales—totally wild animals—choose to seek out the touch of a human hand. Only here in Laguna San Ignacio do whales ever stop swimming and say hello to their human neighbors. Raising their massive heads up out of the water, they come face-to-face with people. Some mother whales even lift their newborns up on their backs to help them get a better view of those who have come to see them. Or maybe they are just showing off, sharing their new baby the way any proud parent would.

The whales have been coming to this lagoon for hundreds of years, and Adelina is proud that her grandfather, Pachico, was the first person to tell of a "friendly" visit with one. She loves to hear him tell the story of that whale and that day. She listens closely as he talks about being frightened, since he didn't know then that the whale was only being friendly. He thought he was in big trouble.

Adelina looks first at the tight, leathery skin of her grandfather, browned from his many years of fishing in the bright tropical sun. From his face she glances down to the small plastic model of a gray whale that he keeps close by. As he begins to tell the story of his first friendly whale encounter, there is a twinkle in his eye and a large smile on his face. Adelina and her father, Runolfo, smile too, listening again to the story that they have heard so many times before.

In a whisper, her grandfather begins to draw them in. Adelina closes her eyes to imagine the calm and quiet on that first afternoon when his small boat was gently nudged by a huge gray whale. As the boat rocked, her grandfather's and his fishing partner's hearts pounded. They held tight and waited, preparing themselves to be thrown into the water by the giant animal. The whale dove below them and surfaced again on the opposite side of their boat, scraping her head along the smooth sides. Instead of being tossed from the boat, they were surprised to find themselves still upright and floating. For the next hour the whale glided alongside them, bumping and bobbing gently— as gently as possible for an animal that is as long as a school bus and as wide as a soccer goal. As the sun started to set behind them, the whale gave out a great blast of wet, snotty saltwater that soaked their clothes and stuck to their skin. The whale then rose up inches away from their boat and dove into the sea. Her first visit was over.

As her grandfather finishes the story, he looks to Adelina, who joins him in speaking the last line of the story: "Well, my friend, no fish today!" they say before breaking into laughter.

After this first friendly visit with the whales, word quickly spread of the unique encounter between a wild fifty-foot whale and a tiny fishing boat. Scientists and whale watchers started to come to Laguna San Ignacio to see the whales themselves. Perhaps word spread among the whales, too, because now dozens of whales began to approach the small boats. With brains as large as a car's engine, gray whales might even have their own language. They "talk" in low rumbles and loud clicks, making noises that sound like the tappings of a steel drum or the ticking that a playing card makes as it slaps against the spokes of a turning bicycle wheel. Maybe they told each other that it was safe to visit here.

Adelina's favorite time of the day is the late afternoon, when her father and grandfather return from their trips on the water, guiding visitors to see the whales. They sit together as the sun goes down behind them, and she listens to stories of the whales. She asks them lots and lots of questions.

Adelina has learned a lot about the gray whales. She knows that when a whale leaps out of the water and makes a giant splash falling back in, it's called breaching. When a whale pops its head straight up out of the water, as if it is looking around to see what is going on, it is called spyhopping. Adelina also learned how the whale's wide, flat tail is called a fluke, and when it raises its tail up in the air as it goes into a deep dive, that is called fluking.

Although her home is a simple shack on a sandy bluff hugging the edge of the Pacific Ocean, Adelina has many new friends who come to share her world. She has met people who come from beyond the end of the winding, bumpy road that rings the lagoon. Some are famous actors. Some are politicians. Some speak Spanish. Some speak English. Those that weigh forty tons speak to her in their own magical style. The whales have taught her that the world is a big place.

Adelina knows that she has many choices in her future. Sometimes she giggles with delight at the idea of being the first girl to captain a panga (a small open fishing boat) and teach people about the whales in the lagoon. Or sometimes she thinks she may become a biologist who studies the ocean and can one day help to unlock some of the mysteries of the whales in her own backyard. Or maybe she will take pictures like the photographer whom she watches juggling his three cameras as he stumbles aboard the whale-watching boat. But no matter what she chooses, the whales will always be a part of her life.

KUYIMA-5

For these three months Adelina knows how lucky she is to live in Laguna San Ignacio, the little corner of Mexico that the gray whales choose for their winter home. This is the place where two worlds join together. She wouldn't trade it for anything.

In the early spring the lagoon grows quiet. One by one the whales swim off, heading north for a summer of feeding.

On their heads and backs they carry the fingerprints of those they met, the memories of their encounters in Mexico. Maybe, as the whales sleep, they dream of the colorful sunsets of Laguna San Ignacio.

Every afternoon Adelina continues to gaze across the water. Sometimes now, when she closes her eyes, she can still see the whales swimming by. And if she listens *really* closely, she can even hear their breathing.

Think, Talk and Write

Talk About It What were your thoughts about gray whales as you read the selection? What would you think if you were to see real gray whales?

1. Why do you think the author tells you about gray whales from Adelina's point of view? **Think Like an Author**

2. A statement of fact can be proved true or false. Which two of the following choices are statements of fact? How do you know? **Fact and Opinion**

   a. The whales go to Laguna San Ignacio to visit Adelina.

   b. Electricity is turned on for only a few hours each day in Laguna San Ignacio.

   c. A whale's wide, flat tail is called a fluke.

3. Create a web to record what you learned about gray whales from the selection. **Graphic Organizers**

4. A description of Laguna San Ignacio would include these Words to Know: *lagoon, tropical,* and *bluff*. What other words from the selection describe the location? **Vocabulary**

TEST PRACTICE

Look Back and Write Reread the question on page 283. How might Adelina answer this question?

Meet author Richard Sobol on page 378.

Summarize

W2.2.a Write responses to literature: Demonstrate an understanding of the literary work.

Writing

Prompt *Adelina's Whales* uses words and pictures to tell about whale migration. Think of a question you have about an animal and its migratory patterns. Now write an expository composition that answers that question.

Writing Trait

Keep your purpose in mind when writing.

Student Model

On the Move

Caribou are related to deer and live in Alaska and Canada. Do these animals migrate? Yes. Every year, thousands of caribou migrate in the spring and then again in the fall. In the spring, after the calves **are born,** herds of caribou begin to walk to the place where they will spend the summer.

During the spring and summer, caribou eat grasses, tree leaves, and other plants. In September, when the temperature starts to drop, caribou move south. They do not always go to the same place for the winter. During the winter, caribou **will eat** lichens.

If you were to draw a straight line between the place where a herd of caribou spends the summer and the place where the herd spends the winter, the distance could be up to 400 miles. But caribou do not walk in straight lines. Scientists **have discovered** that caribou may walk up to 3,000 miles in a year!

Expository nonfiction poses questions and gives answers.

Main and helping verbs are used correctly.

Writer maintains purpose.

Use this model to help you write your own expository composition.

Patterns in Nature

W1.3 Use traditional structures for conveying information (e.g., chronological order, cause and effect, similarity and difference, posing and answering a question).

Strategy Talk

Text Features Authors use text features to help readers understand information. Text features include headings, maps, graphs, illustrations, and captions.

Monitor and clarify is a strategy that is used while reading. Good readers ask themselves questions as they read. If they have trouble understanding something, they can look at the headings throughout the article. This can help them get a better understanding of how the information is organized.

 Ready to Try It?
Read "Sea Animals on the Move." Use the headings in the article to help monitor your comprehension.

Concept Link

Great white sharks migrate thousands of miles every year. Research another animal that migrates. Make a map that shows this animal's migration route.

Sea Animals on the Move

by Joanne Wachter

Some families take a trip to see relatives every Thanksgiving. Other families go to a cabin in the mountains every summer. Certain sea animals take trips to the same place year after year too. The trips these animals take are called *migration.*

Line Up!

One sea animal that migrates is the spiny lobster. Usually, the lobster stays close to its home, a crack in a rock deep in the ocean. When the first winter storm hits, however, something strange happens. The lobster starts a long trip. Groups of up to 60 lobsters line up, head to tail. Then they travel day and night, going 30 or more miles in a few days.

Other sea animals that migrate are sharks, eels, turtles, and whales. Some of these take very long trips. For example, sea turtles may travel more than 7,000 miles, one-third of the way around the Earth. Some fish have special ways to rest on their long trips. Lampreys use their sucking mouths to hold on to rocks for short breaks.

Trips with a Purpose

Why would an animal make such a trip? Some, such as spiny lobsters and sharks, move to warmer or cooler waters when the seasons change. Others, such as flashlight fish, migrate in search of food. The flashlight fish moves from deep to shallow water in order to feed. It uses a light that shines out of its body to find its way.

Many sea animals migrate to find safe places to lay eggs. Salmon live in the salty sea but travel to fresh water to have their young. The fish digs a hole in the river floor with its tail. Then it lays as many as 14,000 eggs. Sea turtles swim thousands of miles to have their babies on the same beaches where they hatched.

Traveling Without a Map

People would get lost very quickly if they tried to swim underwater from place to place. There are no signs or buildings to point the way in the ocean. Surprisingly, however, sea animals do not get lost.

Scientists think that sea animals use their senses to find their way. Some fish use their strong sense of smell. It helps them notice the familiar scents of rocks and plants along the way. Others use their sense of touch. They feel the movement of waves, tides, and currents. These clues help them map their journey.

Scientists have another interesting idea. They think that some sea animals have a sense that people do not. Something in the bodies of these animals may act like a compass. This sense may point them in the right direction.

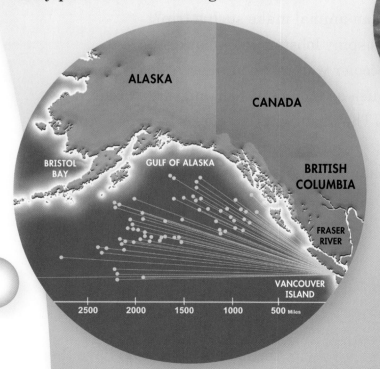

Scientists have tracked the distances traveled by some salmon. These salmon swam from the dots marked in the ocean to Fraser River in Canada.

Tag a Fish

Scientists are trying to learn more about migration. They have invented tools such as tagging to study how sea animals move. Researchers catch a sea animal, glue or strap a small tag to it, and then return the animal to the water. The tag gathers facts about the animal's journey and sends a report to satellites above the Earth. The satellites send the report back to computers on land. People use this information to learn about the patterns of the animals.

Reports about migration are useful. People from different countries are sharing what they learn so that we can all work together to protect sea animals. Dr. Barbara Block is one of these people. She believes, "The first step in protecting their [sea animals'] future on Earth is knowing where they go."

Researchers in Canada tag a sockeye salmon.

A tag on the fin of a loggerhead turtle relays information about the sea turtle's journey.

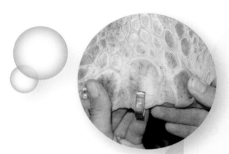

Reading Across Texts

How is Adelina's understanding of migration different from that of the scientists in this article?

Writing Across Texts Tell about an animal from these two selections whose migration you find the most interesting. Include reasons for your choice.

Build Language

Day and Night

Build Vocabulary

Learn ⦿ **Skill Unfamiliar Words** Sometimes when you are reading, you may come to a word you do not know. The context—the words and sentences around the unknown word—may give you clues to the word's meaning.

Practice Read "At the Edge of the Sea" on page 301. Look for context clues to try to figure out the meanings of this week's Words to Know. Use a glossary or a dictionary to make sure your definitions are correct.

Words to Know	brilliant	shimmering	coward
	gleamed	chorus	

On Your Own Reread "At the Edge of the Sea." Imagine you are the coast of a tropical island. Write a letter home describing the island and the sea. Use words from the Words to Know list.

  G3R1.6 Use sentence and word context to find the meanings of unknown words.

At the Edge of the Sea

The two boys hesitated at the edge of the forest. They looked out at the sea. Waves caught the morning sun and sparkled in a thousand points like brilliant jewels. The white sand gleamed as though some servant of the wind had been polishing it all night. The boys knew it would soon be too hot to tread.

Still, they stood gazing out. The scene was like a painting. Its colors were bright and already shimmering with heat. Other than the waves and a few seabirds, nothing moved. It was all too radiant. Perhaps it also did not seem real because a great journey lay ahead of them. They hoped for some omen of good luck.

At their backs, a chorus of birds began their songs. "May your travels be safe," they seemed to chant. "May your hearts be true and brave. May you never know the shame of a coward. Firm in purpose, may you find what you seek."

The boys smiled then. They shifted the canoe on their shoulders and stepped forward onto the white sand.

Need a Review?
For additional help with using context clues to determine the meanings of unfamiliar words, see *Words!* on p. W•7.

Ready to Try It?
Read *How Night Came from the Sea* on pp. 304–317.

Build Comprehension

Learn   ◎ **Skill Generalize**

- A generalization is a broad statement or rule that applies to many examples.

- You can look for clue words such as *most, usually, all*, and *in general* to help you identify generalizations.

- Valid generalizations can be supported by facts, logic, and your own prior knowledge.

- Faulty generalizations cannot be supported.

Generalization	Clue Word

Practice   As you read "Call It a Day" on page 303, look for clue words that identify a generalization.

On Your Own   **Write to Read** Reread "Call It a Day." Using what you learned in the passage, write one valid and one faulty generalization about time.

 Need a Review? See the *Picture It!* lesson on p. PI•7 for additional help with making generalizations.

 Ready to Try It? As you read *How Night Came from the Sea* on pp. 304–317, look for generalizations.

G5R2.4 Draw inferences, conclusions, or generalizations about text and support them with textual evidence and prior knowledge.

Call It a Day

When we say *day*, we often mean daytime, when it is light out—unlike nighttime, when it is dark. The number of hours of daylight a place has depends on where it is and the time of year. Along the equator the number of daylight hours is always the same—about 12 hours.

North or south of the equator, hours of daylight change over the year. In general, the farther north or south you are, the greater the change. The longest day of the year in the Northern Hemisphere is usually June 21. On that day, New York has about 13 hours of daylight. The North Pole has 24!

Of course, "24 hours" is another meaning of *day*. Daytime and nighttime together make up one day. We have day and night because Earth orbits the sun and spins on its axis.

It takes about 24 hours for Earth to complete one full spin. As Earth spins, the side that faces the sun has day. The side that faces away from the sun has night. Earth spins on its axis at a tilted angle. For the half of the year that the Northern Hemisphere tilts toward the sun, daytime there is longer than nighttime.

Skill What generalization does the author make in this paragraph? (*Hint: The clue word is* often.)

Skill What are two generalizations in this paragraph? Which clue words signal them?

Skill Are the two generalizations in this paragraph valid? Use facts from the text and your own knowledge to support your answer.

Genre **Myths** are stories that explain how things in nature came to be. Think about how you would explain the cycle of day and night as you read this story.

How Night Came from the Sea

A Story from Brazil

retold by Mary-Joan Gerson
illustrated by Carla Golembe

Why do we have day—*and* night?

Long, long ago, at the very beginning of time, when the world had just been made, there was no night. It was always daytime.

No one had ever heard of sunrise or sunset, starlight or moonbeams. There were no night creatures such as owls and tigers, and no night flowers that secretly open their petals at dusk. There was no soft night air, heavy with perfume. Sunlight always filled the sky. The light jumped from the coconuts at the top of the palm trees, and it gleamed from the backs of the alligators wading at the edge of the sea. Everywhere there was only sunlight and brightness and heat.

In that time, the great African goddess Iemanjá dwelt in the depths of the sea. And Iemanjá had a daughter who decided to marry one of the sons of the earth people. With sorrow and with longing, the daughter left her home in the deep ocean and came to live with her husband in the land of daylight.

Iemanjá's daughter loved her husband, and she loved the magic of daylight that he showed her: the shimmering sand of the beach, the rows and rows of cocoa and sugarcane baking in sunlight, and the sparkling jewels and feathered costumes worn in harvest festivals.

But with time, the light became too bright and hard for Iemanjá's daughter. The sight of the workers bent over in the fields day after day hurt her eyes and her heart.

And finally even the brilliant colors worn by the dancers at the festivals burned through her drooping lids.

"Oh, how I wish night would come," she cried. "Here there is always daylight, but in my mother's kingdom there are cool shadows and dark, quiet corners."

Her husband listened to her with great sorrow, for he loved her. "What is this night?" he asked her. "Tell me about it, and perhaps I can find a little of it for you."

"Night," she said, "is like the quiet after crying or the end of the storm. It is a dark, cool blanket that covers everything. If only we could have a little of the darkness of my mother's kingdom to rest our eyes some of the time."

Her husband called at once his three most faithful servants. "I am sending you on a very important journey," he told them. "You are to go to the kingdom of Iemanjá, who dwells in the depths of the seas. You must beg her to give you some of the darkness of night so that my wife will stop longing to return to her mother's kingdom and will be able to find happiness on land with me."

The three servants set forth. After a long, dangerous journey through the surging waves of the ocean, over the cliffs of underwater sand, and past the razor-sharp reefs of coral, they arrived at the palace of Iemanjá. Throwing themselves at the feet of the goddess, they begged her for some night to carry back with them. "Stand up, you foolish men," she commanded. "How can you beg a mother whose child is suffering?" And without a second lost, she packed a big bag of night for them to carry through the circling currents of water. "But," she said, "you must not open this until you reach my daughter, because only she can calm the night spirits I have packed inside."

The three servants pulled the big bag alongside them as they swam back through the cool, swirling sea. Finally they emerged into the bright sunlight of the shore and followed the path home, bearing the big bag upon their heads. Soon they heard strange sounds. They were the voices of all the night creatures squeezed inside. The servants had never heard this strange chorus of night screeching before, and they shook with fear.

The first servant stared at the screaming bag of voices and began to tremble.

"Let us drop this bag of night and run away as fast as we can," said the second servant.

"Coward!" said the third, trying to sound brave. "I am going to open the bag and see what makes all those terrible sounds."

He laid the bag on the ground and opened its sealing wax with his teeth. **Out rushed** the **night beasts,** the **night birds,** and all the **night insects. Out jumped** the **stars** and the **moon.** The servants ran terrified into the jungle.

But the servants were in luck, because Iemanjá's daughter
was standing at the shore, waiting and waiting for their return.
Ever since they had set out on their journey, she had stood in
one spot under a palm tree at the edge of the sea, shading her
eyes with her hand and praying for the darkness. And she was
still standing in that spot when the servants let night escape.

"Night has come. Night has come at last," she cried
as she saw the blue-black shadows gather on the horizon.
"I greet you, my kinship spirits." And when she spoke, the
night spirits were suddenly calmed, and there was hushed
darkness everywhere.

Then the gentle hum of the night creatures began, and moonbeams flickered across the sky. The creatures of the night appeared before her: the owl hunting by moonlight and the tiger finding its way through the forest by smelling the dark, damp earth. The soft air grew heavy with the smell of night perfume. To Iemanjá's daughter, this coming of night was indeed like the quiet after crying or the end of the storm. It was like a dark, cool blanket covering everything, and just as if a soft hand had soothed her tired eyes, Iemanjá's daughter fell fast asleep.

She awoke feeling as if she were about to sing. How rested she was after the coolness of her night dreams! Her eyes opened wide to the brightness of the glistening day, and in her heart she knew she would find peace in her husband's land. And so to celebrate the beauty of her new home, Iemanjá's daughter made three gifts.

To the last bright star still shining above the palm tree she said, "Glittering star, from now on you will be our sign that night is passing. You shall be called the morning star, and you will announce the birth of each day."

To the rooster standing by her, she said, "You shall be the watchman of the night. From this day on, your voice will warn us that the light is coming."

And to the birds all about her she called, "You singing birds, you shall sing your sweetest songs at this hour to announce the dawn of each day."

To this day, the gifts of Iemanjá's daughter help celebrate each new sunrise. In Brazil the early morning is called the madragada. As the madragada slides onto the horizon, the morning star reigns in the sky as queen of the dawn. The rooster announces the day's approach to the sleeping birds, and then they sing their most beautiful songs.

And it is also true that in Brazil night leaps out quickly like a bullfrog just as it leapt quickly out of the bag in the beginning of time. The night flowers suddenly open their petals at dusk. And as they do, the owl and tiger begin their hunt for food.

The beasts and birds and insects of the night begin to sing their gentle chorus. And when the dark, cool blanket of night covers everything, the people of the earth take their rest.

Think, Talk and Write

Talk About It Why do you think the servants were so afraid of the bag they were carrying? Would you have been scared? Why or why not?

1. How might the end of the story have been different if Iemanjá had not been nearby when the bag was opened?
Think Like an Author

2. What generalization could you make about the story or one of the characters in it? What examples support that generalization? **Generalize**

3. After the servants let night escape, they run "terrified into the jungle." What might the jungle be like at night? Describe what the servants might feel. **Visualize**

4. Write your own "ode to night," explaining why it is important to you. Use words from the Words to Know list and the story. **Vocabulary**

TEST PRACTICE

Look Back and Write Reread the question on page 305. How is this explanation of day and night in the story different from the scientific explanation of day and night?

Meet author **Mary-Joan Gearson** and illustrator **Carla Golembe** on **page 375.**

Retell

W2.2.a Write responses to literature: Demonstrate an understanding of the literary work.

Writing

Prompt *How Night Came from the Sea* tells how people long ago explained the concept of night and day. Think about how you might explain the pattern of night and day. Now write a myth that includes your explanation.

Writing Trait

Correct **verb tenses** make your writing clear.

Student Model

How We Got Day and Night

Sunna, daughter of Sol, the Giver of Light, met Siran while **he was building** a ladder that would reach the sun. Siran told Sunna stories and made her laugh. She wanted him to spend more time with her. He would always answer, "It's still light outside. I have to keep working."

The story is told in the past tense.

Sunna went to her father and said, "Father, I really like Siran, but he's always working. **He says** he can't stop, because it's still light outside. Can't you do something to make the sun stop shining?" **Sunna was** so unhappy that Sol decided to hide the sun behind a nearby planet for twelve hours each day.

Some **myths** try to explain a natural phenomenon.

"Father, thank you so much!" she cried. On the day that **Sol hid** the sun, Sunna ran to find Siran. As the sun moved behind the planet, the sky grew dimmer. Finally, it was very dark. Sunna asked Siran, "Now will you spend some time with me?" Siran smiled as he put down his tools and took her hand.

Subjects and verbs agree.

Use the model to help you write your own myth.

W2.1.b Write narratives: Provide a context to enable the reader to imagine the world of the event or experience.

Skill Talk

Author's purpose is the reason or reasons an author has for writing. Good readers ask, "Why did the author write this?" Authors often have more than one reason for writing. Four common reasons are to persuade, to inform, to entertain, or to express a mood or feeling. Each text could be a combination of the above reasons.

Ready to Try It?
Read "The Ant and the Bear." As you read the selection, try to identify the author's purpose.

Concept Link

Many ancient civilizations passed down stories to explain changes in nature. Write a paragraph about a story you were told that explained a phenomenon of nature.

THE ANT AND THE BEAR

from SPIRIT OF THE CEDAR PEOPLE

MORE STORIES AND PAINTINGS OF CHIEF LELOOSKA

Into the newly created world came Whone, the Changer. It was he who set the world right. Whone piled up earth and made the mountains. He planted trees on the hills and in the valleys. He planted all the edible roots that we now use for food. Then Whone took a stick and dug the rivers, and he called the salmon forth from the sea to feed the children of men.

After Whone had grown weary of all his good work, he called upon the animal people to help him make rules for the new world. One of the most important decisions was the proper length for the daylight and the dark. For in that time the daylight came and went as it pleased. A day might last a whole season or be as quick as a blink of the eye. Clearly something needed to be done, so Whone chose Ant and Bear for the task.

Bear was big and fat and lazy. He yawned, scratched himself, and looked down at the tiny Ant, the little Sky Yack, and said in a deep, gruff voice, "I am Chetwin! I am the Bear! I think half the year should be dark and half of it light. Then we bears could sleep for half the year and eat for the other half."

Ant was a scrawny little fellow, and he had a habit of tugging nervously at his belt when he talked. But Ant was also proud and stubborn. He was not about to let Bear decide anything for him. Ant pulled himself up as tall as he could and shouted up to the great Bear, "No, no! Never do! Never do! Never do! We must have *kai tacheelah, kai tacheelah, chowow, chaloose!* We must have daylight and dark, daylight and dark, every day!"

Bear, who was used to having his own way, leaned down and stared in Ant's face. "*Yo yoks! Sky ta che!*" he growled. "Half of the year dark and half of it light!"

And so the argument went on. Ant began to jump up and down in excitement, all the while yanking nervously at his belt and squeaking at the top of his voice, "Daylight and dark! Daylight and dark! Every day!"

Bear became very angry. He roared louder and louder, "Half the year dark and half of it light!"

On and on they shouted. How long they argued no one knows because there was no proper length for the daylight and the dark.

At last Bear grew weary. "All right, Ant, have it your way," he said. "Daylight and dark every day. But we bears will have it our way too! We will go into the mountains and sleep for half the year. Then we will wake up and eat."

Bear began to lumber away. Then he turned back to Ant. "And do you know what we will eat, Ant?" asked Bear with a big grin. "We will eat you! And all your relatives! We will tear open the old rotten logs and find you and eat you!"

"No, no, you will not," cried Ant. "We will grow wings and fly away!"

And so little Ant won the argument. There would be daylight and dark every day. Ant was pleased with himself, but then he looked down at his waist. In his excitement and all that yanking on his belt, Ant had cinched himself up so tight that he was almost cut in two. Ant had paid an awful price for his victory. He was left with the little skinny waist that all ants have to this very day.

We know this story must be true because ants do have tiny waists; they do grow wings and fly out of old rotten logs in the late summer; and bears do rumble off into the mountains and sleep for half the year. Most of all, we know it is true because we have daylight and dark every single day!

Reading Across Texts

Both *How Night Came from the Sea* and "The Ant and the Bear" are myths that explain the cycle of day and night. Summarize each explanation.

Writing Across Texts

Which explanation of day and night do you like better? Write a paragraph that tells why you chose the one you did.

Build Language

Storms

Build Vocabulary

Learn   ◉ **Skill** **Root Words** When you come across a word you do not know, try to identify the root word to help you figure out the meaning. For example, the word *construction* has the root *construct*. If you don't know the meaning of the root, you can use a dictionary to check it.

Practice   Use a dictionary to look up this week's Words to Know. Look for root words as you write down the meanings in your journal. Then read "Hurricanes" on page 325.

Words to Know	destruction	surge	forecasts
	shatter	inland	expected

On Your Own   Look for other words with roots as you reread "Hurricanes." See if you can replace the prefixes or suffixes of these words to make new meanings. How many meanings can you make from one root?

R1.3 Use knowledge of root words to determine the meanings of unknown words within a passage.

HURRICANES

A hurricane is a large storm with high winds and heavy rain. It needs heat and moisture to form, so the best hurricane-producing place is a tropical ocean. As warm, moist air rises, cooler air moves in. Then the air begins to spin. The winds spin around a calm center called the eye. The strongest winds are around the eye. They may have speeds of 200 miles per hour. A hurricane's winds may extend 250 miles from the eye.

If a hurricane stays over water, it keeps pulling heat and moisture from the ocean. But it begins to lose power as it reaches land, where the air is cooler and drier. Once it moves over land, it becomes weak very quickly.

The destruction from a hurricane comes from both wind and water. High winds shatter windows and uproot trees. Besides bringing heavy rain, a hurricane can cause a storm surge as winds push ocean water to areas far inland.

Meteorologists watch for and track hurricanes. They issue forecasts telling when a hurricane is expected to arrive so that people can prepare for the storm.

 Need a Review?
For additional help with root words, see *Words!* on p. W·4.

 Ready to Try It?
Read *Eye of the Storm* on pp. 328–339.

Patterns in Nature

325

Build Comprehension

Learn ⊙ **Skill Graphic Sources**

- A graphic source supports information in the text. Pictures, maps, charts, time lines, and diagrams are all examples of graphic sources.

- You can use graphic sources to preview and predict what you will read about.

- Look at the graphic source below. How can you use this diagram to understand hurricanes?

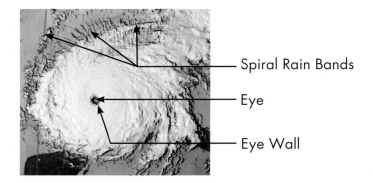

Spiral Rain Bands

Eye

Eye Wall

Practice   Use what you learned about graphic sources as you read "Name That Hurricane" on page 327.

On Your Own   **Write to Read** Reread "Name That Hurricane." Make your own list of hurricane names. Use the same pattern as the list of names shown on the chart.

   Need a Review? See the *Picture It!* lesson on pp. PI•8– PI•9 for additional help with using graphic sources.

▶   **Ready to Try It?** As you read *Eye of the Storm* on pp. 328–339, use what you learned about graphic sources to help you understand the text.

🐻   **G2R2.7** Interpret information from diagrams, charts, and graphs.

NAME THAT HURRICANE

Hurricanes are huge storms with powerful winds that form over the ocean and sometimes hit land. Weather scientists, or meteorologists, track hurricanes and warn people to get to safety. To help talk about these storms, meteorologists name them.

Hurricane names are taken from a list on a six-year cycle. In other words, every six years, meteorologists use the same names. They do not always need every name in a given year. It depends on the number of hurricanes that year.

Some hurricanes have been so destructive that their names have been retired. For example, there will never be another Hurricane Katrina. This large storm slammed into Louisiana, Mississippi, and Alabama in 2005, killing more than one thousand people and causing billions of dollars in damage. The name Katia will be used instead of Katrina.

Skill Look at the graphic sources on this page. Then predict what you will read about.

Skill What is the next year after 2011 that a new chart will be used?

Skill Look closely at this list. What can you tell about the order of the names in general and the order of the boy and girl names in particular? Which letters of the alphabet are not used to name hurricanes?

Atlantic Ocean Hurricane Names for the Year 2011

1. Arlene	8. Harvey	15. Ophelia
2. Bret	9. Irene	16. Philippe
3. Cindy	10. Jose	17. Rina
4. Don	11. Katia	18. Sean
5. Emily	12. Lee	19. Tammy
6. Franklin	13. Maria	20. Vince
7. Gert	14. Nate	21. Whitney

Patterns in Nature

327

Eye of the

by Stephen Kramer
photographs by Warren Faidley

Genre

Expository nonfiction gives information about real people and events. Be prepared for a few surprises as you read about a real person, Warren Faidley, who experiences a real storm, Hurricane Andrew.

Storm

Chasing Storms with Warren Faidley

Is the middle of a hurricane any place for a photographer?

Warren Faidley is a storm chaser. Beginning in April and continuing through November, he can be found on the trail of tornadoes, thunderstorms, and hurricanes, photographing their spectacular beauty and power. When he is not out chasing storms, Warren is at home in Tucson, Arizona, where he sells his photographs through his business, a stock photo agency.

Storm Seasons and Chasing

Storms are caused by certain kinds of weather patterns. The same patterns are found in the same areas year after year. For example, every spring, large areas of cool, dry air and warm, moist air collide over the central United States. If the winds are right, tornado-producing thunderstorms appear. That's why tornadoes in the south central United States are most likely to happen in spring. During July and August, shifting winds push moisture from the south up into the Arizona desert. When the cool, moist air is heated by the hot desert, storm clouds form. That's why Tucson has summer thunderstorms. In the late summer and early fall, when oceans in the northern Atlantic are warmest, tropical storms form off the west coast of Africa. A few of these turn into the hurricanes that sometimes batter the east and gulf coasts of North America.

April	May	June	July	August	September	October	November

Tornadoes

Thunderstorms

Hurricanes

Because Warren is a storm chaser, his life also follows these weather patterns. Each spring, Warren goes on the road, traveling through parts of the United States likely to be hit by tornadoes. During the summer, he stays near Tucson so he can photograph the thunderstorms that develop over the desert. In the late summer and fall, he keeps an eye on weather activity in the Atlantic Ocean, ready to fly to the east coast if a hurricane appears.

Chasing Hurricanes

By the first or second week in September, Tucson's summer thunderstorms are ending. There won't be much lightning until the next summer. But that works out well for Warren, because August through November are months when hurricanes sometimes strike the east and gulf coasts of the United States.

Although Tucson is far from the areas where hurricanes hit, Warren begins his hurricane chases from home. He uses his computer to get information on tropical storms or hurricanes moving toward North America.

"I can't go out and look for a hurricane, or watch one develop, like I can with tornadoes and lightning," says Warren. "When a hurricane is forming, I look at satellite pictures, I listen to weather forecasters talk about it, and I pay attention to what scientists and meteorologists think the hurricane is going to do. Hurricane paths are very hard to predict. Often a hurricane will roar right up to the coast and then stop and go away. So I want to be sure that I'm going to have a storm to photograph before I travel all the way to the east coast!"

When weather forecasters predict that a hurricane will strike the eastern United States, Warren flies to a city near the place the storm is expected to arrive. Flying is faster than driving Shadow Chaser* all the way from Tucson. Besides, a vehicle would not be safe during a hurricane. Branches, boards, and other loose materials carried by hurricane winds quickly shatter windows and damage any cars left outside.

*Shadow Chaser is Warren's specially equipped four-wheel-drive vehicle.

"Hurricanes are the only type of storm where I'm shooting destruction in progress. With tornadoes, you're not usually close enough to shoot the destruction—if you are, you're in a very dangerous place! With hurricanes I'm shooting palm trees bending until they're ready to break and floodwaters splashing over the bank. Those kinds of shots really separate hurricane photos from the others. Most of my hurricane photos are wind shots with heavy rains.

"Finding a place to stay safe while I take hurricane photos is also a challenge. I like to find a solid garage. A good concrete garage is going to be able to withstand the high winds. Another danger with hurricanes is that the powerful winds can lift the seawater and carry it a long ways inland. This is called a storm surge, and it's like a flood from the ocean. When you're picking a spot to stay during the hurricane, you need to have some idea of how high the storm surge might be and how far inland it will go."

Hurricane Andrew

On Saturday, August 22, 1992, after a seven-hour flight from Tucson, Warren arrived in Miami, Florida. He had arranged to meet Mike Laca and Steve Wachholder, two other experienced hurricane chasers. Hurricane Andrew was expected to hit the Florida coast in two days, so Mike, Steve, and Warren had agreed to work together to predict where the storm was going to hit, scout out a safe place to stay, and photograph the storm.

When Warren arrived, the three compared notes. They knew, from weather reports and bulletins from the National Hurricane Center, that Andrew had the potential to become a very dangerous storm. The hurricane was about 520 miles from Miami. It was heading in their direction at about 14 miles per hour. The storm had sustained wind speeds of 110 miles per hour, and they were expected to increase. Warren, Mike, and Steve agreed to get a good night's sleep and meet at noon the next day to go over the latest forecasts. When they had a better idea of where the storm would hit, they could start looking for a safe place to stay.

Mike and Warren found a sturdy, seven-story parking garage in an area called Coconut Grove. It was built with thick concrete walls and looked like a fortress, but the outside walls also had large square openings that could be used for taking pictures. Fort Andrew, as Warren began calling the building, was located on a slight hill, which would help protect it from the storm surge.

Warren, Mike, and Steve find shelter in a seven-story parking garage.

Steve, Mike, and Warren set up a "command center" on the fifth floor of the garage. They stockpiled food, water, rope, and waterproof bags as well as their photography equipment. The three took turns monitoring the latest updates on TV and radios.

As the sun set, Warren and his friends waited anxiously. By 11:00 P.M., there was still no sign of the storm. They began to wonder whether the hurricane had changed direction. But reports on the TV and radio kept saying that Andrew was still headed straight for land—and its strongest winds were expected to hit the area where Warren, Steve, and Mike were staying.

About 2:30 A.M., Hurricane Andrew finally arrived. Warren was watching when bright flashes began appearing in the northeast. The lights looked like fireworks. Actually, they were sparks and explosions as the approaching winds knocked down power lines and transformers. Warren will never forget the sounds of that night:

"At first, there was just the noise of sparking electrical lines and trash cans rolling down the street. But as time passed, the wind just kept getting louder and louder and scarier and scarier."

During the next hour, Steve and Warren tried several times to measure the wind speeds with an instrument called an anemometer. Steve held the instrument out an opening in the wall and Warren used his flashlight to read the dial. When the wind reached 65 miles per hour they gave up.

"I can't hold on anymore," Steve called above the howling winds. "It's too dangerous! I can't hold on!" The winds were carrying raindrops sideways through the air.

"Around 3:45 A.M., we began to hear bursts of breaking glass, as the winds became strong enough to blow in windows. Sometimes the crack of breaking glass was followed by a tinkling sound, like wind chimes, as the wind blew the broken glass along the streets. Inside the garage, car alarm sirens wailed as cars were hit by blasts of wind. Later, even the sound of alarms and the crack of breaking glass disappeared in the roar of the hurricane winds."

As the wind wailed in the darkness, Warren wondered how he was ever going to get any pictures. He worried that by the time it became light, the hurricane winds would die down. He worried about missing the chance to see what was going on outside.

About 5:15 A.M., the hurricane winds reached their peak. The parking garage began to shake. Wind slammed into the concrete walls with the force of bombs. Large sprinkler pipes fastened to the ceilings in the garage began to work their way loose. Several pipes collapsed and fell to the floor.

Now the winds were blowing so hard inside the garage that it was impossible to walk even a few feet in areas that weren't blocked by walls. The roar of the wind turned into a sound like the constant blast of jet engines.

Finally, around 6:00 A.M., with the winds still howling, Warren saw the first faint light of the new day. As the sky gradually turned a strange blue color, Steve, Mike, and Warren looked out on a scene of terrible destruction. Broken boats, and parts of boats, had been carried by the storm surge from the marina almost to the garage. A tree that had been torn from the ground during the night had smashed into the side of a parked truck. Although most of the buildings around the garage were still standing, many had been heavily damaged.

When there was finally enough light for his camera, Warren headed outside. Leaning into the strong winds, he carefully made his way toward the marina. At times, gusts of wind knocked him to the ground. Wreckage from boats and buildings was still flying through the air. Warren took pictures of the wind bending the trees near the marina and the broken boats on the shore.

Warren continued walking along the beach, shooting more pictures as the sky turned light. After about an hour, the wind began to quiet and the rain became more gentle. Now Warren began to wade carefully toward the marina, taking more pictures of the wreckage ahead of him. Other people were arriving to look at the damage and to see if their boats had survived.

After a tour of the marina, Warren went back to the beach. It was littered with boat parts, clothing, and dead fish. There was even a photo album opened to a wet page. More and more people arrived to see what remained of their homes or boats.

Warren finally returned to his motel, where he slept for ten hours. The next day, when he drove back to the Miami airport, his camera bags were filled with rolls of exposed film. His arm ached where the wind had slammed him into a railing after he left the parking garage. Still, as the airplane took off from Miami, it was hard for Warren to imagine that two nights earlier he had been watching, listening to, and photographing the destructive winds of Hurricane Andrew.

Think, Talk and Write

Talk About It When is it wise to chase a storm? When is it foolish? If you went storm chasing with Warren Faidley, would you be wise or foolish? Explain.

1. Were you surprised that the hurricane damaged a thick concrete building? How did the author use details to show you the force of that destruction? **Think Like an Author**

2. The selection's photos and captions are graphic sources. What kinds of information do they provide that the text cannot? How do these features add to your understanding of the selection? **Graphic Sources**

3. Do you think Warren Faidley will continue to chase storms? Why do you think this? **Predict**

4. Make a chart labeled "Sights and Sounds of Hurricane Andrew." Write words and phrases from the Words to Know list and the selection that fit into each category. **Vocabulary**

Look Back and Write Reread the question on page 329. What dangers are there for a person in the middle of a hurricane? Would you want to be in the middle of a hurricane? Why or why not?

Meet author Stephen Kramer on page 376.

Summarize

W2.2.a Write responses to literature: Demonstrate an understanding of the literary work.

Writing

Prompt *Eye of the Storm* describes how a photographer tracks storm patterns. Think of a destructive storm that has been in the news. Using a cause-and-effect structure, write an expository composition that explains the storm's impact on people.

Student Model

Tennessee Tornado

Last spring, a tornado hit outside Nashville, Tennessee. With winds between 150 and 200 miles per hour, the tornado **destroyed** schools, businesses, and homes in the middle of the day. It also turned over cars and **uprooted** trees. Ten people were killed.

This year I saw a story that followed up on some of the people who had experienced the tornado. Many had **rebuilt** their homes. Some had added a special "safe" room, which is a small room built using extra materials, including steel. A safe room **is** strong enough to withstand the strong winds of a tornado. It **will protect** people from debris that can slam into walls and cause damage.

The high winds of a tornado **can be** very dangerous. Buildings and other structures can be completely destroyed by a tornado. Proper shelter can help protect people from harm during a tornado.

The composition describes a cause and its effects.

Past, present, and future verb tenses are used correctly.

Conclusion wraps up the central idea.

Patterns in Nature

Use the model to help you write your own expository composition.

W1.3 Use traditional structures for conveying information (e.g., chronological order, cause and effect, similarity and difference, posing and answering a question).

Severe Weather Safety

Web Site Every Web site has a home page. A home page introduces the site. You can move around a Web site by clicking on links on the home page.

Links are buttons or underlined words or phrases set in a different color. When you click on a link, your computer will open a new Web page that contains the information indicated by the link.

 Ready to Try It?
Read "Severe Weather Safety." As you read, look at the different links that can be accessed.

Concept Link

In the United States, an average of 300 people are injured by lightning each year. Which type of severe weather occurs most often in your area? What things can you do to stay safe when severe weather occurs?

After reading *Eye of the Storm*, Natalia wants to know more about storm safety. Where she lives, in northern Illinois, thunderstorms are frequent during the spring and summer. What should she do if she is caught outside during a thunderstorm, she wonders. And if she is inside during a storm, are there any things she shouldn't do?

for more practice

Get Online!
PearsonSuccessNet.com

Natalia decides to search for information on the Internet. Her search takes her to the Web site of a regional weather service office.

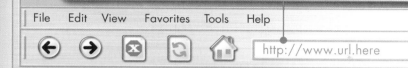

File   Edit   View   Favorites   Tools   Help

http://www.url.here

Regional Weather Service Office

Staying Safe in Severe Weather

Contents

Tornado Safety

Flash Flood Safety

Lightning Safety

Winter Storm/Blizzard Preparedness and Safety

Hurricane Safety

Other Severe Weather Safety Links

In the United States, lightning causes about 100 deaths each year. This is more than tornadoes and hurricanes combined.

Natalia clicks on a link that takes her to a Web page about severe weather safety. After skimming the contents of the page, she decides to click on the Lightning Safety link.

Clicking on the Lightning Safety link opens a new Web page on Natalia's computer screen. As the link indicates, the Web page contains information about lightning safety.

Regional Weather Service Office

Lightning Safety

Do you know what to do if you are caught in the open during a thunderstorm or you feel tingling or your hair is standing on end?

General lightning safety rules:

Natalia reads the information, and then clicks on the General lightning safety rules link. Another new Web page opens on her screen.

Regional Weather Service Office

General lightning safety rules:

When inside:

Do not use the telephone or other appliances.

Do not take a bath or shower.

Regional Weather Service Office

When outside:

Go to a safe place right away, such as inside a strong building. A hard-top automobile with the windows up can also offer fair protection.

If you are boating or swimming, get out of the water right away and move to a safe place away from the water!

If you are in a wooded area, take cover under a thick growth of relatively small trees.

If you feel your hair standing on end, squat with your head between your knees. **Do not lie flat!**

Stay away from: isolated trees or other tall objects, bodies of water, sheds, fences, convertible automobiles, tractors, and motorcycles.

If you are outside and your hair stands on end, squat with your head between your knees.

Reading Across Texts

Both hurricanes and tornadoes produce lightning. Compare the lightning safety tips with how Warren, Steve, and Mike faced lightning in *Eye of the Storm*.

Writing Across Texts Use both selections to prepare a "Lightning Dos and Don'ts" list.

Build Language

Changes in Nature

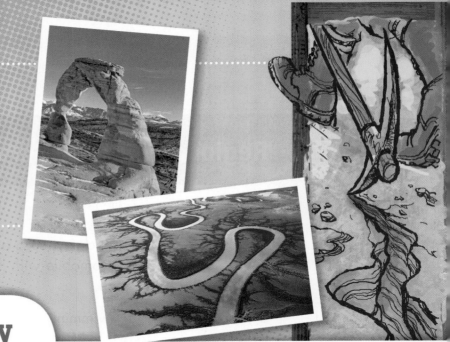

Build Vocabulary

Learn ◉ **Skill** **Suffixes** A suffix is a word part added to the end of a word. When a suffix is added to a base word, it changes the meaning of the word. For example, the base word of *movement* is *move*. The suffix *-ment* describes the result of an action or a condition. So, *movement* means "the act of moving."

Practice Read "Working with Babe" on page 347. Look for words that end with suffixes. Use the suffix to help you figure out each word's meaning. Remember, a dictionary is the best place to find the correct meaning of a word.

Words to Know	lumberjacks	feature	harness
	thaw	untamed	unnatural
	announcement	requirements	

On Your Own Read "Working with Babe" again. Write about a time when you worked hard. How did you feel at the end of the job? Use words from the Words to Know list.

G3R1.8 Use knowledge of prefixes (e.g., *un-, re-, pre-, bi-, mis-, dis-*) and suffixes (e.g., *-er, -est, -ful*) to determine the meanings of words.

Working with Babe

Back in the old days, lumberjacks used oxen to help move logs out of the woods. At first, when Paul Bunyan opened his own logging camp, Babe the Blue Ox did all the work himself. Paul's camp was so successful that Babe soon needed help. At the start of the spring thaw, he put up an announcement calling for oxen to help him.

Besides the obvious feature of being huge, Babe asked that the oxen that applied be

- strong enough to pull logs 300 feet in diameter
- wide enough to hold a 10-foot basket of food on their backs
- tame enough to care for a newborn lamb

Babe did not have time to deal with untamed oxen. He needed them to be able to go right to work. Hundreds of oxen showed up to work. Before being hired, the oxen said they had some requirements of their own. They each wanted ten bags of oats a day. They each wanted a harness lined with the softest fur. And, even though it seemed unnatural, they wanted an endless supply of chocolate chips! It is a well-kept secret that oxen love sweets.

 Need a Review?
For additional help with suffixes, see *Words!* on p. W•6.

 Ready to Try It?
Read "Paul Bunyan" on pp. 350–363.

Patterns in Nature

Build Comprehension

Learn ◉ **Skill Generalize**

- Sometimes when you read, you can make a statement about all people and things in a group. This statement is called a generalization.

- Clue words such as *most, all, always,* and *never* can help you identify generalizations in what you read.

- A valid generalization is supported by specific facts and logic. A faulty generalization is not.

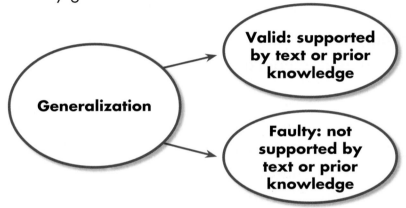

Generalization

Valid: supported by text or prior knowledge

Faulty: not supported by text or prior knowledge

Practice Use what you learned about generalizations as you read "Davy Crockett" on page 349.

On Your Own **Write to Read** Reread "Davy Crockett." Write a journal entry that contains generalizations about Davy Crockett. Make a graphic organizer like the one above to help you list facts from the text that support your generalizations.

 Need a Review? See the *Picture It!* lesson on p. PI•7 for additional help with generalizations.

 Ready to Try It? As you read "Paul Bunyan" on pp. 350–363, use what you know about generalizations to help you understand the text.

G5R2.4 Draw inferences, conclusions, or generalizations about text and support them with textual evidence and prior knowledge.

Davy Crockett

David "Davy" Crockett was born on August 17, 1786, in northeastern Tennessee. As a young man, Crockett spent a lot of time hunting. Most of the food he and his family ate came from the animals he hunted. They ate the meat of deer, elk, turkeys, and bears. One year, Crockett said he shot more than fifty bears.

When Crockett was twenty-eight, he fought against the British in the War of 1812. After the war, he spent time hunting and exploring the forests of Tennessee. In 1821, Davy ran for election to the Tennessee congress. Many people voted for him. He won and was in office for four years. In 1827, Crockett was elected to the U.S. House of Representatives. After losing an election in 1831, he ran again in 1833 and won. He stayed in office until 1835.

After leaving office, Davy traveled to Texas. He fought in a war to make Texas independent from Mexico. Crockett was killed during the Battle of the Alamo in March of 1836.

Davy Crockett had the most exciting and interesting life. He was a skilled rifleman and hunter. He fought in wars and was elected to public office several times.

Skill What clue word signals a generalization? Can it be supported by facts?

Skill Is this a valid generalization? How do you know?

Skill Which statement in this paragraph has a faulty generalization? Explain why.

Patterns in Nature

Genre

Tall tales are humorous stories with characters who have superhuman abilities. As you read, think about how the exaggerated details help explain many of the natural features of the American frontier.

PAUL BUNYAN

BY MARY POPE OSBORNE
ILLUSTRATIONS BY HARVEY CHAN

WHAT DOES IT TAKE TO TAME NATURE?

It seems an amazing baby was born in the state of Maine. When he was only two weeks old, he weighed more than a hundred pounds, and for breakfast every morning he ate five dozen eggs, ten sacks of potatoes, and a half barrel of mush made from a whole sack of cornmeal. But the baby's strangest feature was his big curly black beard. It was so big and bushy that every morning his poor mother had to comb it with a pine tree.

Except for that beard, the big baby wasn't much trouble to anybody until he was about nine months old. That was when he first started to crawl, and since he weighed over five hundred pounds, he caused an earthquake that shook the whole town.

When the neighbors complained, the baby's parents tried putting him in a giant floating cradle off the coast of Maine. But soon a delegation of citizens went to the baby's parents and said, "We're sorry, folks, but you have to take your son somewhere else. Every time he rolls over in his cradle, huge waves drown all the villages along the coast."

So his parents hauled the giant toddler to a cave in the Maine woods far away from civilization and said good-bye. "We'll think of you often, honey," his mother said, weeping. "But you can't come back home—you're just too big."

"Here, son," his father said. "I'm giving you my ax, my knife, my fishing pole, and some flint rocks. Good-bye and good luck."

After his parents left, the poor bearded baby cried for thirty days and thirty nights. He was so lonely, he cried a whole river of tears. He might have cried himself to death if one day he hadn't heard *flop, flop, flop.*

When the baby looked around, he saw fish jumping in his river of tears. He reached for his father's fishing pole and soon he was catching trout. He used his father's knife to clean and scale what he had caught and his father's ax to cut wood for a fire. He started the fire with his flint rocks and cooked his catch over the flames. Then he ate a big fish dinner and smiled for the first time in a month.

That's the story of how Paul Bunyan came to take care of himself in the Maine woods. And even though he lived alone for the next twenty years, he got along quite well. He hunted and fished. He cut down trees and made fires. He battled winter storms, spring floods, summer flies, and autumn gales.

Nothing, however, prepared Paul Bunyan for the wild weather that occurred on the morning of his twenty-first birthday. It was a cold December day, and when Paul woke up, he noticed gusts of snow blowing past the mouth of his cave. That was natural enough. What was unnatural was that the snow was blue.

"Why, that's beautiful!" Paul said. And he pulled on his red-and-black mackinaw coat, his corn-yellow scarf, and his snow boots. Then grinning from ear to ear, he set out across the blue hills.

The snow fell until the woods were covered with a thick blanket of blue. As Paul walked over huge drifts, bitter winds whistled through the trees and thunder rolled in the sky. But he soon began to hear another sound in the wind—"Maa-maa."

"Who's there?" Paul called.

"Maa-maa."

"Who's there?" said Paul again. His heart was starting to break, for the cries sounded as if they were coming from a baby crying for its mother and father.

"Maa-maa."

"Where are you, baby?" Suddenly Paul saw a tail sticking right up out of a blue snowdrift. When he pulled on the tail, out came the biggest baby ox on earth. Except for its white horns, the creature was frozen deep blue, the same color as the snow.

"He-ey, babe!" Paul shouted.

"Maa-maa-maa."

"Hush, hush, hush, babe," Paul whispered as he carried the frozen ox back home.

"There now," he said, setting the blue creature gently down in front of his fire. "We'll get you warmed up all right."

Paul fell asleep with his arm around the giant baby ox. He didn't know if the frozen babe would live or not. But when the morning sun began shining on the blue snow outside the cave, Paul felt a soft, wet nose nuzzling his neck. As the rough tongue licked his cheeks and nose and eyelids, Paul's joyous laughter shook the earth. He had found a friend.

Paul Bunyan and Babe the Blue Ox were inseparable after that. Babe grew so fast that Paul liked to close his eyes for a minute, count to ten, then look to see how much Babe had grown. Sometimes the ox would be a whole foot taller. It's a known fact that Babe's full-grown height was finally measured to be forty-two ax handles, and he weighed more than the combined weight of all the fish that ever got away. Babe was so big that when he and Paul trekked through forests, Paul had to look through a telescope just to see what Babe's hind legs were doing.

In those times, huge sections of America were filled with dark green forests. And forests were filled with trees—oceans of trees—trees as far as the eye could see—trees so tall you had to look straight up to see if it was morning, and maybe if you were lucky, you'd catch a glimpse of blue sky.

It would be nice if those trees could have stayed tall and thick forever. But the pioneers needed them to build houses, churches, ships, wagons, bridges, and barns. So one day Paul Bunyan took a good look at all those trees and said, "Babe, stand back. I'm about to invent logging."

"Tim-ber!" he yelled, and he swung his bright steel ax in a wide circle. There was a terrible crash, and when Paul looked around he saw he'd felled ten white pines with a single swing.

Paul bundled up the trees and loaded them onto the ox's back. "All right, Babe," he said. "Let's haul 'em to the Big Onion and send 'em down to a sawmill."

Since both Babe and Paul could cover a whole mile in a single step, it only took about a week to travel from Maine to the Big Onion River in Minnesota.

"She's too crooked. Our logs will get jammed at her curves," Paul said to Babe as he peered through his telescope at the long, winding river. "Let's see what we can do about that." He tied one end of the rope to Babe's harness and the other around the end of the river. Then he shouted, "Pull! Pull!"

And Babe huffed and puffed until he pulled all the kinks out of that winding water.

"There! She's as straight as a gun barrel now," Paul said. "Let's send down these logs."

After that Paul and Babe traveled plenty fast through the untamed North Woods. They cut pine, spruce, and red willow in Minnesota, Michigan, and Wisconsin. They cleared cottonwoods out of Kansas so farmers could plant wheat. They cleared oaks out of Iowa so farmers could plant corn. It seems that the summer after the corn was planted in Iowa, there was a heat wave. It got so hot the corn started to pop. It popped until the whole state was covered with ten feet of popcorn. The wind blew the popcorn over to Kansas, where it fell like a blizzard. Unfortunately, the Kansas cows thought it *was* a blizzard and immediately froze to death.

When next heard of, Paul and Babe were headed to Arizona. Paul dragged his pickax behind him, not realizing he was leaving a big ditch in his tracks. Today that ditch is called the Grand Canyon.

When they got back from out west, Paul and Babe settled down on the Big Onion River. One night, after the two had spent the day rolling thousands of logs down the river, Paul was so tired he couldn't even see straight. As he lay under the stars, his giant body aching, he said, "Babe, it's time I started me a logging camp. I'm gonna hire a bunch of fellers to help me."

You might say this was a turning point for Paul Bunyan. Not for thirty years, since the day his parents had left him crying all alone in that Maine cave, had he asked a single human being for help. But the next day Paul and Babe hiked all over the northern timberlands, posting signs that said: LOGGERS NEEDED TO WORK FOR PAUL BUNYAN. IF INTERESTED, COME TO BIG ONION, MINNESOTA, TO APPLY.

Word spread fast. Since all the woodsmen had heard of Paul Bunyan, hundreds of thousands of them hurried to Big Onion, eager to be part of his crew.

Paul wanted the biggest and brawniest men for his camp, so he made an announcement to all the men who'd gathered to apply for the job. "There's only two requirements," he said. "All my loggers have to be over ten feet tall and able to pop six buttons off their shirts with one breath."

Well about a thousand of the lumberjacks met those requirements, and Paul hired them all. Then he built a gigantic logging camp with bunkhouses a mile long and ten beds high. The camp's chow table was so long that it took a week to pass the salt and pepper from one end to the other. Paul and Babe dug a few ponds to provide drinking water for everyone. Today we call those ponds the Great Lakes.

But feeding that crew of giants was a bigger problem. One day Paul's cook, Sourdough Sam, said to Paul, "Boss, there's no way I can make enough flapjacks for these hungry fellers. Every morning the ones who don't get seconds threaten to kill me."

The next day Paul built Sam a flapjack griddle the size of an ice-skating rink. Then he lit a forest fire underneath that burned night and day.

"But how'm I supposed to grease this thing?" Sam asked.

"Every morning before dawn we'll get a hundred men to strap bacon fat to the bottoms of their shoes and skate around the griddle till you're ready to cook," Paul said.

Well, after Paul got the flapjack griddle all squared away, he figured he needed a bookkeeper to keep track of all the food bills. So he hired a man named Johnny Inkslinger. Johnny kept the payroll, and he took care of Babe's hay and grain bills, and about ten thousand and two other things. He used a fountain pen that was twenty feet long and connected by a giant hose to a lake filled with ink. It's said that Johnny figured out he could save over four hundred and twenty gallons of ink a year just by not crossing his *t*'s and dotting his *i*'s.

359

Everything at the Big Onion Lumber Company ran pretty smoothly until the year of the Hard Winter. That winter it was so cold that one day Shot Gunderson, Paul's foreman, rode up to Paul's shanty on his saddled bear with a whole list of problems.

"Boss, we've got trouble!" he said. "When the fellers go out to work, their feet are getting so frostbitten, they're starting to fall off."

"That's bad," Paul said, scratching his beard. "Well, tell the fellers to let their whiskers grow. Then when their beards get down to their feet, they can knit them into socks."

"Good thinkin'," said Shot.

"What else?" said Paul.

"The flames for all the lanterns are freezing!"

"Well, just take the frozen flames outside and store them somewhere," Paul said. "Then wait for them to melt in the spring."

"Great idea," said Shot.

"What else?" said Paul.

"Just one more thing—when I give orders to the woods crew, all my words freeze in the air and hang there stiff as icicles."

"Oh, well, get Babe to haul your frozen words away and store them next to the lantern flames. They'll thaw out in the spring too," Paul said.

Sure enough, the beard socks kept the men's feet from freezing and falling off, and the lantern flames and Shot's words all thawed out in the spring. The only problem was that when the lantern flames melted, they caused some mean little brushfires. And when Shot's frozen words thawed, old cries of *"Timber!"* and *"Chow time!"* started to echo throughout the woods, causing all sorts of confusion. But other than that, things ran pretty smoothly at the Big Onion Lumber Company until the spring of the China Rains.

One day that spring, Shot Gunderson burst into Paul's shanty with his pant legs soaking wet. "Boss, we've got a problem! The rains are starting to come *up* from the ground instead of down from the sky."

"They must be coming from China," said Paul. "Order two thousand umbrellas. When they come, cut the handles off and replace them with snowshoe straps."

Shot did as Paul said, and soon all the loggers were wearing umbrellas on their shoes to keep the China Rains from shooting up their pant legs.

Unfortunately, the China Rains caused a crop of ten-foot mosquitoes to attack the camp. The men tried using chicken wire for mosquito nets. Then they started barricading the doors and windows of the bunkhouse with two-ton boulders to keep them out. Finally they had to vacate the bunkhouse altogether when the mosquitoes tore off the roof.

"Get some giant bumblebees," Paul ordered Shot. "They'll get rid of the mosquitoes."

Shot did as Paul said. The only problem was, the bees and the mosquitoes fell madly in love, and soon they were having children. Since the children had stingers on both ends, they caught the loggers both coming and going!

But Paul finally outsmarted the bee-squitoes.

"If there's one thing a bee-squito loves more than stinging, it's sweets," Paul said. So he got them to swarm to a Hawaiian sugar ship docked in Lake Superior. And when the whole bunch got too fat to move, he shipped them to a circus in Florida.

Well, there's stories and stories about Paul Bunyan, Babe the Blue Ox, and the Big Onion Lumber Company. For many years, old loggers sat around potbellied stoves and told about the good old times with Paul. They told how Paul and Babe logged all the trees in Minnesota, then moved on to Washington, Oregon, and Alaska. And when last heard of, the two were somewhere off the Arctic Circle.

The old loggers are all gone now, but many of their stories still hang frozen in the cold forest air of the North Woods, waiting to be told. Come spring, when they start to thaw, some of them might just start telling themselves. It's been known to happen.

Think, Talk and Write

Talk About It As you read this tall tale, what did you think about the exaggeration?

1. A tall tale uses common speech and exaggerated details to tell a humorous story. What are some examples of common speech in the story? What expressions would you have used? **Think Like an Author**

2. Use details from the story to support the generalization that Paul Bunyan and Babe the Blue Ox were inseparable. **Generalize**

3. The basic elements of a story include a problem, or conflict, rising action, a climax, and a resolution, in which the conflict is resolved. Does "Paul Bunyan" have all the basic elements of a story? Explain. **Story Structure**

4. What suffix does the word *announcement* contain? What does this suffix mean? List other words you know that use this suffix. **Vocabulary**

Look Back and Write Reread the question on page 351. Can one man tame nature? Why or why not?

Meet author Mary Pope Osborne on page 377.

Retell

W2.2.a Write responses to literature: Demonstrate an understanding of the literary work.

Writing

Prompt "Paul Bunyan" is a tall tale about the adventures of a man who uses his enormous size and strength to conquer nature. Think about the adventures of another bigger-than-life character. Now write a tall tale about that person.

> **Writing Trait**
>
> **Strong verbs** help readers imagine the story.

Student Model

How Lake Superior Was Made

Most people know that Paul Bunyan **dug** Lake Michigan so that his huge blue ox, Babe, could have a place to drink. But not many people know the story of how Paul **made** Lake Superior. Lake Superior is the largest of the Great Lakes. If all the water from all the swimming pools around the world **were** poured into the lake, it still wouldn't be full!

Babe hated the summer heat. Paul tried all kinds of ways to help Babe cool down. He even **let** Babe stand under Niagara Falls, but to the giant ox, it was like running through a sprinkler. Nothing seemed to help.

Finally, Paul dug a hole big enough for Babe to swim in. When the huge ox waded into the cool waters of Lake Superior, he was so happy, he slapped his tail against the water's surface like a beaver. Water **flew** so high into the air that it rained for days afterward. Whenever Babe **swam** in the lake, rivers that flowed into the lake **ran** in the opposite direction.

Irregular verbs are correctly used.

The main characteristic of a **tall tale** is exaggeration.

Vivid word choice includes strong verbs.

Patterns in Nature

Use the model to help you write your own tall tale.

 W2.1.a Write narratives: Relate ideas, observations, or recollections of an event or experience.

Skill Talk

Compare and contrast is a skill readers use to find similarities and differences between things or ideas in a text. Sometimes clue words such as *like, unlike, however,* or *similarly* can help you find a comparison or contrast while you read. Other times, you will have to find a comparison or contrast without clue words.

 Ready to Try It?
Read "A Very Grand Canyon." As you read the selection, try to identify some comparisons and contrasts in the text.

Concept Link

Wind, water, glaciers, and gravity are natural forces that cause weathering and erosion on Earth's surface. However, people have changed Earth's surface too. Make a list of ways that humans have changed Earth's surface.

A Very

The Colorado River slices through the Grand Canyon.

Grand Canyon

by Ann Gadzikowski

It is huge and deep and was formed millions of years ago. People who visit have trouble finding the right words to describe it. Words like *impressive, incredible, fantastic*, and *awesome* are not enough. Just as surprising as its size are its many rocks of different colors and shapes. What is it? It's the Grand Canyon!

The Grand Canyon, located in the state of Arizona, is 277 miles long as measured in river miles. That river is the Colorado River, which flows along the canyon floor.

In some places, the canyon is more than a mile deep from rim to bottom and more than ten miles wide. Today most of the Grand Canyon and the area around it is called the Grand Canyon National Park.

Long ago, the Colorado River flowed over a flat plain. Like many other canyons, over the course of millions of years, the flow of water caused the dirt and rock to wear away. Little by little, the natural process of erosion formed

impressive, incredible, fantastic

the Grand Canyon. Some kinds of rock wear away more quickly than others. This uneven erosion causes shapes to form, such as cliffs and slopes.

Along the walls of the Grand Canyon, you can see lines. These colored stripes show the layers of different kinds of rock. The layers come in many different colors, including shades of red, green, blue, and yellow. As the sun moves across the sky, the changing light and shadows cause the colors to appear to magically change.

Geologists study rocks. Imagine how interested they must be in the Grand Canyon. Its rock layers hold evidence of the early geological history of North America. The layers of rock in the Grand Canyon are made of limestone, sandstone, shale, granite, and schist. Many layers of rock in the Grand Canyon are from the Paleozoic Era (about 500 million years ago) and the Precambrian Era (almost two billion years ago). The oldest rocks in the canyon walls are at the bottom. Unlike the newest rocks, which are at the top.

Nearly five million people visit the Grand Canyon every year. Most visitors view the canyon from the top. Others make a trip all the way to the bottom. There are no roads, just trails. So the only way to get there is by hiking or riding a mule. Although it is a mile straight down from the rim to the bottom, it is a long, hard seven miles of winding trails to get there.

awesome, fantastic

However, some people visit the bottom of the Grand Canyon by boat. They take rafts or canoes down the Colorado River. This can also be a difficult trip. It takes at least two days to travel into the Grand Canyon on the river.

The Grand Canyon continues to grow and change. What do you think the Grand Canyon will look like a million years from now?

Flowing water helped form these caverns.

Some rafting tours can take up to three weeks to complete.

Reading Across Texts

Both "Paul Bunyan" and "A Very Grand Canyon" provide explanations of how the Grand Canyon was formed. Make a chart to compare and contrast these two explanations.

Writing Across Texts Which explanation did you like better? Write a paragraph that tells why you chose the one you did. Use the chart you made to help you plan your paragraph.

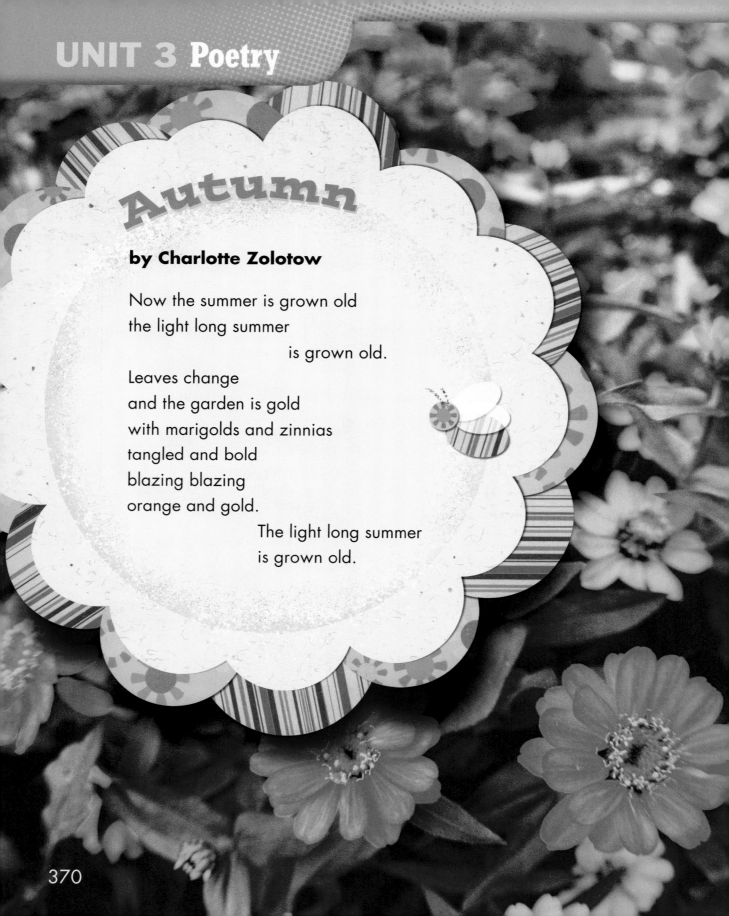

Autumn

by Charlotte Zolotow

Now the summer is grown old
the light long summer
                    is grown old.
Leaves change
and the garden is gold
with marigolds and zinnias
tangled and bold
blazing blazing
orange and gold.
            The light long summer
            is grown old.

Falling Snow

author unknown

See the pretty snowflakes
    Falling from the sky;
On the walk and housetop
    Soft and thick they lie.

On the window-ledges
    On the branches bare;
Now how fast they gather,
    Filling all the air.

Look into the garden
    Where the grass was green;
Covered by the snowflakes,
    Not a blade is seen.

Now the bare black bushes
    All look soft and white,
Every twig is laden—
    What a pretty sight!

Spring meadow
a child's bicycle
tied to a tree

by Yu Chang

Weather

by Eve Merriam

Dot a dot dot...dot a dot
Spotting the windowpane.
Spack a spack speck...flick a flack fleck
Freckling the windowpane.

A spatter a scatter...a wet cat a clatter
A splatter a rumble outside.
Umbrella umbrella umbrella umbrella
Bumbershoot barrel of rain.

Slosh a galosh . . .slosh a galosh
Slither and slather a glide
A puddle a jump a puddle a jump
A puddle a jump puddle splosh
A juddle a pump aluddle a dump a
Puddmuddle jump in and slide!

Author Study

Do you have a favorite selection? Make a note of the author's name and look for books by that author. You will probably enjoy other works by him or her.

Try It

- Find three or four works by one author.
- Read the book jackets or use the Internet to learn about the author's life to see what may have influenced his or her writing.
- Read the author's works.
- Compare topics, genres, and so on.
- Tell which work is your favorite and why.

Read this author study of Charles R. Smith Jr.

Charles R. Smith, Storyteller and Poet

Charles R. Smith has three loves—photography, writing, and basketball. It makes sense that he has written stories and poems about basketball and has illustrated them with his photographs. His story "What Jo Did" is about a girl who can dunk a basketball, much to the surprise of some neighborhood boys. Mr. Smith also writes poems about basketball. They have short lines that rhyme to match the fast pace of a basketball game. Both his story and his poems are fun to read.

Authors and Illustrators

Don Abramson
The author of *Scene Two*, p. 188

Don Abramson first got involved in theater as a high school freshman. Since then he has directed and acted in plays as well as designed and built theatrical sets. He has also written plays for both children and adults, which have been performed in various cities in the United States as well as in London, England.

Michael Austin
The illustrator of *The Horned Toad Prince*, p. 92

"*The Horned Toad Prince* stood out to me right away because of its personality and energy," Michael Austin said. As an artist, Mr. Austin has always had a "strange point of view." He enjoys drawing because it gives him a chance to "draw things my own way, strange or not." **Another book: *Late for School***

Mary-Joan Gerson
The author of *How Night Came from the Sea*, p. 304

Mary-Joan Gerson and her husband served with the U.S. Peace Corps in Nigeria. After returning to the United States, Ms. Gerson wanted to write children's books so that American children could learn more about life in Africa. Ms. Gerson still travels to learn about other cultures for her books. How Night Came from the Sea grew out of a trip to Brazil, where she went to experience the Yoruba culture. **Other books: *People of Corn* and *Why the Sky Is Far Away***

Carla Golembe
The illustrator of *How Night Came from the Sea*, p. 304

Carla Golembe is an artist, writer, and teacher. Her paintings have been displayed in art galleries. Of her art she says, "My paintings are the product of my dreams and experiences." Ms. Golembe loves to travel to warm places. When she paints jungles or oceans, she thinks of her experiences in Mexico, Belize, and Hawaii. **Other books: *People of Corn* and *Why the Sky Is Far Away***

Lisa Halvorsen
The author of *Letters Home from Yosemite*, p. 114

Lisa Halvorsen has visited more than 40 countries on six continents. "Writing opens up a lot of doors," says Ms. Halvorsen. "It gives me a chance to travel, learn about places, and meet people I might not meet if I weren't a writer." **Other books: *Letters Home from the Grand Canyon* and *Letters Home from Yellowstone***

Jackie Mims Hopkins
The author of *The Horned Toad Prince*, p. 92

Jackie Mims Hopkins got the idea for *The Horned Toad Prince* when she was researching horned toads for another book. "I realized there weren't many stories about them. I decided it was time to write a story about the little critters," she says. "I started thinking about which fairy tale could be used with a horned toad as the main character. 'The Frog Prince' was a perfect match." **Another book: *The Three Armadillies Tuff***

Robert Kausal
The author of *Scene Two,* p. 188

Robert Kausal first started working in theater during high school. Since then he has acted in local theater before eventually becoming a high school English teacher. Mr. Kausal says, "My students always enjoyed reading and performing plays, so when I had the opportunity to work with Don Abramson on *Scene Two,* I jumped at it." This is his first attempt at writing a play.

Stephen Kramer
The author of *Eye of the Storm*, p. 328

Stephen Kramer says, "I write science books because I love science and want to share my excitement with young readers. I also hope that my books might inspire some of my readers to become scientists!" **Other books: *Caves* and *Hidden Worlds***

Lensey Namioka
The author of *Yang the Youngest and His Terrible Ear,* p. 28

Lensey Namioka was nine when she moved to the United States from China. In her books for young people, such as *Yang the Youngest and His Terrible Ear* and *Yang the Third and Her Impossible Family,* she draws upon her Chinese heritage.   **Other books: *Half and Half, Yang the Third and Her Impossible Family***

Mary Pope Osborne
The author of "Paul Bunyan," p. 350

Mary Pope Osborne has always been attracted to adventure. After graduating from college she lived in a cave on a Greek island. Then she traveled with a group of young people all through Asia and the Middle East. Her books for young people are as adventure-packed as her life.
Other books: *Monday with a Mad Genius, American Tall Tales*

Kate Petty
The author of *Horse Heroes:*
True Stories of Amazing Horses, p. 210

Kate Petty has published more than a hundred children's books. She enjoys making information helpful and useful, while making sure kids will enjoy reading the information. She won the Royal Society/Aventis Foundation prize for science writing for her book *The Global Garden,* and says that she is extremely pleased with the honor because children are the ones who make the final decision for this award.

Joan Sandin
The author and illustrator of *Coyote School News,* p. 162

Joan Sandin grew up in Tucson, Arizona. *Coyote School News* is based on a real school newspaper called *Little Cowpuncher.* Schoolchildren in southern Arizona wrote articles for the paper from 1932 to 1943. Their teacher was Eulalia Bourne. Ms. Sandin explains, "Coyote School is a fictionalized school with fictionalized students, but it was inspired by the *Little Cowpuncher* papers."   **Other books about school papers: *The Young Journalist's Book* and *Extra! Extra!***

Authors and Illustrators

Allen Say
The author and illustrator of *Grandfather's Journey*, p. 70

Allen Say was born in Japan. When he was 16, he moved to California. Remembering his grandfather's tales, he was excited about the move. But when he arrived, he was lonely and unhappy. Mr. Say often writes about people who are part of two cultures. **Other books: *Tea with Milk* and *The Lost Lake***

David Small
The illustrator of *So You Want to Be President?* p. 232

David Small draws political cartoons for newspapers and illustrates children's books. *So You Want to Be President?* was a perfect opportunity for him to combine these two interests. "I hope readers will laugh first, and then begin to think a little more deeply," Mr. Small says. "Caricatures are not only funny pictures of people. The best ones make us see familiar faces in a new way." **Another book: *Imogene's Antlers***

Charles R. Smith Jr.
The author and photographer for "What Jo Did," p. 142

Charles R. Smith Jr. loves photography, writing, and basketball. These three interests came together for his book *Tall Tales: Six Amazing Basketball Dreams.* "What Jo Did" is just one of the stories in this book. Sometimes he uses infrared film for the photographs in his books. This special film responds to heat and makes unusual colors. You can see the results in "What Jo Did." **Another book: *Loki & Alex: The Adventures of a Dog & His Best Friend***

Richard Sobol
The author and photographer of *Adelina's Whales*, p. 282

Richard Sobol got the idea for *Adelina's Whales* while in Baja California, where Adelina's father was his whale guide. Mr. Sobol hopes his books inspire kids to value and protect the gray whale and other endangered animals. **Other books: *An Elephant in the Backyard* and *Seal Journey***

Judith St. George
The author of *So You Want to Be President?*, p. 232

Judith St. George first discovered writing when she wrote a play in sixth grade. After publishing several books about American history, she decided to write about the presidency. She thought, *How about making my book on Presidents amusing and fun as well as informative?* **Another book: *So You Want to Be an Inventor?***

Jerry Stanley
The author of *Hurry Freedom*, p. 50

Jerry Stanley's nonfiction books for young people have been praised for their careful attention to historical detail. They have also won several awards. Mr. Stanley has written about cowboys, migrant farm workers, California Indians, Japanese immigrants—and, in *Hurry Freedom*, the California Gold Rush. Besides writing about U.S. history, he teaches courses on the American West, the American Indian, and California history at California State University in Bakersfield. **Other books by Jerry Stanley: *Cowboys and Longhorns* and *Children of the Dust Bowl***

Chris Van Allsburg
The author and illustrator of *The Stranger*, p. 258

Chris Van Allsburg started out as a sculptor, drawing only in the evenings for fun. One day an author and artist friend came for dinner and saw Mr. Van Allsburg's drawings. He thought they were amazing and showed them to his editor. Before long, Mr. Van Allsburg published his first picture book, *The Garden of Abdul Gasazi.* **Other books: *The Wretched Stone* and *Zathura***

Authors and Illustrators

Glossary

How to Use This Glossary

This glossary can help you understand and pronounce some of the words in this book. The entries in this glossary are in alphabetical order. There are guide words at the top of each page to show you the first and last words on the page. A pronunciation key is at the bottom of every other page. Remember, if you can't find the word you are looking for, ask for help or check a dictionary.

The entry word is in dark type. It shows how the word is spelled and how the word is divided into syllables.

The pronunciation is in parentheses. It also shows which syllables are stressed.

Part-of-speech labels show the function or functions of an entry word and any listed form of that word.

an·ces·tor (an′ses′tər), *NOUN.* person from whom you are descended, such as your great-grandparents: *Their ancestors had come to the United States in 1812.* ❑ PLURAL **an·ces·tors.**

Sometimes, irregular and other special forms will be shown to help you use the word correctly.

The definition and example sentence show you what the word means and how it is used.

Aa

ac·count (ə kount′), *NOUN.* statement telling in detail about an event or thing; explanation: *We gave them an account of everything that had happened.* ❑ PLURAL **ac·counts.**

ad·vice (ad vīs′), *NOUN.* opinion about what should be done; suggestion: *My advice is that you study more.*

a·maze (ə māz′), *VERB.* to surprise greatly; strike with sudden wonder; astound: *He was amazed at how different the strand of hair looked under a microscope.* ❑ VERB **a·mazed, a·maz·ing.**

am·bi·tion (am bish′ən), *NOUN.* something for which you have a strong desire: *Her ambition is to be an oceanographer.*

an·nounce·ment (ə nouns′mənt), *NOUN.* a public or formal notice: *The announcement was published in the newspapers.*

announcement

ar·gu·ment (är′gyə mənt), *NOUN.* discussion by persons who disagree; dispute: *She won the argument by producing facts to prove her point.*

ar·range·ment (ə rānj′mənt), *NOUN.* adjustment, settlement, or agreement: *No arrangement of the dispute could possibly please everybody.* ❑ *PLURAL* **ar·range·ments.**

as·sort·ment (ə sôrt′mənt), *NOUN.* collection of various kinds: *These scarves come in an assortment of colors.*

au·di·ence (ȯ′dē əns), *NOUN.* group of people gathered to hear or see something: *The audience at the theater enjoyed the play.*

au·di·tion (ȯ dish′ən), *NOUN.* act of hearing to test the ability, quality, or performance of a singer, actor, or other performer.

Bb

bar·gain (bär′gən), *NOUN.* agreement to trade or exchange; deal: *You can't back out on our bargain.*

bawl (bȯl), *VERB.* to shout or cry out in a noisy way: *a lost calf bawling for its mother.* ❑ *VERB* **bawled, bawl·ing.**

be·wil·der (bi wil′dər), *VERB.* to confuse completely; puzzle: *bewildered by the confusing instructions.* ❑ *VERB* **be·wil·dered, be·wil·der·ing.**

bi·ol·o·gist (bī ol′ə jist), *NOUN.* a scientist who studies living things, including their origins, structures, activities, and distribution.

bluff¹ (bluf), *NOUN.* a high, steep slope or cliff.

bluff² (bluf), *verb.* to fool or mislead, especially by pretending confidence: *She bluffed the robbers by convincing them that the police were on the way.*

bluff (def. 1)

bril·liant (bril′yənt), *ADJECTIVE.* shining brightly; sparkling: *brilliant sunshine.*

Cc

cho·rus (kôr′əs), *NOUN.* anything spoken or sung all at the same time: *The children greeted the teacher with a chorus of "Good morning."*

Con·sti·tu·tion (kon′stə tü′shən), *NOUN.* the written set of fundamental principles by which the United States is governed.

a in hat	ėr in term	ô in order	ch in child	ə = a in about
ā in age	i in it	oi in oil	ng in long	ə = e in taken
â in care	ī in ice	ou in out	sh in she	ə = i in pencil
ä in far	o in hot	u in cup	th in thin	ə = o in lemon
e in let	ō in open	ů in put	ŧH in then	ə = u in circus
ē in equal	ȯ in all	ü in rule	zh in measure	

Glossary

con·trac·tor (kon′trak tər or kən trak′tər), *NOUN.* someone who agrees to supply materials or to do work for a certain price: *My family hired a contractor to build our new house.*

cow·ard (kou′ərd), *NOUN.* person who lacks courage or is easily made afraid; person who runs from danger, trouble, etc.

coy·o·te (kī ō′tē or kī′ōt), *NOUN.* a small, wolflike mammal living in many parts of North America. It is noted for loud howling at night.

coyote

Dd

de·scend·ant (di sen′dənt), **1.** *NOUN.* person born of a certain family or group: *a descendant of the Pilgrims.* **2.** *NOUN.* offspring; child, grandchild, great-grandchild, and so on: *You are a direct descendant of your parents, grandparents, and earlier ancestors.* ❏ *PLURAL* **de·scend·ants.**

de·struc·tion (di struk′shən), *NOUN.* great damage; ruin: *The storm left destruction behind it.*

dis·hon·est (dis on′ist), *ADJECTIVE.* not honest; tending to cheat or lie: *A person who lies or steals is dishonest.*

dis·tinc·tion (dis tingk′shən), *NOUN.* something that makes you especially worthy or well known; honor: *He has the distinction of being the best chess player in his school.*

draft (draft), **1.** *NOUN.* current of air: *I caught cold by sitting in a draft.* **2.** *NOUN.* a rough copy: *She made two drafts of her book report before she handed in the final form.*

dude (düd), **1.** *NOUN.* in the western parts of the United States and Canada, person raised in the city, especially an easterner who vacations on a ranch. **2.** *NOUN.* guy; fellow (slang). ❏ *PLURAL* **dudes.**

Ee

em·ploy·ment (em ploi′mənt), *NOUN.* work; job: *She had no difficulty finding employment.*

etch (ech), **1.** *VERB.* to engrave a drawing or design on a metal plate, glass, etc. **2.** *VERB.* to impress deeply: *Her face was etched in my memory.* ❏ *VERB* **etched, etch·ing.**

etch (def. 1)

ex·pect (ek spekt′), *VERB.* to think something will probably happen: *They expected the hurricane to change directions.* ❏ *VERB* **ex·pect·ed, ex·pect·ing.**

Ff

fas·ci·nate (fas′n āt), *VERB.* to interest greatly; attract very strongly; charm: *She was fascinated by the designs and colors in African art.* ❑ *VERB* **fas·ci·nat·ed, fas·ci·nat·ing.**

fa·vor (fā′vər), *NOUN.* act of kindness: *Will you do me a favor?*

fea·ture (fē′chər), **1.** *NOUN.* part of the face: *Your eyes, nose, mouth, chin, and forehead are your features.* **2.** *NOUN.* thing that stands out and attracts attention: *Your plan has many good features.*

fore·cast (fôr′kast′), *NOUN.* statement of what is coming; prediction: *What is the weather forecast today?* ❑ *PLURAL* **fore·casts.**

foul (foul), *VERB.* to make an unfair play against. ❑ *VERB* **fouled, foul·ing.**

frost (frȯst), **1.** *NOUN.* a freezing condition; temperature below the point at which water freezes: *Frost came early last winter.* **2.** *NOUN.* moisture frozen on or in a surface; feathery crystals of ice formed when water vapor in the air condenses at a temperature below freezing: *On cold fall mornings, there is frost on the grass.*

Gg

gla·cier (glā′shər), *NOUN.* a great mass of ice moving very slowly down a mountain, along a valley, or over a land area. Glaciers are formed from snow on high ground wherever winter snowfall exceeds summer melting for many years.

gleam (glēm), *VERB.* to flash or beam with light: *The car's headlights gleamed through the rain.* ❑ *VERB* **gleamed, gleam·ing.**

Hh

hard·ware (härd′wâr′), *NOUN.* articles made from metal. Locks, hinges, nails, screws, and so on, are hardware.

har·ness (här′nis), **1.** *NOUN.* the leather straps, bands, and other pieces used to hitch a horse or other animal to a carriage, wagon, plow, etc. **2.** *NOUN.* any similar arrangement of straps, bands, etc., especially a combination of straps by which a parachute is attached to someone.

harness (def. 1)

home·land (hōm′land′), *NOUN.* country that is your home; your native land.

hoop (hůp or hüp), *NOUN.* ring; round, flat band: *a hoop for embroidery, a basketball hoop.*

howl·ing (hou′ling), *ADJECTIVE.* very great: *a howling success.*

hum·ble (hum′bəl), *ADJECTIVE.* not proud; modest: *to be humble in spite of success.*

Ii

im·pres·sive (im pres′iv), *ADJECTIVE.* able to have a strong effect on the mind or feelings; able to influence deeply.

in·fest (in fest′), VERB. to spread in great numbers throughout an area and cause harm: *Mosquitoes infest swamps.* ❏ VERB **in·fest·ed.**

in·land (in′lənd), ADVERB. in or toward the interior: *He traveled inland from New York to Chicago.*

in·sult (in sult′), VERB. to say or do something very scornful, rude, or harsh: *She insulted me by calling me a liar.* ❏ VERB **in·sult·ed.**

Jj

jer·sey (jėr′zē), NOUN. shirt that is pulled over the head, made of soft, knitted cloth: *Members of the hockey team wear red jerseys.*

Ll

la·goon (lə gün′), NOUN. pond or small lake, especially one connected with a larger body of water.

land·slide (land′slīd′), NOUN. mass of earth or rock that slides down a steep slope.

landslide

las·so (la′ sō), VERB. to catch with a long rope with a loop on one end. ❏ VERB **las·soed, las·so·ing.**

long (lȯng), **1.** ADJECTIVE. measuring a great distance from end to end: *A year is a long time.* **2.** VERB. to wish very much; desire greatly: *long to see a good friend.* ❏ VERB **longed, long·ing.**

lum·ber·jack (lum′bər jak′), NOUN. person whose work is cutting down trees and sending the logs to the sawmill; woodsman; logger. ❏ PLURAL **lum·ber·jacks.**

lumberjack

Mm

mar·vel (mär′vəl), VERB. to be filled with wonder; be astonished: *She marveled at the beautiful sunset.* ❏ VERB **mar·veled, mar·vel·ing.**

mas·sive (mas′iv), ADJECTIVE. big and heavy; bulky: *a massive boulder.*

mood·y (mü′dē), ADJECTIVE. sunk in sadness; gloomy; sullen: *They sat in moody silence.*

Nn

nat·ur·al·ist (nach′ər ə list), NOUN. person who makes a study of living things.

Oo

of·fend (ə fend′), VERB. to hurt the feelings of someone; make angry; displease; pain: *My friend was offended by my laughter.* ❏ VERB **of·fend·ed, of·fend·ing.**

Pp

par·lor (pär′lər), **1.** *NOUN.* formerly, a room for receiving or entertaining guests; sitting room. **2.** *NOUN.* room or set of rooms used for various business purposes; shop: *a beauty parlor, an ice cream parlor.*

pol·i·tics (pol′ə tiks), *NOUN SINGULAR OR PLURAL.* the work of government; management of public business: *Our senior senator has been engaged in politics for many years.*

prair·ie (prâr′ē), **1.** *NOUN.* a large area of level or rolling land with grass but few or no trees, especially such an area making up much of central North America. **2.** *NOUN.* (regional) a wide, open space.

prairie (def. 1)

praise (prāz), *VERB.* the act of saying that a thing or person is good. ❑ *VERB* **prais·es.**

pre·serve (pri zėrv′), *VERB.* to keep from harm or change; keep safe; protect: *Good nutrition helps preserve your health.* ❑ *VERB* **pre·served, pre·serv·ing.**

Qq

quick·sand (kwik′sand′), *NOUN.* a very deep, soft, wet sand that will not hold up a person's weight: *Quicksand may swallow up people and animals.*

Rr

re·hears·al (ri hėr′səl), *NOUN.* act of rehearsing; process of preparing for a public performance: *The rehearsal for the show was a disaster, but the performance was great.*

re·quire·ment (ri kwīr′mənt), *NOUN.* a demand; thing demanded: *That school has a requirement that students wear uniforms.* ❑ *PLURAL* **re·quire·ments.**

re·sist·ance (ri zis′təns), *NOUN.* thing or act that resists; opposing force; opposition: *Air resistance makes a feather fall more slowly than a pin.*

re·spon·si·bil·i·ty (ri spon′sə bil′ə tē), *NOUN.* the act or fact of taking care of someone or something; obligation: *We agreed to share responsibility for planning the party.*

rick·et·y (rik′ə tē), *ADJECTIVE.* liable to fall or break down; shaky; weak: *a rickety old chair.*

rim (rim), *NOUN.* an edge, border, or margin on or around anything: *the rim of a wheel, the rim of a glass.*

riv·er·bed (riv′ər bed′), *NOUN.* channel in which a river flows or used to flow.

riverbed

Glossary

385

roam (rōm), *VERB.* to go about with no special plan or aim; wander: *roam through the fields.* ❏ *VERB* **roamed**

round·up (round′up′), *NOUN.* act of driving or bringing cattle together from long distances.

rum·ble (rum′bəl), *VERB.* to make a deep, heavy, continuous sound: *Thunder was rumbling in the distance.* ❏ *VERB* **rum·bled, rum·bling.**

Ss

script (skript), *NOUN.* manuscript of a play, movie, or radio or TV show.

sculp·ture (skulp′chər), **1.** *NOUN.* the art of making figures by carving, modeling, casting, etc. Sculpture includes the cutting of statues from blocks of marble, stone, or wood, casting in bronze, and modeling in clay or wax. **2.** *NOUN.* sculptured work; piece of such work. ❏ *PLURAL* **sculp·tures.**

sculpture (def. 2)

shat·ter (shat′ər), *VERB.* to break into pieces suddenly: *A stone shattered the window.* ❏ *VERB* **shat·tered, shat·ter·ing.**

shim·mer (shim′ər), *VERB.* to gleam or shine faintly: *Both the sea and the sand shimmered in the moonlight.* ❏ *VERB* **shim·mered, shim·mer·ing.** ❏ *ADJECTIVE* **shim·mer·ing.**

shriek (shrēk), *VERB.* to make a loud, sharp, shrill sound. People sometimes shriek because of terror, anger, pain, or amusement. ❏ *VERB* **shrieked, shriek·ing.**

slope (slōp), *NOUN.* any line, surface, land, etc., that goes up or down at an angle: *If you roll a ball up a slope, it will roll down again.* ❏ *PLURAL* **slopes.**

snag (snag), *NOUN.* a hidden or unexpected obstacle: Our plans hit a snag.

sol·emn·ly (sol′əm lē), *ADVERB.* seriously; earnestly; with dignity.

spe·cies (spē′shēz), *NOUN.* a set of related living things that all have certain characteristics: *Spearmint is a species of mint.*

speech·less (spēch′lis), *ADJECTIVE.* not able to talk: *He was speechless with wonder.*

spur (spėr), *NOUN.* a metal point or pointed wheel, worn on a rider's boot heel for urging a horse on. ❏ *PLURAL* **spurs.**

spur

stern (stėrn), *ADJECTIVE.* harshly firm; hard; strict: *a stern parent.*

still (stil), **1.** *ADJECTIVE*. staying in the same position or at rest; without motion; motionless: *to stand or lie still. The lake is still today.* **2.** *VERB*. to make or become calm or quiet: *The father stilled the crying baby.* ❑ *VERB* **stilled, stil·ling.**

surge (sėrj), *NOUN*. a swelling motion; sweep or rush, especially of waves: *Our boat was upset by a surge.*

swat (swät), *VERB*. to hit sharply or violently: *swat a fly.* ❑ *VERB* **swat·ted, swat·ting.**

sym·pa·thet·ic (sim′pə thet′ik), *ADJECTIVE*. having or showing kind feelings toward others; sympathizing: *She is a sympathetic friend.*

Tt

ter·ror (ter′ər), *NOUN*. great fear: *The dog has a terror of thunder.*

thaw (thȯ), *VERB*. to make or become less cold: *After shoveling snow, I thawed my hands and feet in front of the fire.*

tim·id (tim′id), *ADJECTIVE*. easily frightened; shy: *The timid child was afraid of the dark.*

tow·er·ing (tou′ər ing), **1.** *ADJECTIVE*. very high: *a towering mountain peak.* **2.** *ADJECTIVE*. very great: *Developing a polio vaccine was a towering achievement.*

trop·i·cal (trop′ə kəl), *ADJECTIVE*. of or like the regions 23.45 degrees north and south of the equator where the sun can shine directly overhead: *tropical heat.*

Uu

un·be·liev·a·ble (un′bi lē′və bəl), *ADJECTIVE*. incredible; hard to think of as true or real: *an unbelievable lie.*

un·com·fort·a·ble (un kum′fər tə bəl), *ADJECTIVE*. uneasy; not comfortable: *I felt uncomfortable when they stared at me.*

un·nat·ur·al (un nach′ər əl), *ADJECTIVE*. not natural; not normal.

un·tamed (un tāmd′), *ADJECTIVE*. wild; not domesticated: *Untamed animals are wary of people.*

Vv

vain (vān), *ADJECTIVE*. having too much pride in your looks, ability, etc.: *a good-looking but vain person.*

vast (vast), *ADJECTIVE*. very great; immense: *Texas and Alaska cover vast territories.*

Ww

wage (wāj), *NOUN*. the money paid for work done, especially work paid for by the hour: *His wages average $450 a week.* ❑ *PLURAL* **wages.**

wil·der·ness (wil′dər nis), *NOUN*. a wild, uncultivated region with few or no people living in it.

wilderness

Word List
English/Spanish

Unit 1

Yang the Youngest and His Terrible Ear
*insulted / insultado
audience / público
rehearsal / ensayo
praises / alaba
moody / taciturno
*audition / audición
uncomfortable / incómodo
sympathetic / compasivo

Hurry Freedom
*employment / empleo
assortment / surtido
hardware / ferreteía
contractor / contratista
accounts / informe
distinction / mérito
wages / salario

Grandfather's Journey
amazed / maravillaban
bewildered / desconcertaban
homeland / tierra natal
longed / deseaba
sculptures / esculturas
still / calmar
towering / imponentes

The Horned Toad Prince
bargain / pacto
*favors / favores
lassoed / enlazó
*offended / ofendida
prairie / pradera
riverbed / lecho
shrieked / chilló

Letters Home from Yosemite
*glacier / glaciar
*impressive / impresionante
*naturalist / naturalista
*preserve / preservar
slopes / laderas
species / especies
wilderness / zona silvestre

Unit 2

What Jo Did
fouled / hizo una falta
hoop / aro
jersey / camiseta
*marveled / se maravillaban
rim / canasta
speechless / estupefactos
swatted / le dio
unbelievable / increíble

Coyote School News
bawling / berreando
*coyote / coyote
dudes / dandis
roundup / rodeo
spurs / espuelas

388

* English/Spanish Cognate: A **cognate** is a word that is similar in Spanish and has the same meaning in both languages.

Scene Two

script / guión
arrangements / arreglo
advice / consejo
*dishonest / deshonesto
argument / discusión
snag / tropiezo
*descendants / descendientes

Horse Heroes

vast / extenso
*ambition / ambición
roamed / vagó
rickety / desvencijado
quicksand / arena movediza
*resistance / resistencia
infested / plagó
landslide / desprendimiento de tierra

So You Want to Be President?

*Constitution / Constitución
howling / rotundo
humble / humildes
*politics / política
*responsibility / responsabilidad
*solemnly / solemnemente
*vain / vano

Unit 3

The Stranger

draft / corriente vde aire
etched / grabadas
*fascinated / fascinaba
frost / escarcha
parlor / salón
*terror / terror
*timid / tímido

Adelina's Whales

*biologist / bióloga
bluff / despeñadero
*lagoon / laguna
massive / inmensas
rumbling / retumbante
*tropical / tropical

How Night Came from the Sea

*brilliant / brillante
chorus / coro
coward / cobarde
gleamed / relucía
shimmering / centelleante

Eye of the Storm

*destruction / destrucción
expected / esperaba
forecasts / pronósticos
inland / tierra adentro
shatter / hace añicos
surge / oleada

Paul Bunyan

feature / rasgo
unnatural / artificial
harness / arnés
untamed / indomable
announcement / anuncio
requirements / requisitos
lumberjacks / leñador
thaw / calentar

Reading

1.0 Word Analysis, Fluency, and Systematic Vocabulary Development

Students understand the basic features of reading. They select letter patterns and know how to translate them into spoken language by using phonics, syllabication, and word parts. They apply this knowledge to achieve fluent oral and silent reading.

Word Recognition

1.1 Read narrative and expository text aloud with grade-appropriate fluency and accuracy and with appropriate pacing, intonation, and expression.

Vocabulary and Concept Development

1.2 Apply knowledge of word origins, derivations, synonyms, antonyms, and idioms to determine the meaning of words and phrases.

1.3 Use knowledge of root words to determine the meanings of unknown words within a passage.

1.4 Know common roots and affixes derived from Greek and Latin and use this knowledge to analyze the meanings of complex words (e.g., international).

1.5 Use a thesaurus to determine related words and concepts.

1.6 Distinguish and interpret words with multiple meanings.

2.0 Reading Comprehension

Students read and understand grade-level-appropriate material. They draw upon a variety of comprehension strategies as needed (e.g., generating and responding to essential questions, making predictions, comparing information from several sources). The selections in *Recommended Literature, Kindergarten Through Grade Twelve* illustrate the quality and complexity of the materials to be read by students. In addition to their regular school reading, students read one-half million words annually, including a good representation of grade-level-appropriate narrative and expository text (e.g., classic and contemporary literature, magazines, newspapers, online information).

Structural Features of Informational Materials

2.1 Identify structural patterns found in informational text (e.g., compare and contrast, cause and effect, sequential or chronological order, proposition and support) to strengthen comprehension.

Comprehension and Analysis of Grade-Level-Appropriate Text

2.2 Use appropriate strategies when reading for different purposes (e.g., full comprehension, location of information, personal enjoyment).

2.3 Make and confirm predictions about text by using prior knowledge and ideas presented in the text itself, including illustrations, titles, topic sentences, important words, and foreshadowing clues.

2.4 Evaluate new information and hypotheses by testing them against known information and ideas.

2.5 Compare and contrast information on the same topic after reading several passages or articles.

2.6 Distinguish between cause and effect and between fact and opinion in expository text.

2.7 Follow multiple-step instructions in a basic technical manual (e.g., how to use computer commands or video games).

3.0 Literary Response and Analysis

Students read and respond to a wide variety of significant works of children's literature. They distinguish between the structural features of the text and the literary terms or elements (e.g., theme, plot, setting, characters). The selections in *Recommended Literature, Kindergarten Through Grade Twelve* illustrate the quality and complexity of the materials to be read by students.

Structural Features of Literature

3.1 Describe the structural differences of various imaginative forms of literature, including fantasies, fables, myths, legends, and fairy tales.

Narrative Analysis of Grade-Level-Appropriate Text

3.2 Identify the main events of the plot, their causes, and the influence of each event on future actions.

3.3 Use knowledge of the situation and setting and of a character's traits and motivations to determine the causes for that character's actions.

3.4 Compare and contrast tales from different cultures by tracing the exploits of one character type and develop theories to account for similar tales in diverse cultures (e.g., trickster tales).

3.5 Define figurative language (e.g., simile,

metaphor, hyperbole, personification) and identify its use in literary works.

Writing

1.0 Writing Strategies
Students write clear, coherent sentences and paragraphs that develop a central idea. Their writing shows they consider the audience and purpose. Students progress through the stages of the writing process (e.g., prewriting, drafting, revising, editing successive versions).

Organization and Focus
1.1 Select a focus, an organizational structure, and a point of view based upon purpose, audience, length, and format requirements.
1.2 Create multiple-paragraph compositions:
    a. Provide an introductory paragraph.
    b. Establish and support a central idea with a topic sentence at or near the beginning of the first paragraph.
    c. Include supporting paragraphs with simple facts, details, and explanations.
    d. Conclude with a paragraph that summarizes the points.
    e. Use correct indention.
1.3 Use traditional structures for conveying information (e.g., chronological order, cause and effect, similarity and difference, posing and answering a question).

Penmanship
1.4 Write fluidly and legibly in cursive or joined italic.

Research and Technology
1.5 Quote or paraphrase information sources, citing them appropriately.
1.6 Locate information in reference texts by using organizational features (e.g., prefaces, appendixes).
1.7 Use various reference materials (e.g., dictionary, thesaurus, card catalog, encyclopedia, online information) as an aid to writing.
1.8 Understand the organization of almanacs, newspapers, and periodicals and how to use those print materials.
1.9 Demonstrate basic keyboarding skills and familiarity with computer terminology (e.g., cursor, software, memory, disk drive, hard drive).

Evaluation and Revision
1.10 Edit and revise selected drafts to improve coherence and progression by adding, deleting, consolidating, and rearranging text.

2.0 Writing Applications (Genres and Their Characteristics)
Students write compositions that describe and explain familiar objects, events, and experiences. Student writing demonstrates a command of standard American English and the drafting, research, and organizational strategies outlined in Writing Standard 1.0.

Using the writing strategies of grade four outlined in Writing Standard 1.0, students:
2.1 Write narratives:
    a. Relate ideas, observations, or recollections of an event or experience.
    b. Provide a context to enable the reader to imagine the world of the event or experience.
    c. Use concrete sensory details.
    d. Provide insight into why the selected event or experience is memorable.
2.2 Write responses to literature:
    a. Demonstrate an understanding of the literary work.
    b. Support judgments through references to both the text and prior knowledge.
2.3 Write information reports:
    a. Frame a central question about an issue or situation.
    b. Include facts and details for focus.
    c. Draw from more than one source of information (e.g., speakers, books, newspapers, other media sources).
2.4 Write summaries that contain the main ideas of the reading selection and the most significant details.

Written and Oral English Language Conventions

The standards for written and oral English language conventions have been placed between those for writing and for listening and speaking because these conventions are essential to both sets of skills.

1.0 Written and Oral English Language Conventions

Students write and speak with a command of standard English conventions appropriate to this grade level.

Sentence Structure

1.1 Use simple and compound sentences in writing and speaking.

1.2 Combine short, related sentences with appositives, participial phrases, adjectives, adverbs, and prepositional phrases.

Grammar

1.3 Identify and use regular and irregular verbs, adverbs, prepositions, and coordinating conjunctions in writing and speaking.

Punctuation

1.4 Use parentheses, commas in direct quotations, and apostrophes in the possessive case of nouns and in contractions.

1.5 Use underlining, quotation marks, or italics to identify titles of documents.

Capitalization

1.6 Capitalize names of magazines, newspapers, works of art, musical compositions, organizations, and the first word in quotations when appropriate.

Spelling

1.7 Spell correctly roots, inflections, suffixes and prefixes, and syllable constructions.

Listening and Speaking

1.0 Listening and Speaking Strategies

Students listen critically and respond appropriately to oral communication. They speak in a manner that guides the listener to understand important ideas by using proper phrasing, pitch, and modulation.

Comprehension

1.1 Ask thoughtful questions and respond to relevant questions with appropriate elaboration in oral settings.

1.2 Summarize major ideas and supporting evidence presented in spoken messages and formal presentations.

1.3 Identify how language usages (e.g., sayings, expressions) reflect regions and cultures.

1.4 Give precise directions and instructions.

Organization and Delivery of Oral Communication

1.5 Present effective introductions and conclusions that guide and inform the listener's understanding of important ideas and evidence.

1.6 Use traditional structures for conveying information (e.g., cause and effect, similarity and difference, posing and answering a question).

1.7 Emphasize points in ways that help the listener or viewer to follow important ideas and concepts.

1.8 Use details, examples, anecdotes, or experiences to explain or clarify information.

1.9 Use volume, pitch, phrasing, pace, modulation, and gestures appropriately to enhance meaning.

Analysis and Evaluation of Oral Media Communication

1.10 Evaluate the role of the media in focusing attention on events and in forming opinions on issues.

2.0 Speaking Applications (Genres and Their Characteristics)

Students deliver brief recitations and oral presentations about familiar experiences or interests that are organized around a coherent thesis statement. Student speaking demonstrates a command of standard American English and the organizational and delivery strategies outlined in Listening and Speaking Standard 1.0.

Using the speaking strategies of grade four outlined in Listening and Speaking Standard 1.0, students:

2.1 Make narrative presentations:
  a. Relate ideas, observations, or recollections about an event or experience.
  b. Provide a context that enables the listener to imagine the circumstances of the event or experience.
  c. Provide insight into why the selected event or experience is memorable.

2.2 Make informational presentations:
  a. Frame a key question.
  b. Include facts and details that help listeners to focus.
  c. Incorporate more than one source of information (e.g., speakers, books, newspapers, television or radio reports).

2.3 Deliver oral summaries of articles and books that contain the main ideas of the event or article and the most significant details.

2.4 Recite brief poems (i.e., two or three stanzas), soliloquies, or dramatic dialogues, using clear diction, tempo, volume, and phrasing.

Acknowledgments

Text

28: From *Yang The Youngest and His Terrible Ear* by Lensey Namioka. Copyright © 1992 by Lensey Namioka. Reprinted by permission of Lensey Namioka. All rights are reserved by the Author

50: From *Hurry Freedom* by Jerry Stanley, copyright © 2000 by Jerry Stanley. Used by permission of Crown Publishers, an imprint of Random House Children's Books, a divison of Random House, Inc

70: From *Grandfather's Journey* by Allen Say. Copyright © 1993 by Allen Say. Reprinted by permission of Houghton Mifflin Company. All rights reserved

92: *The Horned Toad Prince* © 2000 by Jackie Mims Hopkins. Illustrations © 2000 by Michael Austin. Reprinted by permission from Peachtree Publishers

114: *Letters Home from Yosemite* by Lisa Halvorsen. Copyright © 2000. Used by permission of Lisa Halvorsen

132: "We're All In the Telephone Book," from *The Collected Poems of Langston Hughes* by Langston Hughes, edited by Arnold Rampersad with David Roessel, Associate Editor, copyright © 1994 by The Estate of Langston Hughes. Used by permission of Alfred A. Knopf, a division of Random House

133: "Speak Up" by Janet S. Wong. Reprinted with the permission of Margaret K. McElderry Books, an imprint of Simon & Schuster Children's Publishing Division from *Good Luck Gold and Other Poems* by Janet S. Wong. Copyright © 1994 Janet S. Wong

134: "City I Love" by Lee Bennett Hopkins. Copyright © 2002 by Lee Bennett Hopkins. First appeared in *Home to Me: Poems Across America*, published by Orchard Books. Reprinted by permission of Curtis Brown, Ltd

135: "Midwest Town" by Ruth De Long Peterson from *The Saturday Evening Post*, © 1954 Saturday Evening Post Society. Used by permission of Saturday Evening Post Society

142: "What Jo Did," from *Tall Tales: Six Amazing Basketball Dreams* by Charles R. Smith Jr., copyright © 2000 by Charles R. Smith Jr. Used by permission of Dutton Children's Books, A Division of Penguin Young Readers Group, A Member of Penguin Group (USA) Inc., 345 Hudson Street, New York, NY 10014. All rights reserved

162: *Coyote School News* by Joan Sandin. Text and Illustrations copyright © 2003 by Joan Sandin. Reprinted by permission of Henry Holt and Company, LLC

210: From *Horse Heroes: True Stories of Amazing Horses* by Kate Petty. Copyright © 1999 Dorling Kindersley Limited. Reprinted by permission

232: From *So You Want to Be President?* by Judith St. George, illustrated by David Small, copyright © 2000 by Judith St. George, text. Copyright © 2000 by David Small, illustrations. Used by permission of Philomel Books, A Division of Penguin Young Readers Group, A Member of Penguin Group (USA) Inc., 345 Hudson Street, New York, NY 10014. All rights reserved

248: "His Hands," from *My Man Blue* by Nikki Grimes, copyright © 1999 by Nikki Grimes. Used by permission of Dial Books for Young Readers, A Division of Penguin Young Readers Group, A Member of Penguin Group (USA) Inc., 345 Hudson Street, New York, NY 10014. All rights reserved

249: "Homework" from *Egg Thoughts and Other Frances Songs* by Russell Hoban. Used by permission of David Higham Associates

250: "Lem Lonnigan's Leaf Machine" from *Here's What You Do When You Can't Find Your Shoe* by Andrea Perry. Reprinted with the permission of Atheneum Books for Young Readers, an imprint of Simon & Schuster Children's Publishing Division. Text copyright © 2003 by Andrea Perry

258: From *The Stranger* by Chris Van Allsburg. Copyright © 1986 by Chris Van Allsburg. Reprinted by permission of Houghton Mifflin Company. All rights reserved

282: From *Adelina's Whales* by Richard Sobol, copyright © 2003 by Richard Sobol. Used by permission of Dutton Children's Books, A Division of Penguin Young Readers Group, A Member of Penguin Group (USA) Inc., 345 Hudson Street, New York, NY 10014. All rights reserved

304: *How Night Came from the Sea* retold by Mary-Joan Gerson, illustrations by Carla Golembe. Text copyright © 1994 by Mary-Joan Gerson. Illustrations copyright © 1994 by Carla Golembe. Reprinted by permission of Goodman Associates Literary Agents as authorized agent for Mary-Joan Gerson and Carla Golembe

320: "The Ant and the Bear" from *Spirit of the Cedar People: More Stories and Paintings of Chief Lelooska* edited by Christine Normandin. A DK Inc Book, 1998. Reprinted by permission of the Estate of Don Lelooska Smith, Lelooska Foundation

328: From *Eye of the Storm* by Stephen Kramer, copyright © 1997 by Stephen Kramer, text. Used by permission of G.P. Putnam's Sons, A Division of Penguin Young Readers Group, A Member of Penguin Group (USA) Inc., 345 Hudson Street, New York, NY 10014. All rights reserved

350: "Paul Bunyan" from *American Tall Tales* by Mary Pope Osborne, copyright © 1991 by Mary Pope Osborne. Illustrations copyright © 1991 by Michael McCurdy. Used by permission of Alfred A. Knopf, an imprint of Random House Children's Books, a division of Random House, Inc.

370: "Autumn" from *River Winding*. Copyright © 1970 by Charlotte Zolotow. Used by permission of Scott Treimel NY.

372: "spring meadow" by Yu Chang. Used by permission of the author.

373: "Weather" from *Catch a Little Rhyme* by Eve Merriam. Copyright © 1966 by Eve Merriam. Used by permission of Marian Reiner.

Illustrations

Cover: Tim Jessell

PI1-PI15 Bill McGuire

66, 73 Allen Say

115 Amanda Hall

182 Sachiko Yoshikawa

184-200 Jimmy Holder

204 Shelly Hehenberger

236, 247 Peter Bollinger

248, 250 Lee White

312 Macky Pamintuan

338 Brent Campbell

350-362 Harvey Chan

W1-W15 Leslie Harrington

Photographs

Every effort has been made to secure permission and provide appropriate credit for photographic material. The publisher deeply regrets any omission and pledges to correct errors called to its attention in subsequent editions.

Unless otherwise acknowledged, all photographs are the property of Scott Foresman, a division of Pearson Education.

Photo locators denoted as follows: Top (T), Center (C), Bottom (B), Left (L), Right (R), Background (Bkgd)

24 (C) Alamy Images, (TR) Comstock Images

25 ©Steve Skjold/Alamy Images

33 ©Mina Chapman/Corbis

44 (CC) The Granger Collection, NY, (TC) Getty Images, (TCR) Getty Images, (B) Getty Images

45 (BR) ©Bettmann/Corbis, (CR) Getty Images

46 (C) ©Rick Gomez/Corbis, (TR) ©Krista Kennell/ZUMA/Corbis, (R) ©Courtesy of the Bancroft Library, University of California, Berkeley

47 (CR) ©Hulton-Deutsch Collection/Corbis, (TR) ©photolibrary pty. ltd./Index Open

55 (T) ©Bryce Flynn Photography Inc/Getty Images, (CR) ©Culver Pictures/The Art Archive

56 ©Courtesy of the Bancroft Library, University of California, Berkeley

58 Image B-01601/Courtesy of British Columbia Archives

59 ©Courtesy of the Bancroft Library, University of California, Berkeley

60 ©Courtesy of the Bancroft Library, University of California, Berkeley

61 ©Courtesy of the Bancroft Library, University of California, Berkeley

62 Courtesy of the California History Room, California State Library, Sacramento, California

64 (T) Courtesy of the Society of California Pioneers, San Francisco, (B) de Young Collection, FN-19961/California Historical Society

65 ©Courtesy of the Bancroft Library, University of California, Berkeley

66 (R) Gift of Templeton Crocker, FN-39709/California Historical Society, (C) ©Michael DeYoung/Corbis, (TR) ©Randy Faris/Corbis

70 (CR) ©Lowell Georgia/Corbis, (Bkgd) ©Bettmann/Corbis

71 (BR) ©Bettmann/Corbis, (CR) Corbis/Jupiter Images

75 (Bkgd) ©Joseph Sohm/Visions of America/Corbis

84 (TR) © Dallas and John Heaton/Corbis, (BR) © Roger Ressmeyer/Corbis

87 (TL) Dex Image, (TR) © Orion Press/Getty Images, (CL) © Roger Ressmeyer/Corbis, (CR) © Ken Biggs/Getty Images

88 (C) ©age fotostock/SuperStock, (TR) ©Russ Bishop/Stock Connection/Jupiter Images

110 (C) ©Christopher Rennie/Robert Harding/Jupiter Images, (TR) ©Daniel J. Cox/Getty Images

114 (C) © David Muench/Corbis, (TL, TR, CR) Getty Images

115 Getty Images

116 (Bkgd) Getty Images, (BR) ©Royalty-Free/Corbis

117 (CR) Getty Images, (BC) Corel, (TR) ©Royalty-Free/Corbis

118 (TC, BL) Corel

119 (TL) Digital Vision, (TR) ©Royalty-Free/Corbis, (BR) Corel

120 (C) © Harvey Lloyd/Getty Images

121 (TC, BR) Corel, (CR) ©Royalty-Free/Corbis

122 (TL) © Boyle & Boyle/Animals Animals/Earth Scenes, (CR) © Don Mason/Corbis

123 (C, BL) Getty Images

124 ©Royalty-Free/Corbis

125 (TC) Corel, (TR) Getty Images, (CR) © Phil Schermeister/Corbis

134 USDA

135 (TR) image100/Jupiter Images, (TL) ©Diane Cook & Len Jenshel/Corbis, (Bkgd) © Don Mason/Corbis

136 (T) USDA, (Bkgd) ©Bill Ross/Corbis

138 (TR) Getty Images, (C) ©Image Source Limited, (CR) Mike McMillan/Spotfire Images

147 ©Tracy Kahn/Corbis

154 ©NBAE/Getty Images

155 ©NBAE/Getty Images, (BC) Getty Images

156 ©Andrew D. Bernstein/NBAE/Getty Images

157 Getty Images

158 (TR) Jupiter Images, (C) Getty Images

184 (TR) Brand X Pictures, (C) Corbis/Jupiter Images

187 (B) ©Jamie & Judy Wild/Danita Delimont/Digital Railroad, (TR) ©Gabriel Bouys/AFP/Getty Images

191 ©Bettmann/Corbis

206 (C) ©tbkmedia.de/Alamy Images, (TR) ©Prenzel Photo/Animals Animals/Earth Scenes

210 National Science Foundation

213 (TR) ©Image Source, (CR) ©Brandon Benson/Reuters/Corbis, (TC) Jupiter Images

215 Marital Colomb/Photodisc/Getty Images

218 ©Bob Langrish/Animals Animals/Earth Scenes

220 (BC, BR) Private Collection, Peter Newark American Pictures/Bridgeman Art Library

221 Private Collection, Peter Newark Western Americana/Bridgeman Art Library

222 (TL) ©North Wind Picture Archives/Alamy Images, (CL) Private Collection, Peter Newark American Pictures/Bridgeman Art Library, (B) ©Mary Evans Picture Library/Alamy Images

223 Private Collection, The Stapleton Collection/Bridgeman Art Library

226 ©Bob Langrish

227 (T) ©Gary Braasch/Getty Images, (B) ©Arco Images/Alamy Images

228 (T) ©Robert Landau/Corbis, (B) The Kobal Collection, (TR) ©Brooks Kraft/Corbis, (C) Getty Images

229 (R, BC) Ronald Grant Archive

230 ©Phil Schermeister/Corbis

231 ©Bettmann/Corbis

WORDS!

A Vocabulary Handbook

Antonyms

An antonym is a word that has the opposite meaning of another word. *Day* is an antonym for *night*.

Day

Night

Antonym = Opposite.

Strategy for Antonyms

1. Identify the word for which you want to find an antonym.
2. Think of other words or phrases that have the opposite meaning.
3. Use a thesaurus to help you find antonyms.
4. Use a dictionary to check the antonyms' meanings so that you use the words that best communicates your ideas.

Synonyms

A synonym is a word that has almost the same meaning as another word. *Hot* is a synonym for *scorching*.

Hot

Scorching

Synonym = Same.

Strategy for Synonyms

1. Identify the word for which you want to find a synonym.
2. Think of other words or phrases that have the same, or almost the same, meaning.
3. Use a thesaurus to help you find more synonyms, and make a list.
4. Use a dictionary to find the word that best communicates your ideas.

Base Words/Root Words

A base word, also called a root word, is a word that can't be broken into smaller words. *Friend* is a root of *friendly* and *friendship*.

Earth

Unearthly

Earth is the base word.

Strategy for Base Words

1. Look for a base word in the unknown word.
2. Determine the meaning of the base word.
3. Guess the meaning of the unfamiliar word. Does it make sense in the sentence?
4. Check the meaning in a dictionary.

Prefixes

A prefix is a word part added to the beginning of a base word to form a new word.

Wrap

Unwrap

Common Prefixes and Their Meanings

Prefix	Meaning
un-	not
re-	again, back
in-	not
dis-	not, opposite of
pre-	before

Strategy for Prefixes

1. Look at the unknown word and identify the prefix.
2. What does the base word mean? If you're not sure, check the dictionary.
3. Use what you know about the base word and the prefix to figure out the meaning of the unknown word.
4. Use a dictionary to check your guess.

Suffixes

A suffix is a word part added to the end of
a base word to form a new word.

Shoe

Shoeless

Common Suffixes and Their Meanings

-ly	characteristic of
-tion	act, process
-able	can be done
-ment	action or process
-less	without

Strategy for Suffixes

1. Look at the unknown word and identify the suffix.
2. What does the base word mean? If you're not sure, check a dictionary.
3. Use what you know about the base word and the suffix to figure out the meaning of the unknown word.
4. Use a dictionary to check your guess.

Context Clues

Context clues are the words and sentences found around an unknown word that can help you understand a word's meaning. Use context clues to figure out what a fireworm is.

I can't decide whether to write my underwater-creature report on a starfish, dolphin, fireworm, or octopus.

Strategy for Context Clues

1. Look for clues in the words and phrases around the unknown word.
2. Take a guess at the word's meaning. Does it make sense in the sentence?
3. Use a dictionary to check your guess.

Word Families

Word families are related words that all have the same base word.

Cycle

Bicycle

Cyclist

Strategy for Word Families

1. Find the base word in your unknown word.
2. Identify the meaning of the base word.
3. Guess the meaning of the unfamiliar word. Does it make sense in the sentence?
4. Use a dictionary to check your guess.

Word Origins: Roots

Many English words contain Greek and Latin roots.

Telephone

Dentures

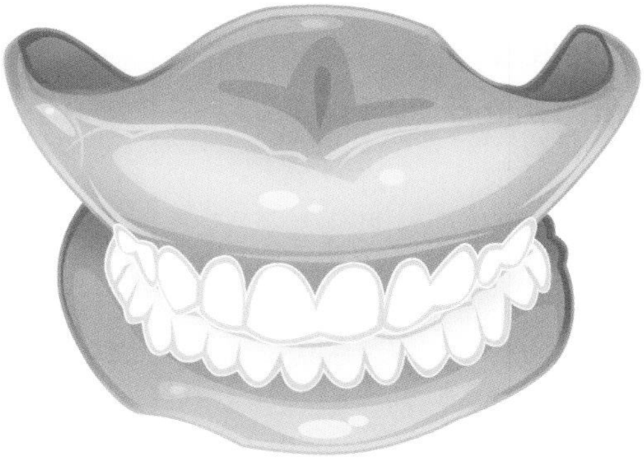

Tractor

Latin Roots

dent	tooth
dict	to say; to speak
scrib	to write
sub	under; below
tract	to pull
vis	to see

Greek Roots

auto	self
bio	life
micro	very small
ology	the study of
phon	sound; voice
scope	see
tele	far

Strategy for Roots

1. Use what you know about Greek and Latin roots to guess the meaning of the unknown word.
2. Does your guess make sense in the sentence?
3. Use a dictionary to check your guess.

Multiple-Meaning Words

Multiple-meaning words are words that have different meanings depending on how they are used. Homonyms, homographs, and homophones are all multiple-meaning words.

Homographs

Homographs are words that are spelled the same but have different meanings and sometimes different pronunciations.

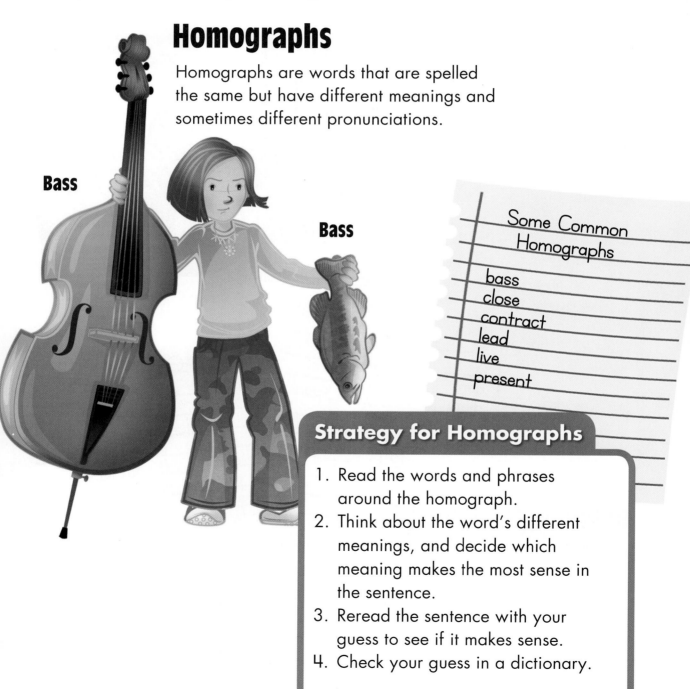

Bass

Bass

Some Common Homographs

bass
close
contract
lead
live
present

Strategy for Homographs

1. Read the words and phrases around the homograph.
2. Think about the word's different meanings, and decide which meaning makes the most sense in the sentence.
3. Reread the sentence with your guess to see if it makes sense.
4. Check your guess in a dictionary.

Homonyms

Homonyms are words that are pronounced the same and have the same spelling, but their meanings are different.

Squash

Squash

Some Common Homonyms

pen
duck
mail
ear
bank
bark

Strategy for Homonyms

1. Read the words and phrases near the homonym.
2. Think about the word's different meanings, and decide which one makes the most sense.
3. Reread the sentence with your guess to see if it makes sense.
4. Use a dictionary to check your guess.

Homophones

Homophones are words that are pronounced the same way but have different spellings and different meanings.

Ball

Bawl

Some Common Homophones

ate	eight
bored	board
brake	break
knight	night
weight	wait

Strategy for Homophones

1. Think about the different spellings and meanings of the homophone.
2. Check a dictionary for definitions of the words.
3. Use the word that best fits your writing.

This chart can help you remember the differences between homonyms, homographs, and homophones.

Understanding Homographs, Homonyms, and Homophones

	Pronunciation	Spelling	Meaning
Homographs	may be the same or different	same	different
Homonyms	same	same	different
Homophones	same	different	different

Homograph

present

present

bark

Homonym

bark

aisle **Homophone** isle

Dictionary

A dictionary is a reference book that lists words alphabetically. It can be used to look up definitions, parts of speech, spelling, and other forms of words.

punc·tu·al ❶ (pungk′ chü əl), ❷ ADJECTIVE. ❸ prompt; exactly on time: ❹ *He is always punctual.* ❺ □ ADVERB **punc′tu·al·ly.**

❶ Pronunciation

❷ Part of speech

❸ Definitions

❹ Example sentence

❺ Other form of the word and its part of speech

Strategy for Dictionary

1. Identify the unknown word.
2. Look up the word in a dictionary. Entries are listed alphabetically.
3. Find the part of the entry that has the information you are looking for.
4. Use the diagram above as a guide to help you locate the information you want.

Thesaurus

A thesaurus is a book of synonyms. Sometimes it will also contain antonyms. Look through the synonyms to find one with the best meaning by using a dictionary.

cute
adjective
attractive, appealing, amusing, charming, adorable, enchanting.
ANTONYMS: ugly, dull, unappealing

Strategy for Thesaurus

1. Look up the word in a thesaurus. Entries are listed alphabetically.
2. Locate the synonyms for your word.
3. Find the word with the exact meaning you want.

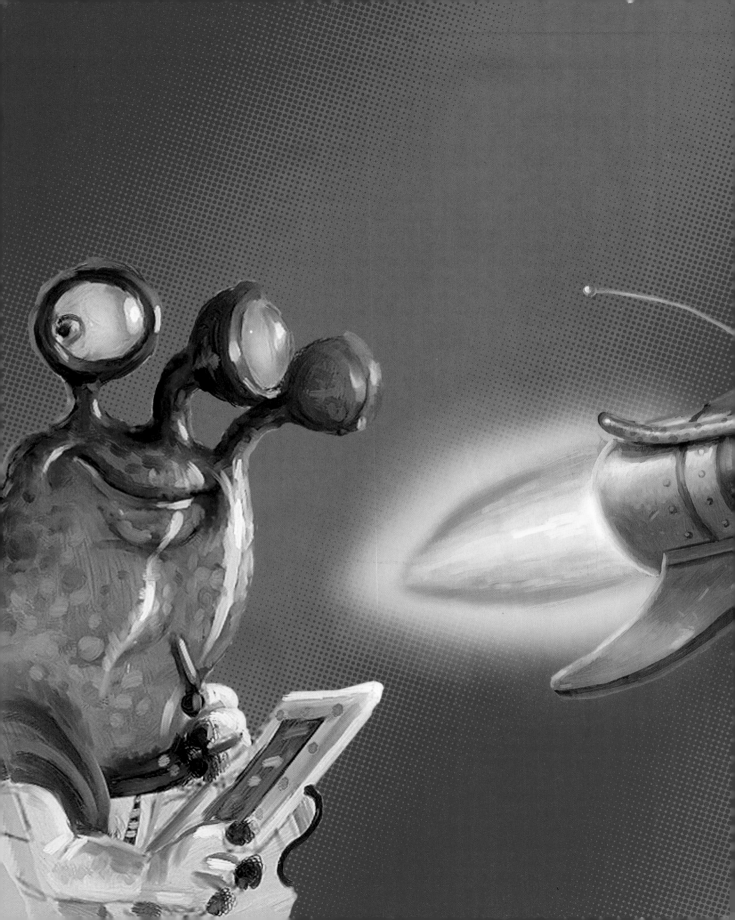

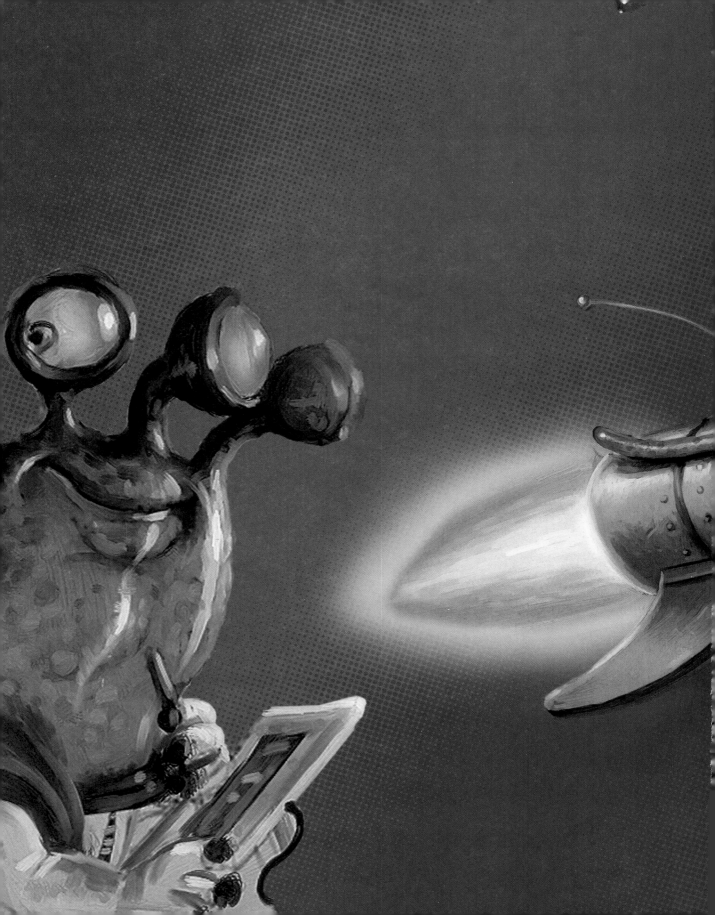